The Book of
Cullompton

Celebrating a Devonshire Market Town

Compiled by the People of the Parish

HALSGROVE

First published in Great Britain in 2001

British Library Cataloguing-in-Publication Data
A CIP record for this title is available from the British Library

ISBN 1 84114 1178

HALSGROVE
PUBLISHING, MEDIA AND DISTRIBUTION

Halsgrove House
Lower Moor Way
Tiverton, Devon EX16 6SS
Tel: 01884 243242
Fax: 01884 243325
email: sales@halsgrove.com
website: http://www.halsgrove.com

Frontispiece photograph: *Fore Street, early 1900s.*

Printed and bound in Great Britain by Bookcraft Ltd, Midsomer Norton.

FOREWORD

I call upon you, my readers, to play your personal part in promoting the well-being of our Parish. Let none say, 'I mind my own business, that's enough for me.' That is a sentiment utterly selfish, and wholly unworthy of a Christian or good citizen. The 'common good' should have our constant and warmest concern. He is no true 'Cullomptonian' who does not aim at making Cullompton the best and brightest township in the County of Devon. 'Vivat Cullomptonia'

Revd G. Forrester in St Andrew's Parochial Magazine, *March 1903.*

The Book of Cullompton, Celebrating a Devonshire Market Town has been collated by a small group from the Town Council, with contributions from many local people. Over the years, quite a few booklets have been published which cover aspects of the town's history and there is a wealth of other material available. One of our millennium projects was to bring together as much as we could in one book. We set out not just to recall the past, but also to record the present, so that future generations can see what Cullompton was like in the year 2000. We have tried to include as much detail as possible but this book is not just a collection of dates, names, facts and figures; it also contains stories of daily life, snatches from history, thoughts, memories and recollections.

We have used many sources of information and have tried to ensure the accuracy of the content by checking as thoroughly as possible, but sometimes this is easier said than done. We are sorry if we have made mistakes or left something out. Memories play tricks on us and even published texts differ, so inevitably there will be details with which the reader will disagree, and there will be many areas that we have not been able to cover in the space available. It is our hope, therefore, that the research we have completed for this book will be the start of an archive of material, photographic and textual, which can be catalogued and stored for the benefit of the town. We welcome any additional information you may be able to provide for this.

Gathering the information has been a tremendous task, but those of us involved have had a most exciting time sifting through it all. It has offered many people the opportunity to reminisce, to share common experiences and relate personal memories. Whilst researching the history of the town's schools we came across the following paragraph in a booklet published by the Girls' Convent High School. It was written around 1936, the writer is unknown, but obviously thought highly of the town:

Cullompton is a quaint, lovely little town. Its water Conduit, due to the munifence of one of the early Abbots of Buckland, is unique and the pride of the people. The shops are fine, its people charming. Business is brisk and the service up-to-date. Every public want is catered for, not in a mediocre way, but exceptionally well. The Hotels are very comfortable and the surrounding country a dream of beauty. There are two excellent glove factories.

We hope you enjoy the book and that it will become a source of interest and reference for all of us, our children and grandchildren for many generations to come.

Cullompton Town Council, 2001

Making a farm track in the 1930s.

Mr Stafford Hill, 1934. The Aberdeen Angus heifer won 2nd prize at Exeter Show and was later shown at Smithfield where it won 1st prize.

CONTENTS

Foreword 3
Acknowledgements 7
Introduction 9
Chapter One: Childhood & School Days *by Linda Holloway* 13
Chapter Two: Land & Buildings *by Judy Morris* 39
Chapter Three: Churches *by Various Contributors* 49
Chapter Four: Shops & Businesses *by Various Contributors* 59
Chapter Five: Inns of the Parish *by Judy Morris* 75
Chapter Six: Transport *by Various Contributors* 79
Chapter Seven: Heat, Light & Water *by Various Contributors* 85
Chapter Eight: Trade & Industry *by Various Contributors* 89
Chapter Nine: Carnivals, Festivals & Fêtes *by Various Contributors* 95
Chapter Ten: Wartime *by Various Contributors* 105
Chapter Eleven: Emergency Services *by Various Contributors* 113
Chapter Twelve: Sporting Life *by Various Contributors* 119
Chapter Thirteen: Clubs & Organisations *by Various Contributors* 129
Chapter Fourteen: Life in a Country Town *by Various Contributors* 139
Chapter Fifteen: 2000 & Beyond *by Various Contributors* 153

In Conclusion *156*
Subscribers *158*

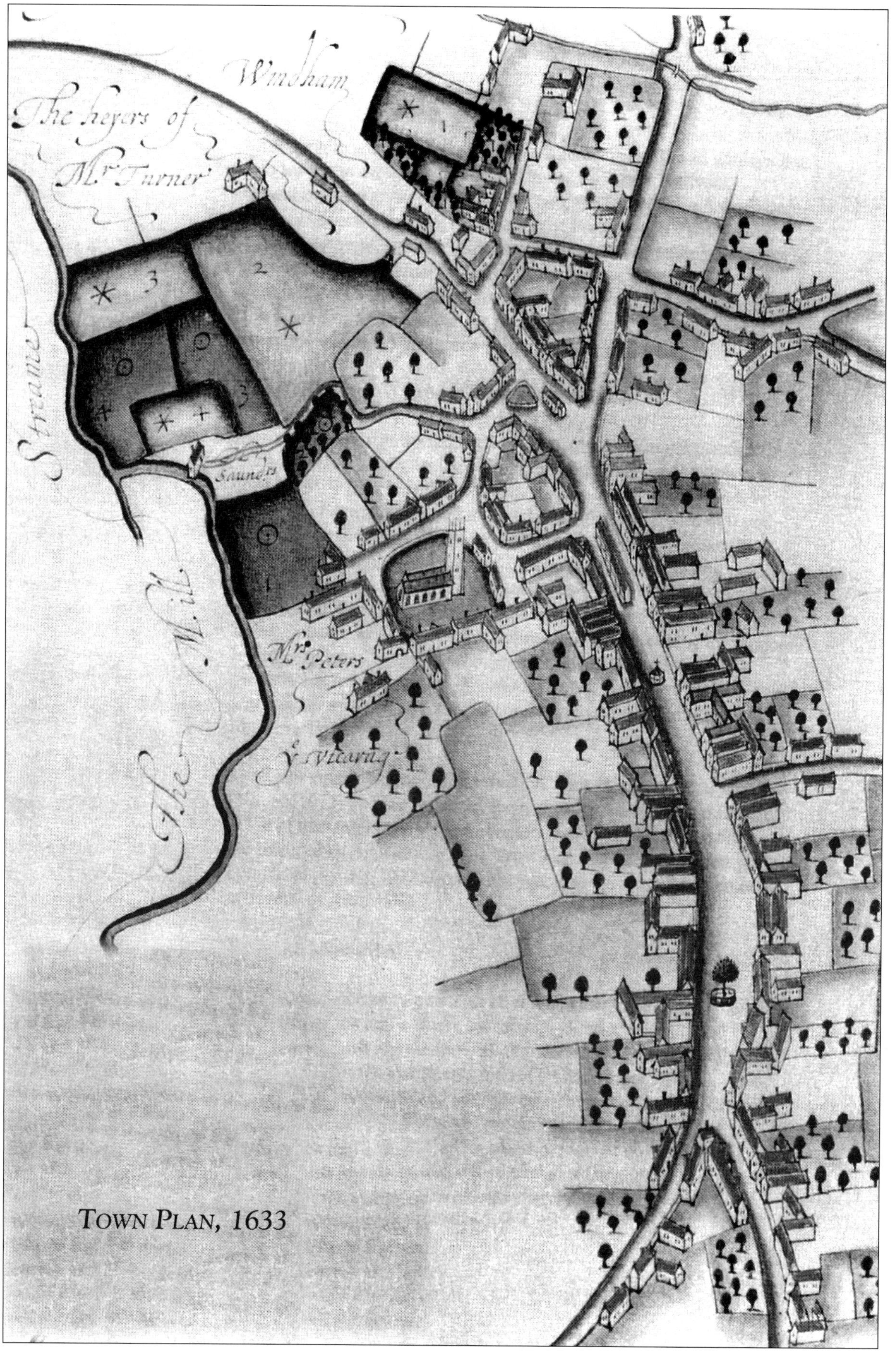

Town Plan, 1633

ACKNOWLEDGEMENTS

Many people have helped us by loaning photographs, providing information and assisting in other ways. Our thanks go to the following and anyone else whose name we have inadvertently overlooked:

Mrs Eileen Andrews, Mrs Linda Ayres, Mr Mike Baker, Mr Peter Batten, Mrs Bennett, Mrs Margaret Bradbeer, Mr Richard Bradbeer, Mr Jim Brooks, Mrs Joan Broom, Mrs Queenie Broom, Mr David Broom, Mrs M.R. Broucke, Mr Derek Budd, Mrs Jane Campbell, Mr Jack Cann, Mrs Marjorie Chapman, Mr John Chard, Mr Richard Chard, Mr Joe Chowings, Mr B. Chubb, Mrs Clark, Mr Dave Clode, Mrs Liz Cole, Miss Susan Coles, Mrs Katie Coombes, Mrs Muriel Coxhead, Mrs Barbara Crispin, Mr Crispin, Mr Percy Cross, Mrs Teresa Cummings, Mr Tony Dobson, Mrs Fay Down, Mr Chris Down, Mrs Marian Dummett, Mr and Mrs Edmunds, Mr Kenneth Edwards, Mrs Jane Fenlon, G.D.V. Glynn Esq., Mrs Mandy Goff, Mr Goff, Mrs Kay Gordon, Mrs Betty Greening, Mrs Groves, Mr Ron Hake, Mrs Alice Harris, Mr David Hathaway, Mr John Hawke, Mrs Wendy Hawke, Mr Norman Hellier, Mr Steve Hellier, Mr Philip Herring, Ms Bridget Hill, Mr Peter Hill, Mr Mike Hines, Mr Michael Hitt, Mr C. Hodge, Mrs Linda Holloway, Mr Dave Hopper, Mr Brian Hooper, Mrs Carol Jolliffe, Mrs Dorothy Julian, Mr Terry Kerslake, Mr Peter Labdon, Mrs Elizabeth Labdon, Mr Bernard Land, Mrs Wendy Land, Mr Mick Lawrence, Mr Norman Lindsell, Mrs Lyle, Mrs Jean Manfield, Revd John Mapson, Mr Ross McBride, Mrs Judy Morris, Mr Geoff Munn, Mr Clive Nicholas, Mrs Joyce Owens, Mr Ron Parker, Mrs Pike, Mr David Pugsley, Mr Roger Mudditt, Mrs Margaret Russ, Miss June Severn, Mr Sid Russ, Mr Marcus Scott, Miss Marjorie Shere, Mrs Thelma Shere, Mr M. Smith, Mr Alan Spear, Mr Sid Staddon, Mrs Dawn Stevens, Mrs Marion Stone, Revd Alan Taylor, Mr Mike Thompson, Mr John Vicary, Mrs Wellington, Mr Whitfield, Mr Bob Whitell, Jenny Wood, Mrs Louise Younger.

Visit of General Sir Redvers Buller, 1906.

Section of the Second Edition Ordnance Survey Map of Cullompton, 1904.

INTRODUCTION

Cullompton, or 'Cully' as the town is affectionately known to those that live there or know it well, is a small inland Devon market town half way between Exeter and Taunton close to the M5 motorway. Its 2001 estimated population is approximately 7600. It was recorded in the Domesday Book in 1086 but at that time was just a small settlement. We know very little of Cullompton's early history but it was built on the site of a much older settlement.

The parish is primarily green and fertile farmland with a town at its heart, surrounded on three sides by hills which ensure its identity is preserved by creating a protective barrier. Incorporating the hamlets of Langford, Mutterton and Westcott within its bounds, it covers nearly 8000 acres and extends seven miles along the Culm Valley. It is located between high ground in the south, west and north-east, and a corridor of flat land to the east which accommodates the River Culm, the main railway line and the M5. From the hills on the edge of the town a habitation surrounding the medieval church of St Andrew's can be clearly seen. From Old Hill it is possible to differentiate between the old town and the new estates, but from the hills behind Growen and Bunnyford's Cross all that can be seen is a small group of houses nestling in a valley interwoven with trees.

By the mid-17th century the town's population was almost 3000 and it remained at about this level until the early 1970s, since when, due mainly to residential development, it has gradually increased.

There have been over 40 different spellings of its name. In AD549 St Columba, an Irish saint, preached in the area and is thought to have given the settlement its name. (Columda is the Latin for dove.) 'Columtune' became part of the private property of the House of Wessex by the time of the Saxon king Alfred the Great, who in 872 bequeathed Columtune and its lands to his son Ethelward.

In 1020 the manor and lands of Cullompton, which was then known as Colitina, belonged to the Lady Gytha, a Danish princess who was the widow of Earl Godwin and the mother of King Harold (who was later defeated and killed at the Battle of Hastings in 1066). In 1087 William the Conqueror passed though the 'villa' of 'Colitina' on his way to besiege Exeter and Lady Gytha fled to that city, where she held a great deal of land. Exeter fell 18 days later to the Norman soldiers of William I who then divided up the land he had confiscated giving it to his Norman barons. He gave the manor of Cullompton (Colitina), together with Langford and Ponsford, to Baldwin, the favourite nephew of his wife. It was later granted by King Richard I to Richard de Clifford and in 1199 or 1200 by King John, to his brother, Walter de Clifford. The Earls of Devon held it for many years and in 1278 Amicia, Countess of Devon, willed it to the Abbot and Convent of Buckland Monochorum. This bequest was confirmed by her daughter, Isabella, and by Edward I in the eighth year of his reign.

At the Dissolution it was surrendered into the king's hands and purchased by Sir John St Leger. At some stage it was sold by Sir George St Leger to Thomas Risdon and later sold to the Hillersdon family, from whom the Hillersdon estate takes its name.

Various sections of the troops visited Cullompton during the Civil Wars. Charles I passed through with his troops on 20 September 1644 and on 12 October 1645 Sir Thomas Fairfax arrived from Honiton. There was sporadic action thereafter in the neighbourhood before the surrender of Exeter at Poltimore House in April 1646. Four decades later St Andrew's Church housed Monmouth's rebels on their way to trial and in 1688 a small force of the Dutchman's soldiers was stationed in the town during William of Orange's progress from Brixham to London.

The Cullompton Company of Volunteers was one of the first few raised in England for the defence of the kingdom during the latter part of the 18th century. The first were enrolled in 1794 and gradually increased until three companies were quartered in the town. All of the volunteers in the Hundred of Heyridge were formed into one regiment with their headquarters at The Green (between New Cut and Shortlands). The company was disbanded in 1810 but in 1859 was formed again and the company was then named the Upper Culm Vale Rifle Corps, 5th Devon, and Mr John N. Walrond was elected Captain. The armoury was in a room where the present-day Town

Boiler waiting in Fore Street to go to the Axle Works at the bottom of Middle Mill Lane, c.1900.

G. Shore's sawmills in Station Road (see map on page 8), c.1913.

Hall now stands and the company is still in existence although its name has changed several times and was eventually transferred to G. Co. 4th Devonshire Territorials. In 1909 a Cyclist Company was also established and had their drill hall in the Old Workhouse.

During the 19th century, the wool trade – largely carried on as a cottage industry or in a factory at Shortlands which was demolished to make way for the Hammett Road flats – began to decline, but other sources of employment, including the paper and flour mills, the tanyard and foundry, and a pattern of light industry and agriculture, continued.

The medieval street plan of the town has changed very little over the years. The majority of the town's shops are on Fore Street, a narrow street which leads into High Street, and both are contained within the Conservation Area. There are many courts behind these two streets, linked by alleyways which originally accommodated the weavers and other workers. High Street benefited from an enhancement scheme in 1992 and an open-air market is held here every Wednesday.

Higher Mill Lane, Middle Mill Lane and Lower Mill Lane connect High Street and Fore Street with the Mill Leat, a man-made tributary of the River Culm which powered the corn mills at Higher, Middle and Lower Mill. Middle Mill later became an axle works powered by steam. A public footpath now makes up the River Walk leading to the sports clubs and community fields.

What follows is an extract from an article written by R.S. Harris, who left Cullompton for Australia in July 1854, returning for a visit after 37 years away. It appeared in the *Standard* under the heading 'Tiverton Gazette and East Devon Herald of Nov 8':

I arrived at Cullompton on 1 May... on my first walk through the streets of the town I noticed great improvements had been made to its general appearance and comfort. The old rough-stone pitched side-walks have given place to nice smooth square tiles. Gas has taken the place of oil, though in my boyhood the street lamp-posts were not illuminated with any kind of light. The tree planting in High Street is also another step in the right direction. In a few years, when the trees are larger, they will make this pretty street still more attractive. I think the trees should have been planted further from the street line by six or eight feet, for, when they have grown to their usual size, their branches will be, I fear, too close to the buildings. I noticed some addition had been made to the town in the way of buildings, notably Mr Pidgeon's pretty terrace [Belle Vue Terrace], *built of brick, in Lower Street, and many old dwellings had been renovated and beautified. Others, again, had been replaced by houses built of brick and free stone, modelled on the modern development of architecture. It speaks well for the public spirit of the proprietors and the good taste displayed by the local architect, for the neat and pretty designs introduced.*

When I reached Church Street I was pained to find a very old house, opposite the late Dr Porter's residence, had been pulled down. This house was occupied by John Lane, between the years 1500 and 1550, who, during that time, built and gave the additions to the church, called Lane's Aisle. Our family dwelt in this house for over 100 years; I believe my grandfather, Thomas Middle and all his children (7) were born there, also Mr Henry Middle of Cullompton, and myself, representatives of the third generation. Although sorry I could not renew my acquaintance with the old house, I confess its removal has improved the appearance of the street.

From a sanitary point of view, I observed that the small streets and by-ways had not been neglected, but my greatest pleasure was to know that the domestic position of the working people had kept pace with the town. They appeared happy, better clad and better fed; in fact a butcher friend told me that the consumption of meat in the town was now 100 per cent more than 40 years ago, with 600 less in the population now than then.

Though time has wrought many changes, I found that a few scions of old Cullompton families still resided there, notably descendants of Francis Colman, who once owned and resided at Hillersdon; John Blackmore of Moorhayes, who inherited this estate 1711; and the Upcotts, of Shortlands, my respected friend, Mr John S. Upcott, of Master House, being the survivor of the third generation of successful manufacturers for over a century, in Cullompton, of woollen stuffs, such as cloth, blankets and serge.

The last, but not least, I may be allowed to refer to, is John Shute, for Worth, in his History of Devon *says:- 'Nicholas Hilliard, the most distinguished English portraits of royalty, and members of distinguished families. Hilliard's only recorded predecessor in Devonian art, was John Shute, of Cullompton, who also worked in miniature, and who died in 1563.'*

During my visit I travelled upwards of 5,000 miles over England, Ireland, Scotland and Wales and I say that during my travels I saw no twelve-to-fourteenth century town of its size, or even larger, to equal or to approach Cullompton for good buildings, compactness and cleanliness, with such copious supply of water running in open gutters in every street and such good natural drainage making it one of the healthiest and prettiest of little towns, and around it, where can you find its equal for rural scenery?

When I commenced this letter I intended to have spoken of the May fair of 1891, and the May fairs, as I saw them in the thirties; also my visit to the first Cullompton races last year... But, I fear I have trespassed too much already on your valuable space... Ever faithful to the home of my birth,

Yours R.S. Harris
Warrnambool, Victoria, Australia, 24 September 1892.

THE TOWN CRIER

The Cullompton Town Crier is a wonderful advert for the town; as well as supporting all kinds of events, he shouts about Cullompton wherever he goes. With his sense of humour and willing and helpful nature, he brings colour and ceremony to many occasions. Here is his story:

My name is Gordon Pring and I am the Cullompton Town Crier. My interest began in 1982 when I divorced after 35 years and three daughters. My best pal was Dougie Fletcher, who was at that time the Town Crier of Topsham, and I started going around the country with him to competitions. I became more and more involved and made many Town Crier friends – not only from this country but from all over the world.

On many occasions I joined in as a guest crier, not having been appointed by any town or authority. Many of my crier friends advised me to try and get a town to officially appoint me so in 1987 I applied to Cullompton Town Council but at that time they were not interested in having a crier for the town. I still kept on with my travels and on several occasions I was appointed to act as one of the judges at competitions. Then in 1989 I wrote again to Cullompton Town Council explaining some of the advantages of having a crier for the town. I was then of an age to join the ranks of senior citizens and went off to see my eldest daughter in Adelaide, South Australia.

On my return I was invited to attend a Council meeting on 14 February 1990 when I again explained what town crying was all about and the advantages of having a crier. This must have impressed them because when the vote was taken I was officially appointed there and then.

Since then I have travelled all over the country and indeed all over the world, promoting Cullompton and the surrounding countryside. I have visited Australia, Canada twice, Vancouver Island, Anacortes in Washington State USA, France, Holland, and Belgium six times. I have also been to Jersey and Guernsey on courtesy visits.

As well as being Cullompton's Crier I was made the honorary Town Crier of Adelaide by the Lord Mayor and also honorary Town Crier of Exeter which is also in South Australia.

I have been the Devon Champion Town Crier on four occasions, Lancashire Open Champion, West of England Champion twice and Wessex Champion, as well as many more successes including a 5th place at Niagara Falls in a Nine Country International in 1993.

I still enjoy representing and promoting Cullompton wherever I go and hope to for a few more years yet!

God Save the Queen
Gordon Pring

The inauguration of the first Town Mayor of Cullompton, 7 January 1995. Left to right: Deputy Town Mayor Councillor Mrs Jane Campbell, Town Mayor Councillor Mrs Marian Dummett and Cullompton Town Crier Mr Gordon Pring. (Cullompton Town Council elected a Chairman annually until May 1994, after which date the Chairman of the Council also acquired the title of Cullompton Town Mayor.)

*Gordon Pring (*left*) outside Buckingham Palace during a Queen's birthday cry and (*right*) at the Town Crier World Championships, August 1999, held at Vancouver Island, Canada.*

Chapter One

Childhood & School Days

The National Schools

In 1816 two schoolrooms were erected – one for poor boys and one for poor girls – on land belonging to the Revd Walter Gray MA, a former vicar of the church. He donated the land six years later in 1822. The cost of building and equipping the schools was £500, and the sum was made up from a gift of £200 from Henry Bratton Esq., a donation of £200 from a fund left by a Miss E. Pryor for benevolent purposes and a grant of £100 from the National Society. The general upkeep was maintained by voluntary subscriptions, school fees and Government grants.

The trustees were the Revd Walter Gray, Sir Thomas Dyke Acland and Francis Huyshe; also Revd John Templer, Revd William Barker and Revd James Townsend Lewes (Vicar of Cullompton, Rector of Broadclyst and Vicar of Halberton respectively). Parts of the premises were to be used as residences for the master and mistress. Church-of-England principles were to be taught, along with reading, writing and arithmetic and, in addition, for the girls, needlework.

In 1872 new schools were erected at a cost of £2315, the sum being raised from voluntary subscriptions, grants, church collections and the proceeds from the sale of the old school premises. The new schools came under the head of non-provided or denominational schools. The annual examination of the school was reported in the *Parish Magazine*. An example from 1892 states that the Senior Inspector for the Diocese the Revd R.J.E. Baggis carried out the inspection of 534 children; 175 boys, 158 girls and 201 infants. The Boys' School was reported upon thus:

> *... very good, discipline is thoroughly maintained, and the boys have been taught with much ability... The Catechism, however, wants fuller explanation and illustration, and the Prayer Book subject has not received sufficient attention, but otherwise the work of the school is excellent.*

The Girls' School was said to be 'in admirable order' with 'much attention [being] devoted to the instruction'.

In the *St Andrew's Parochial Magazine* of March 1903 there is an account of 'an Entertainment given by the School Children' which on 18 February had 'packed the large Infant Schoolroom to overflowing'. So popular was the event that: 'A large number who sought admission could not be accommodated, much to their vexation, and to the sincere regret of those conducting the entertainment.' Those fortunate to find seats were treated to fine performances:

> *Songs and Recitations by the tiniest mites, were given with faultless memory, with the utmost intelligence, with clearest enunciation, which could only have been secured by great skill and untiring patience on the part of those who undertook the task of training. Not less admirable were the several displays of Musical Drill and Gymnastics Exercises given by the Boys and Girls, performed with a perfection of time and a beauty of grace, which justly called forth the heartiest applause.*

There was praise too for 'the Instrumentalists, the young Pianists and the three Violinists, for their pleasing contributions to the evening's enjoyment.' And thanks were added to Mrs Sanders 'who laboured so earnestly to promote the success of the Entertainment', and to Miss Smale 'who played the accompaniments'.

G. Forrester, writing in the *Parish Magazine* of February 1903 commented that under the new Education Bill:

> *... the Church Schools will be rendered yet more efficient, whilst the Clerical influence, such as it is, will in most instances, be materially lessened. The conscientious religious scruples of the parents will be met yet more effectually than at present...*

Until this time the Church Voluntary Schools were built, and almost exclusively maintained, by Church people, and parishioners were exempt from paying the sometimes heavy rates entailed by Board Schools in other parishes. The new Education Act meant that all ratepayers would be liable for their proportionate share in the support of the education given in these elementary schools. However, if the Authority

Above: *Cullompton School, 1930. Left to right, back: ?, ?, ?, ?, ?, Walter Clarke, ?, ?; middle: Margaret Taylor, ?, ?, Douglas Heale, Bernard Owens, Ken Saunders, Tony Stuart, Tom Wotton, ?, Roy Rutley, ?, Joan Mitchell, ?; front: ?, Joan Cook, ?, Margery Clark, ?, ?, Gwen Widgery, ?; cross-legged; Harold White, ?.*

Right: *Cullompton School prefects. Left to right, back: Colin Jolliffe, Pat Evans, Norman Hellier, Shirley Blake, Mr Francis Chapman (headteacher, known to the pupils as 'Chipples'); front: Kathleen Greenaway, Alan Stops, Dorothy Daniel, Doreen Lock.*

Left: *Cullompton Senior School, 1935. Left to right, back: ?, ?, ?, Kathleen Sellick, Margery Caines, Gladys Sellick, ?, Margery Osmond, Phyllis Heard, ?, ?, ? Radford; 3rd row: Ken Saunders, ?, ?, Grace Whitton, Betty Smith, ?, Marjorie Harding, Gwen Widgery, ?, Phyllis Denner, ?, Maurice Gould, Ralph Mitchell; 2nd row: Miss Beatrice Labdon (teacher), Gordon Hiscox, ?, ?, Betty Brooks, Joan Cook, ?, Walter Clarke, ?, Bernard Owens, ?, Mr Francis Chapman (head); front: Roy Rutley, ?, Tom Wotton, Francis Venner, ?, John Hopkins, ?, ?.*

required improvements, alterations or enlargements to the buildings or playgrounds, the costs would have to be met out of voluntary subscriptions as before. The Managers would still have to look to the generosity of the parishioners to meet such outlays. The Managers at that time were Messrs Turner, Sellwood, T.P. Grant, E. Lawrence junr (elected to represent the Parish Council), A.W. Hopkins (representative on the County Education Committee) and G. Forrester.

By June 1903 the number of children on the school register had fallen to 510 but standards were high. The annual inspection saw high praise for the girls in particular:

The girls throughout have a very full and intelligent knowledge of Christian Faith and Duty, the result evidently of earnest and painstaking teaching and of loving care for their moral and spiritual well-being.

Mr Swell took over as headteacher from Mr Saunders in 1923 followed by Mr Francis Chapman in 1931. He was respected by all and his insistence on good manners had a notable effect on the general atmosphere of the school.

During the Second World War most male teachers were away on war service. The school also doubled in size when children from Westfield School in Kent were evacuated to the town. The headmaster's office and the staffroom were in the peak of the roof over the centre of the hall and were accessed by a narrow staircase. They were both extremely cramped and utilitarian.

Games were played on the field in Duke Street and the asphalted playgrounds were used for netball and gymnastics. At that time Mrs Margaret Bradbeer was a teacher of domestic science at the school. She recalls that the equipment in 1949 was 'ancient and minimal'. Her classes consisted of up to 22 girls so she was permitted to purchase a dozen brown glazed mixing bowls for 3 shillings each and three aluminium saucepans with lids from Mr William Denner's one-room hardware shop nearby. She also recalls the difficulties which she faced whilst providing instruction in even the most basic household chores:

Cooking apparatus consisted of an industrial gas cooker and an uncontrollable electric stove which incinerated anything put in its oven, so some time later a solid-fuel York Vale was installed which eased matters. Laundry work was a nightmare – there were about fifteen rusty flat irons and three electric ones without thermostats. The gas boiler had a rubber wringer but there was a half inch gap in the middle of the mangle roller.

The children were not used to luxuries, but in spite of rationing and other shortages at that time they turned out quite a wide range of bakery. They were allowed to talk quietly as they worked but were expected to be silent instantly when asked.

Once a week, on Fridays, girls from Culm Valley Schools were driven in for domestic science and hygiene. They covered a much shortened course but it was better than nothing!

Assembly was held each morning. Two partitions were moved to make room for the whole school, then replaced after prayers to form three classrooms. Evening classes were run in various subjects such as woodwork, which were open to boys and girls. On one occasion a man wanted to make a five-barred gate for his field, and others made simple furniture or turned rolling pins and bowls on the lathe.

When Mr Ken Edwards arrived in 1963 he remembers that the first thing he had to do was to have the ceiling beam in the head's office removed. He says it would have decapitated him – Mr Edwards was considerably taller than his predecessor Mr Chapman! The name of the school was changed from 'Cullompton Senior Secondary Modern School Mixed' to 'Cullompton School'.

As there were no changing rooms, the boys removed their football mud at one basin in a corridor outside the needlework room. The toilets were across the playground and very draughty. There was no lab, just a collection of batteries and jars, but there were areas for woodwork, needlework and cookery.

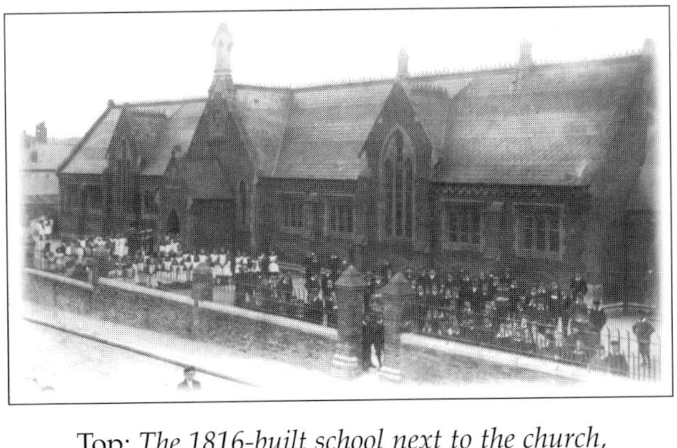

Top: *The 1816-built school next to the church, demolished after this picture was taken.*
Above: *Cullompton School built on the site of the present-day Magistrates Court in 1872.*

The New School

Left: *Cullompton Community College officially opened on 9 February 1965.*

Below, group of four: *Pupils demonstrating equipment and facilities at the new Cullompton School, c.1965.*

Right: *Pupils setting off for a week's camping at Greatwood Forest Camp on the Quantocks in 1968. They slept in log cabins in a valley beside a stream in the middle of a forest.*

THE NEW CULLOMPTON SCHOOL

When Mr Edwards arrived the old premises could not be adapted to provide modern facilities for secondary education, so a brand-new school was being built and equipped in Exeter Road. The accommodation consisted of a hall/gymnasium, library, science laboratory, housecraft and needlework rooms, art room, handicrafts room, history and geography rooms and six classrooms. There was also additional space for music and technical drawing. The building cost £132 000.

Mr Edwards remembers that for the actual move in the summer of 1964, they were left to their own devices. They worked out 'Operation Exodus' to 'the Promised Land' and staff and pupils rallied round to carry equipment to the new school. The new building was not completely ready, but they moved anyway, as Ken recalls:

The hall couldn't be used until the end of October so assemblies were held outside – Harvest on the front steps. There were pneumatic drills and concrete mixers, painters and carpenters everywhere, but when it was all done it was wonderful. It seemed to have a very healthy effect on the children themselves as well as on their educational opportunities. It was nick-named 'The Palace'. To have a fully-equipped lab, well-stocked library full of books, a gym and changing rooms with showers was quite beyond their experience.

Some of the pupils took a while to accept the showers, and this wasn't helped when a group of Governors decided to inspect a fault in the shower installation:

Suddenly the changing room filled with girls who began to strip off, trapping the Governors in the cubicles. The Chairman, Colonel Bird, ex Indian Army, led the charge to the door crying, "It's all right girls, I'm a grandfather myself!"

A new uniform was introduced, chosen by the children. There were no caps for the boys. Instead of blazers, the girls chose what was then a very trendy sleeveless jacket with a choice of skirt or trousers – in 1964 this was avant-garde! Later, as the fifth form developed, they were allowed to choose two colours for their year and then wear anything in those colours. There could have been some freakish outfits, but instead there were several boys who wore stylish suits. Ken Edwards remembers that there were just three school rules: 'Don't run inside the buildings, show consideration for others and use your common sense.' He said, 'I was chuffed when an advisor once said, "We know your school as the one where pupils open doors for visitors."'

A ceremony was held on Tuesday 9 February 1965 when Cullompton School was officially opened by Brigadier E.H.C. Frith. The school settled into its new surroundings and routine. All the members of staff were enthusiastic but the music mistress was quite exceptional. She ran a wind band, orchestra, pop group, junior choir, senior choir and all sorts of smaller groups. She held two rehearsals at lunchtimes and another after school. Christmas productions became quite a feature of school life; they involved around 200 pupils and were popular with the community. There was even one written by a talented father about body snatching! These were early days for computers and the school kept in the forefront of development by being hooked by phone to a main-frame computer at East Devon College.

The delay in the school becoming comprehensive was due to the fact that Mrs Thatcher, the then Minister of Education, could not believe that smaller schools could offer a sufficient number of subjects, but when a team of Her Majesty's Inspectors (HMIs) visited, they found that if anything the school was offering too many. At that time, when a Spanish family arrived in town, the head of modern languages taught herself Spanish and bought a teaching pack of tapes to enable two girls to take their native language to CSE (Certificate of Secondary Education) level. On more than one occasion the headteacher taught Latin to two girls on a one-to-one basis. This just could not be done now.

When the school leaving age was raised to 16 the staff worked very hard to overcome the difficulties of the reluctant fifth former. They were given their own day room and other privileges. Special courses were devised for them called 'Learning for Life', involving subjects like parenthood, getting on with other people and safety at home, on the roads and at work. However, when the students came to make their choices, they picked the traditional subjects. Another new venture was work experience where arrangements were made for pupils to work in local businesses for several weeks before they left school. This is now quite common in schools, but Cullompton School was a pioneer in this field and there were many legal and financial problems to sort out with Government departments and employers before the scheme could get under way.

When a minibus was purchased it was in much demand by academic and sports staff who wanted to take students to fixtures or places of special interest. For many years 48 first-year pupils would be taken to the Scripture Union Greatwood Forest Camp during the Easter holiday. There would be campfire concerts, midnight hikes to Dead Woman's Ditch and wonderful walks across the Quantocks to the Bristol Channel. Later the camp took place at Pixies' Holt at Dartmeet with training in rock climbing and abseiling. There was also the tradition of the ghost story night hike, which centred on the tale of a monk's body being carried across the moor for burial when suddenly he returned to life. As the walkers passed a pool of floodwater, a hooded figure ringing a bell arose from the icy waters – the intrepid PE master was playing his part!

As the Modern Language Department grew, pupil exchanges took place with St Joseph's School at Ploudalmezeau in Brittany. The headteacher at the time was M. Augebin. Pupils continue to enjoy the experiences of annual exchanges with both St Joseph's and also a school in Germany.

In 1974, the school underwent another building programme as it became a comprehensive. There were many who had misgivings about the system, but with the premises, equipment, staff and enthusiasm, the whole venture seemed to be a success.

When Ken Edwards retired in 1980 there were some 600 students attending the school and 50 teaching and non-teaching staff. Some members of staff stayed for many years: Mr Frank Baker spent his whole teaching career at the school and Derek Kellaway was a pupil, workshop technician and subsequently a member of the teaching staff. Mr Keith Turner came to Cullompton School in 1980 and remains at the school more than two decades later, along with the Secretary Mrs Jenny Browning, and humanities teacher Mr Russell Clark. In 1994 the school was designated as a community college and, although it still only accepts students between the ages of 11–16, this has meant improved integration with the local community.

In 1991 the outdoor swimming pool at the school was re-opened, having been closed for five years and threatened with filling in as the school could not afford the repair bills. Cullompton Town Council was persuaded to contribute £6000 to refurbish the pool and bring it into public use. Additional funding came from the County and District Councils, the Culm Valley Swimming Club and the Cullompton Community Association. Unfortunately in 2001 it was vandalised and did not open for the summer.

A new design and technology block was completed in 1998 at a cost of approximately £750 000. A floodlit, all-weather sports pitch was added in 1999, after successful applications for grants from the National Lottery and the Foundation for Sports and the Arts. The latter was a partnership project with Devon County Council and Mid Devon District Council and the pitch is available for use by the community as well as the school. The project included improved cricket and athletics facilities, additions to the Culm Valley Sports Centre and improved changing rooms.

The hall and dining area were refurbished in 2000 and provided facilities which can be used as a theatre by both the college and the community. The PTFA contributed £3300 towards the cost of new curtains for the refurbished hall and the members continue to run monthly bingo sessions and an annual Summer Fayre, together with other fund-raising events to purchase items of additional equipment for the school. As well as the curtains, during 2000, they also paid for an overhead projector and a video camera and made a contribution to the Homework Club.

There are now over 700 students on the school roll, and this number is predicted to rise to 800. With this in mind, plans are being drawn up to construct a new science block which, it is hoped, will also provide disabled access to the first floor. There are hopes that the school will eventually be able to offer education for over-16s.

From September 2001 the young people will no longer wear white shirts, ties and black jumpers; instead both girls and boys will wear a black sweatshirt and a white polo shirt. The new minibus, purchased in May 2001, proudly displays the recently changed school logo.

Universal Cultural Exchange Evening, October 1995. Students from Thailand visited Cullompton, staying with pupils' families for three weeks. The Thai children organised an evening of their national food, singing and dancing and made a presentation to the Chairman of Mid Devon District Council, Mr Derrick Allen (centre). On his right is Deborah Booth (Deputy Head) and on his left is the teacher from Thailand with the Thai students and host families.

ST ANDREW'S SCHOOL

The school was built in 1937 and Mr Ashford, the first headmaster, would ride to school on his bike with his books in a wooden box attached to the carrier. Each day he pushed his bicycle along the corridor and politely acknowledged everyone, tipping his hat and greeting them with 'good morning' and again at the end of the day, wishing them 'goodnight'.

School dinners cost 1d. and many a parent was happy to see their child have a hot midday meal. When, a year or two later, male teachers were appointed to the staff (Mr Baker, Mr Ellis and Mr Clements) pupils were told that this was because the children were so unruly! In 1957 when Barbara Crispin joined the staff as teacher of the Infant 2 Class, other staff included Mrs Ashford, Miss Joyce Scorse, Mrs Joan Bryant, Miss Cole, Mr Tony Dobson, Mr Pike and Mr Terry Kerslake.

In the very bad winter of 1963 the school remained open, even though Mr Dobson remembers his class had 14 absentees, there were no Ash Thomas children and the playground was out of use for three weeks.

Tony Dobson remembers when Linda Whittaker brought a jam jar containing a moth into school. It turned out to be a Silver-striped Hawk Moth – very rare and only the second one recorded in Devon. It is now in the Devon Collection of the Exeter Museum in Queen Street. This find prompted the setting up of an Insect Club the following year.

There were of course the usual incidents that occur at a junior school – crayon up nose, knee between the drainpipe and the wall, needle between front teeth. There was also the time when a pupil's head was jammed through the gap in the back of the chair and couldn't be released. Mr Clarke, the caretaker, was summoned to bring a hacksaw, but instructed not to let the child see it!

Mr Ashford was succeeded in September 1963 by Mr Martin Neeves. Miss Terry Yells, later Rutter, also joined the staff to take the Reception Class. Mr Neeves was a forward-looking man who suggested that a swimming pool was needed. A committee of 33 was formed made up of one person from each area of the town. Thus the Parent Teacher Association (PTA) was born. The group was wholeheartedly supported by the parents, and fêtes, fairs and coffee mornings were organised – anything to raise money. Each December Father Christmas sat in his grotto, sometimes in a wood and once under the sea! Roy Hudd was once due to open the school fête, but failed to turn up. However, two broadcasts of 'Any Questions' were made from the school with David Jacobs in the chair. On other occasions the Welsh Fusiliers gave concerts to help raise funds.

This was before the motorway was built and the committee served all-night breakfast for holidaymakers passing through Cullompton. The Town Council would not allow use of the Parish Hall for this, for fear of upsetting the local traders, so Mr and Mrs Skinner's house in Higher Bullring was established as a base.

The PTA was not just a fund-raising group but also the family's social life; babysitters were unheard of and leisure had to involve the whole family. There was a lot of enjoyment but also a feeling of community spirit – everyone was working for the common good. The outcome of all of this hard work was that a starter swimming pool was built. It cost £600 and was a wonderful asset which was much used, not just by pupils for lessons, but on occasions such as the School Summer Fair and the Leavers' Summer Barbecue. Sadly it is no longer with us. So much damage was caused to the liner by vandals that the PTA and the school found the expense of rising insurance premiums and constant repairs too heavy a burden. The considerable expense of covering the pool was not an option. The spiralling repair costs, together with the limited number of warm days the pool could be used, led to the reluctant decision not to continue with expensive maintenance and the pool was eventually filled in during the early 1990s.

The PTA, or PTFA (Parent, Teacher and Friends Association) as it became known, continued its hard work. Changes in the funding of schools meant that extra money for basic equipment and library books was very much appreciated. However, the aim was not only to organise events to raise money, but also to promote the social side of these occasions. Bingo sessions were very popular and a great money-spinner for many years. Quiz nights were always very entertaining, although they could become extremely competitive as the evening wore on and it became more important to win! There were barn dances led by the head Brian Hooper, exhausting occasions but great fun, and of course the auctions with Clive Madge, when you inevitably went home with more than you had hoped to sell. The termly Friday-night discos for the children were never to be missed, unless you were a parent stuck in an extremely hot kitchen for three hours serving squash, hot dogs and crisps, and looking after purses. Children always loved the balloon races and in the early '80s the school hall was even made into an ice rink for a weekend of ice skating.

The search for original fund-raising ideas goes on and the PTFA also continues to play a direct supporting role to the school by providing refreshments at Sports Day and for evening events and meetings.

Mr Neeves was succeeded as head by Mr Derrick Allen in April 1971. He was very much a 'three R's' man and was also very keen on drama so there were more school productions and themed carol services. It was at this time that the school became very overcrowded as the number of pupils gradually increased to over 500. For one term Mrs Barbara Crispin's classroom was the library and the children did their

St Andrew's School, 1954.
Left to right, back: Malcolm Hutchings, Bob Walters, Phillip Whitton, Basil Potter, ?, Gwyneth Chapman, John Perryman, Chris MacDonald, ?, Graham Parsons, ?;
3rd row: ? Radford, David Owens, ?, Michael Knight, ?, ?, ?, Roger Hillman, ?, ?, Richard Miller, Paddy Lane;
2nd row: ?, ?, Susan Marks, Pam Jones, Julie Andrews, ?, ? Radford, ?, ?;
front: ? Aldridge, ?, Mary Hines, ?, Jane Reynolds, ?, ?, Howard Whitton, Clive Fowler.

PTFA Summer Fayre, c.1969. From left to right, middle: Marian Dummett, Mrs Whitton, Mrs Martinscroft, John Doyle (who opened the Fayre), Mr Neeves (head), Mrs Ford, Doreen Hilton, children from St Andrew's.

Above: *Pupils at Cullompton Station waiting to go to Plymouth on a school visit in 1952.*

Right: *St Andrew's Primary School Sports Day on Upcott Field, 1996. Note the old toilet block prior to demolition, and the entrance before improvements were carried out.*

Below: *St Andrew's School PTFA Christmas Fayre, c.1971. Left to right: Marian Dummett, V. Clarke, Joan Ellis, M. Stone, E. Hunnings, B. Clist, B. Budd, P. Broom, D. Glass, M. Broom, P. Tilley, I. Farmer; front: Hansel and Gretel, D. Tolley and E. Coxhead.*

St Andrew's School Staff, mid 1960s.
Left to right, back: Terry Rutter, Meryl Schouten, Mrs Neeves, Joan Bryant, Barbara Crispin; front: Jean Norman, Tony Dobson, Terry Kerslake, Martin Neeves, Joyce Scorse, Clifford Pike, Edna Bland.

St Andrew's School PTFA serve breakfast to holidaymakers passing through Cullompton on their way to South Devon and Cornwall, c.1968. Left to right: Muriel Coxhead, Dorothy Glass, Joan Ellis, ?, Marian Dummett, Mrs Webber, Mrs Farmer, Mrs Sheila Smith, Mrs Marion Skinner.

painting, etc. in the corridor. It was even suggested that she should take a class of infants in the Parish Rooms, but she finally used the school hall as a classroom for four terms – with 15 children on the stage and 15 on the hall floor.

During this time the plans were being drawn up for the new infants' school, although there were concerns from the very beginning as to whether it would be large enough.

Mr Brian Hooper replaced Mr Derrick Allen in 1981, staying at the school until 1993. Mr Gordon Guest then took on the role of acting head until Mr Bob Whitell was appointed in 1994.

In 1996 St Andrew's became a primary school again and celebrated its 60th birthday in style in 1997. A *Yearbook* was produced by Dawn Stevens and Alison Palmer, which provides a wonderful record of a year in the life of a busy school. A week full of events was organised, culminating in a party when more than 200 former teachers, staff and pupils enjoyed an evening of reminiscing, looking at the changes in the buildings, a buffet and anniversary cake.

St Andrew's pupils continue to enjoy the residential trips which have become the school's hallmark over the years. For many children, their first experience of being away from home and family was their Year 3 trip to Slapton Sands (glow-worms in the dark), or their stay at the Beaford Arts Centre in Year 4 (first attempts at throwing a pot). Those lucky enough to go to Paignton Zoo for a week in Year 4 have Ian Murray to thank – when one of Bradninch Primary School's teachers fell ill, he was chosen to accompany the trip. He thought the experience was so educationally worthwhile that he started it at St Andrew's, some time around 1982. For many years Ian Murray has also taken on the main responsibility for organising the Year 6 residential trips to Dartmoor and London.

St Andrew's Staff in the early 1970s.
Left to right, back: Ian Murray, ?, Rob Shipton, Judy Cunliffe, Stan Newberry, Linda King, Jack Gates, Terry Rutter, Jane Graham, Howard Lovell;
middle: Edna Bland, Jill Huber, Terry Kerslake (deputy head), Derrick Allen (head), Barbara Crispin (head of infants), Sheila Cummins (née Cotton), Joan Bryant;
front: Judith Bardsley, Ann Broven, Rachel Middlemiss, Jane Corkhill, Pat McClellan (parent-helper).

Class of 2000, St Andrew's Primary School.
Left to right, back: Luke Hayes, Emmy Goodall, Harrison Worley, Daniel Metcalf, Luke Burke, Bethany Davis;
middle: Ashley Ayres, Courtney Rees-Peters, Ryan Lee, Katie Somerton, Jake Somerwill, Ryan Mitchell, Sam Chilcott;
front: Oliver Greening, Joel Standford, Adam Meffe, Jack Greenall.

Willowbank Infants School Choir: Devon Schools Prom, 1989. The children sang 'Children of the World' and Mrs Crispin's composition 'The World is Big'. Left to right, back: Marc Jones, Michael Weedon, Rebecca Hobbs, Thomas Quick, Lloyd Gibb, Kelly Gillett, David Firkins, Bonnie Webber, Stuart Maynard; middle: Beth Elstone, Michelle Andrews, Tina Maunder, John Vigar, Katie Young, Davey Jones, Kathryn Holloway, Emma Marshall, Mrs Barbara Crispin; front: Jessica Hunter, Claire Maynard, Clare Pollard, Judy Chan, Haydn Murphy, Wendy Mogford, Helen Westlake, Katrina Gubb, Bonita Cross.

Barbara Crispin retired in 1993 after 40 years of teaching, 36 of these in Cullompton's St Andrew's and Willowbank Schools. In that time she was absent through illness for only two days – when she was sent home because she had shingles! To mark the end of her teaching career a 'Stirling Salute' was made by TV presenter Ian Stirling and this tribute to her was shown on the local evening news on ITV.

WILLOWBANK SCHOOL

With St Andrew's School becoming so crowded in the late 1970s, teachers, children and parents were eagerly awaiting the completion of the new infants school in Manitoba Gardens.

Willowbank County Infants School cost £262 000 to build and opened its doors in September 1980, but despite years of planning and preparation the first days were not without problems. Teachers arriving before the start of term found to their dismay that there weren't enough classrooms! The school was to accommodate 240 pupils and should have had eight units for 30 children each, but only seven were built, causing problems with space right from the start.

Then when the pupils turned up they found no chairs, even though they had been ordered more than a year earlier. The delivery van had left Norfolk at 8a.m. the previous day and Cullompton should have been its first drop but as the first school day was starting, the 270 children's chairs, 70 stools and 30 chairs for staff were said to be 'somewhere in Devon'. Two hours later the van arrived. The *Express and Echo* carried an article titled 'The Seat of the Trouble – School chairs hitch leaves 200 on the mat', showing a picture of pupils unwrapping the chairs. There were no cloakrooms, so nowhere for the children to hang their coats, and hooks were installed down each side of the main corridor at a conveniently reachable height for the children. Unfortunately this turned out also to be the average pupil's eye level. Until their removal in the early '90s, these remained a worry to every member of the Governing Body. Their removal was made possible when the central outside play area was covered over to provide a beautiful new library, allowing the original unit library areas to be made into cloakrooms.

Mrs Margaret Hulme was the first headteacher of this new school, and other members of staff, some of whom had transferred from St Andrew's, included Miss Joan Cudmore, Ann Broven, Barbara Crispin, Jane Graham, Bill Laws, Brenda Stone, Linda King, Terry Rutter and Alex Bellashenko.

The children were divided into age groups called the Ash, Beech and Chestnut Units. The school was of an open-plan design, common among junior schools being built at that time, but unusual for an infant school. Many parents who had experienced traditional schooling found this a difficult concept to accept and many reservations were expressed; how on earth could teachers and pupils work in rooms with no doors, centred around shared practical areas which were a constant hive of activity? Innovative though this was, the teachers were committed to this

Willowbank School in the 1980s before the leaking roof lights of the school hall were removed and the new junior block replaced the mobile huts. The wildlife garden was under construction when this photograph was taken.

style of teaching and with careful shared unit planning it seemed to produce good results. When the children progressed to St Andrew's Junior School many of them found it very strange to be taught in classrooms with doors!

By the 1990s, however, closed classrooms were again the order of the day and gradually, as the opportunities arose, each of the open areas was enclosed and given its own door.

When Mrs Hulme left Willowbank in 1984, Miss Joan Cudmore took on the role of acting head until Miss Sue Coles took up her first headteacher post in January 1985. Although aware that Cullompton was a growing town, she had no idea just how much the school would change in the years to follow. Children at the school at this time will remember the Easter bonnet parades, the treacherous bank of nettles next to the playground, lessons by the pond in the wildlife garden, and trips to Ashclyst Forest, Sandy Bay and Watermouth Castle. Another highlight was when in 1985 Barbara Crispin's choir was asked to join 18 other schools to perform in the Devon Schools Prom in The Great Hall at Exeter University. They excelled, and, being the only infants out of the 530 musicians, received tremendous applause. The School Choir participated in six Proms over the next eight years.

In 1987 additional space was needed to accommodate children from the new housing estate at Headweir Road. The children were horrified when the gates were cut down to allow the crane to bring in the two new mobile classrooms. By 1989 the school roll had grown from 180 pupils to 270.

In the early '90s it was suggested that St Andrew's Junior School and Willowbank Infant School should reorganise into two primary schools. Change is not always well received but there were plenty of opportunities to discuss the proposals and after careful consideration of the implications, the Secretary of State approved the change of status in 1992 with effect from 1994. However, financial constraints at county level delayed the implementation until September 1996.

Between 1995 and 1997 additional buildings to accommodate the rising numbers of children were completed on both sites. At Willowbank the mobile classrooms were moved to the other side of the grounds so that a new four-class block for the junior children could be added. At St Andrew's School, the 'beloved' old toilet block was demolished; a gallery of spectators stood and watched as, within the space of a few minutes, the 'bête noire' was laid to rest! It made way for the magnificent new Early Years Unit, library and IT area. Since then, some of the very old mobile classrooms (huts!) have been removed – they were so rotten they were literally falling down.

Cullompton's schools continue to work hard to meet the particularly challenging requirements of the modern education system. There have been countless changes brought about by each new government in the constant drive for improvement. Each school has a governing body, which is responsible for ensuring the school provides a good quality education. It must include parents elected by other parents of children at the school, teachers elected by their colleagues and usually the headteacher. Other members include representatives of local councils, the church and business interests. All school governors give their time voluntarily.

The Governing Body's responsibilities increased considerably during the late 1980s and into the '90s. It is accountable for the performance of the school and makes decisions on the school's budget and staffing, ensuring that the National Curriculum is taught and that the school provides for all its pupils, including those with special educational needs. It also decides how the school can encourage pupils' spiritual, moral and cultural development. It sets the school aims and policies together with the head. The head is responsible for the day-to-day management but he or she is chosen by the Governors and must work closely with them. Schools now make decisions on how to spend their budgets.

The National Curriculum provides the framework of what is to be taught. Weekly planning based on termly schemes of work ensures that the curriculum is covered. Some educationalists regret the rigidity of modern education methods and feel that there is now less opportunity for teachers to cover related aspects of interest in detail, unless they are included in the schemes of work.

The recent introduction of the 'literacy hour' and 'numeracy hour' over the last two years has meant that there is even more to be accommodated in the school day. On the whole though, the move has been welcomed by most teachers and parents as a much-needed focus on grammar, spelling, knowledge of arithmetic tables and so on. Some feel this is a return to the 'three R's' approach; the methods may be different, but improved results are already evident. Monitoring and recording of pupils' progress is more regular and detailed. The introduction of Standard Assessment Tests (SATs) for children at ages 7, 10 and 14 provides the basis for the controversial 'league tables' showing each school's level of achievement in the core subjects of English, mathematics and science.

The headteacher's role has changed considerably – having trained as teachers they are now more office-based. They act as an accountant, personnel officer and administrator. Because of this changing role, there are some class teachers who feel they would never wish to pursue promotion to the position of headteacher or deputy head as it would inevitably mean little or no time in the classroom. Many can foresee the time when a trained school manager will take on these duties.

By the year 2001, there were 320 pupils on the roll at Willowbank and 280 at St Andrew's.

Our Lady of Dolours Convent School

The aim of the Sisters in their teaching was to educate in the true sense, respecting their pupils' religious tenets but teaching them reverence to God, for their parents and for authority. The Sisters came to Cullompton at the request of Revd A.M. Bouchier, MC. They bought the residence of Dr Gustavus Gidley (Heyford House) for the purpose of establishing the school. It prospered from the beginning and throughout the 1930s. The feelings between the Sisters and the townsfolk were described as 'most cordial and delightful'.

An increase in the numbers of scholars and staff necessitated the 'taking' of The Walronds belonging to A. Burrow Esq., solicitor. It 'came into the Sisters' hands through the courtesy of this gentleman who has been kindness itself.' By all accounts, the school taught a 'wide and varied' curriculum. The school closed towards the end of the Second World War.

Gurdlestone School

In the mid 1930s Miss Gaynor Roberts and Miss Winstone ran Gurdlestone School. It moved around the town to a variety of buildings, rarely staying on one site for more than a term or two. At one time it was housed at Church Street, at the Glen on Willand Road, in Sellwood House and at The Barons in Queen's Square. It was then taken over by Mrs Lucy Hill and transferred to St George's House.

Glanherne School

William Hill, husband of Lucy, bought Victoria Hall in Tiverton Road in 1938. Their daughter Barbara set up Glanherne School there. The school was for boys and girls and they were taught in the main hall which was divided in two by a curtain. The infants were in a small adjoining room.

Sports days were held at the Cricket Club with the usual running, jumping, egg-and-spoon race, slow-bicycle race, etc. The rooms were very cramped and the pupils and staff were delighted when the school transferred to Heyford House in 1946 or 1947. Miss Hill married a Mr Brocklehurst and the school continued under a new headmistress called Miss Ewart. The establishment closed in the early 1960s and for a time the property became Dr Hammond's surgery.

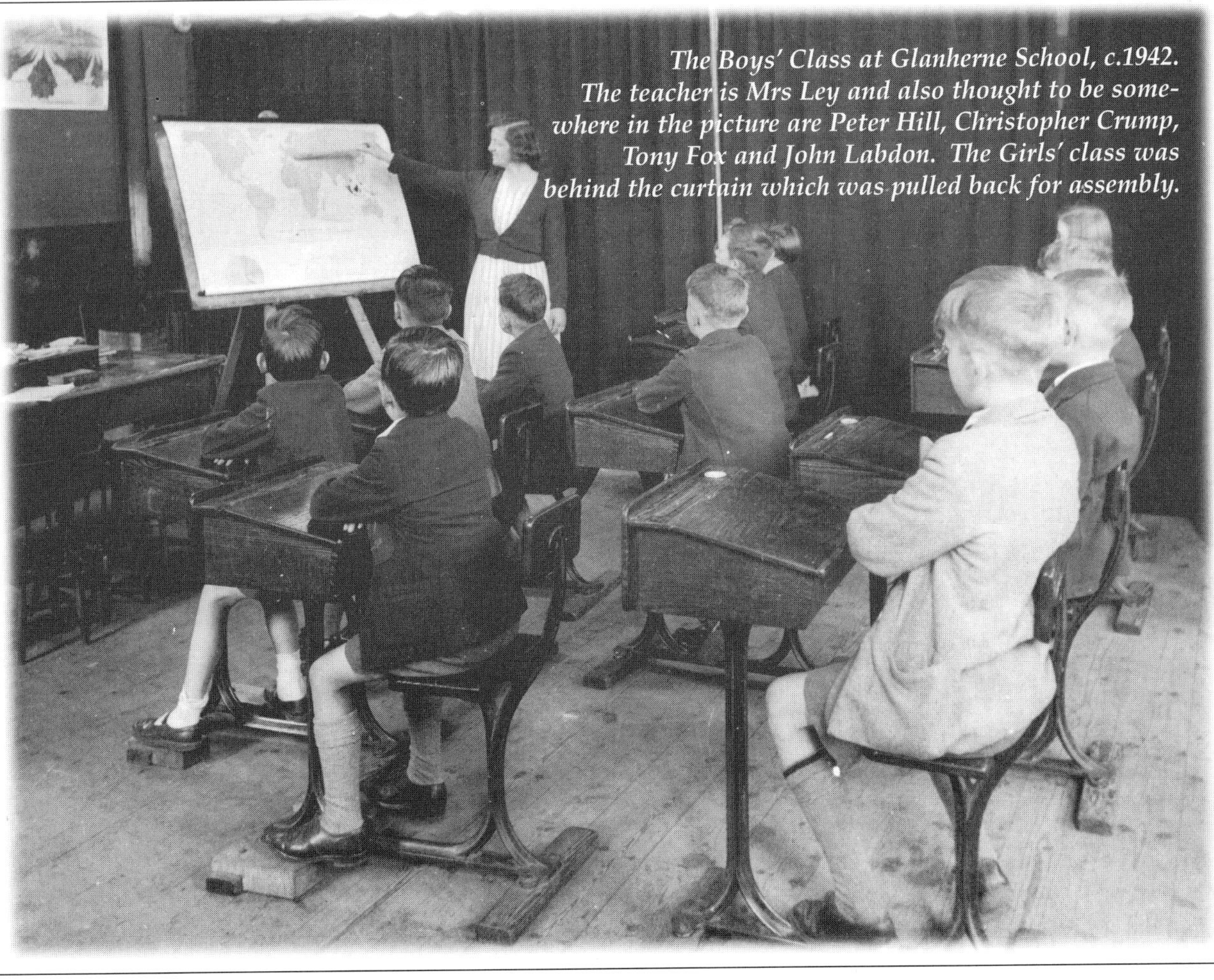

The Boys' Class at Glanherne School, c.1942. The teacher is Mrs Ley and also thought to be somewhere in the picture are Peter Hill, Christopher Crump, Tony Fox and John Labdon. The Girls' class was behind the curtain which was pulled back for assembly.

Glanherne School when it was situated at Heyford House, c.1958.
On the left are Miss Stella Bowles and Miss Davies and on the right are Miss Scales, Mrs Ley and Miss Ewart. The other teachers' names are not known.

The gymnasium and theatre at Our Lady of Dolours Convent School.

Cullompton Pre-School

by Sue Henderson (past Chairman and administrator)

Cullompton Pre-school was established in 1971 by a group of parents who wanted their children to meet and have fun together. The group was originally known as Cullompton Playgroup and met in several places before ending up at its present location. The first meeting place was the Town Hall (then known as the Parish Rooms). The next location was Community House, on the corner of High Street and Church Street, where activities were organised by parents on a roster basis. With the building of new houses and the influx of young families wanting more playgroup places, it soon became apparent that bigger premises were needed. The group had grown so large that it required its own building.

Sarah Duffin, one of the founder members of the group, heard that a school in Exmouth had a large wooden hut surplus to requirements. The hut, appropriately named 'Devon Lady', had a hall with space for storage, two toilets, and more importantly, a large, airy room with windows along each side. What was needed was a suitable location and this was provided by Cullompton Community College (then known as Cullompton School). The school and Devon County Council allowed the playgroup to site the building on a corner of land, over the bridge, next to Brook Road. In 1982 they moved to the Baptist Church to make use of their larger facilities, while the foundations and necessary pipes and cables were laid on the new site.

Fire Service (Welliphant) visits Cullompton Pre-school, 1987.

The playgroup held various events to raise the necessary funds. A charitable trust, which included Sarah Duffin, Mr Keith Turner (head of Cullompton Community College) and parents, was formed. This allowed the playgroup to apply for grants and a bank loan to locate and equip the building. Fencing was erected around the perimeter to ensure a safe outdoor play area for the children and a large five-barred gate hung at the entrance to the site. The fact that one had to cross the bridge over the brook and enter this gate, gave rise to the playgroup also being known locally as Brookgate Playgroup – which has confused many a postman and parent!

At first the playgroup operated on a part-time basis, offering sessions on particular days of the week. However, with more and more children wanting to attend, over the years the sessions have been extended to include mornings and afternoons on Monday to Friday during term time. The building itself has not changed, apart from having a new floor and necessary maintenance. The outside play area has changed in that the boundaries have been moved.

The front boundary fence was moved back towards the building to allow vehicular access for the construction of the all-weather pitch at the Community College and the widening and deepening of the brook. This latter work was carried out after Cullompton saw an unusual sight in August 1997, with the flooding of many parts of the town when the Pre-school sat, as if on an island, completely surrounded by water. Luckily, because the building is raised off the ground, damage was minimal.

The rear boundary fence was also moved. This allowed for a larger play area to the back of the building and was an ideal spot for the swings, climbing frames and slides.

Although there have not been many changes to the structure of the building, what goes on inside has changed in many ways. The original concept of the Pre-school was to provide an opportunity for children to meet, play together and do things which they might not have the opportunity to do at home. The children were supervised by parents and then, later, some paid staff with parents acting as helpers. Now the Pre-school has a team of specialist trained and experienced staff who provide a specially tailored curriculum to meet the individual needs of each child. Previously the Pre-school was allowed to have 26 children at each session. However, with the introduction of the Children's Act of 1989 and the rules regarding a minimum amount of space per child, this was reduced to 20. Under the terms of this Act the Pre-school is inspected annually by Devon County Council Social Services to ensure that high standards of the staff, premises, equipment and the environment are properly maintained.

With the introduction of Nursery Vouchers or 'free' places, the Pre-school is inspected by the Office for Standards in Education (OFSTED) as part of the continuing programme of inspection. The curriculum and quality of education is assessed to make sure that children attain a desirable level of learning before they reach school age. The 'free' places, funded by the Government via the County Council, have changed the system of funding of places and put the Pre-school on a more sound financial footing.

Cullompton Pre-school, 1994; 'We all took guy to the bonfire'.

The Pre-school is, and has been for many years, a member of the Pre-schools Learning Alliance (PLA), a national organisation that offers practical advice, up-to-date information and training in the field of child education and care. The Pre-school has also gained PLA Accreditation, which is a nationally recognised standard of quality assurance for early-years provision.

Although rules and regulations have been introduced to many of the Pre-school's activities since it started, there are some things that have not changed. The Pre-school is still run by an elected committee of parents which ensures that major decision-making is placed in their hands. The Pre-school is still very much a community group, having regular contacts with local schools and visits to and from organisations such as the Fire Brigade, Police, etc.

One thing that has not changed over the years is the meeting of children to have fun together. The aim of the Pre-school continues to be the provision of a safe, secure and stimulating environment where children can learn through play.

There were many people involved in the establishment of Cullompton Pre-school and, over the 30 years since it started, there have been many more who have given of their time and efforts to help make the group the success it is today. Unfortunately there are too many names to mention and there is the danger of causing offence by omitting someone. Suffice to say that as long as parents want their children to have a pre-school education and are willing to contribute their time and energy towards this goal, Cullompton Pre-school will go from strength to strength.

Culm Vale Playgroup

by Linda Holloway

Culm Vale Playgroup was started in about 1965 by Elizabeth Cummings at East Culm. An old barn was used, which was converted into a large playroom with an outside play area which was separated from the business premises. Jane Dunning, Elizabeth Cummings and Joan Ellis were three of the original play leaders. There were approximately 20 children in attendance every day and in 1977 the playgroup transferred to a temporary building next to Hayne Barton Farm, which was owned at that time by Liz and Andy Cole. They were founder members of the playgroup on this new site, along with George and Veronica Mills.

The playgroup was formed to develop social behaviour between the children and to enable them to enjoy the company of others the same age. The committee raised money to buy indoor and outdoor equipment by holding the usual jumble sales, coffee mornings and so on. Supervisors of the sessions in the early days included Jane Dunning and Sue Clements.

Hayne Barton Farm is on the Bradfield Road and as not many families had more than one car there would have been transport problems for many mums. One of the attractions of attending the Culm Vale Playgroup was that a minibus would pick up the children from the Bullring and bring them back at the end of the morning. Leaving mum behind and stepping onto the minibus was a major step along the road to independence; this was a very exciting experience for the three- and four-year-olds. When the bus was late because of cows blocking the lane, this just added to the excitement. At calving time there was always a stable door to peep over to see the newborn, and the children soon learnt to keep all the gates between the fields and the play area closed.

In the early '90s the number of children dropped as more playgroups were established in the villages and in Cullompton itself. In that decade the Government introduced legislation which required an increase in the level of formally-trained staff and made the playgroups more accountable. They were also subject to inspection much like schools. The playgroup adjusted to take on board this new framework, but reduction in demand continued until it was no longer viable to keep the group open. Culm Vale Playgroup closed in December 1997.

Promoting Culm Vale Playgroup outside the Baptist Church, 1985. Supervisors and helpers: Jane Dunning, Kay Gordon and Sandy Maidment.

NOAH'S ARK PLAYGROUP

by Wendy Land

The aim of Noah's Ark Playgroup has always been to give each child a wide range of educational and social experiences, without discrimination. The playgroup is based in the schoolrooms at the Cullompton Baptist Church and is supported by the church, both by volunteers and committee members. Although it is based at the Baptist Church, the group welcomes children of all cultures, backgrounds and religions.

Nikki Phillips has been involved with the group since it was formed in 1991, firstly as a committee member, then parent helper, play assistant and finally as playleader until 1999. She remembers that initially there were six children who attended the three morning sessions a week. Now, a decade later, the playgroup opens for seven sessions in total and has more than 40 children registered.

One of the play assistants has these memories of the group:

In previous years Noah's Ark Playgroup was as lively a group as it is today. The minister and his wife, who wished to do something for the community, originally set it up. Nikki Phillips, Liz Alvis, Jane Ellis and myself – Maureen Pendle – thoroughly enjoyed the start of such a strong team. I still bring one of my four children here. I am pleased to see it is still as successful today as it was then.

The playgroup currently employs nine staff and is fortunate enough to have two very skilled playleaders and excellent support staff. Deborah House, one of the playleaders, notes:

As today's current playleader I am constantly overjoyed by the wonderful sense of community which is generated by Noah's Ark Playgroup. I love to see the happy faces of our little children when I walk through Cullompton. It is such a pleasure to see the progress of such an enthusiastic group of individuals. We are blessed with a lively and intelligent staff that truly love the work that they do. One could not ask for better.

Noah's Ark Playgroup currently opens three mornings and three afternoons a week. There is also the Rainbow Mother and Toddler Group for children from birth to five years, open Monday afternoons during term time.

Noah's Ark Playgroup, end of term, July 1993.
Left to right, back: Nikki Phillips, Liz Alvis (holding John Carpenter), Sharon ?;
middle: James Fox, Matthew Gleeson, Lydia Pavia, Hayley Hawkins, Annabelle Ellis;
front: John Pavia, Becky Ellis, Simon Hawkins, Marc Bastow, Victoria Finlayson, Ellie ?, Oliver Taylor, Michael ?, Russell Phillips, Samantha Finlayson.

Girl Guides

Below: *The 1st Cullompton Rainbow Unit which opened 22 April 1999. This picture is of the first promise ceremony in May 1999. It was the first such unit in the Cullompton and Culm Valley area.*

Above: *Knightshayes Girl Guide Camp, 1940. Left to right, back: Phyllis Wyatt, Margaret Broom, Betty Radford (Captain), Thora Hellier (Lieutenant), Margery Heard, Muriel Terry; seated: Joyce Heard, Pat Tancock, Angela Glass, Eileen Kerslake, ?, Edna Mitchell, Veronica Miller, Pat Dyer, ?, ?, Peggy Hooper.*

Right: *'Thinking Day', 1970. Left to right, back: Karen Greening, Jill Cowley, Linda Clarke, Gillian Heard, Christine Clarke, Wendy Walker, Susan Hilton, ?, Linda Manfield, Penny Staddon, ?, Jane Heard, Carolyn Hodge, Lesley Kemp, ?, Mandy Burnette, Linda Discombe, Tryphena Gillard; 3rd row: Amanda Ellis, Katherine Frost, Shirley Harris, Dawn Ellis, Marion Hilton, Sharon Rew, Anna Wall; 2nd row: ?, Stella Broom, Hayley Tankard, Ann Manfield, Trudy Radford, Julie Westcott, Burnette twins, Christine and Lesley Brooks, Gill Gibbs, Nicky Maddocks, Caroline Evans; front: Janet Board, Heather Foster, Jill Stanley, Helen McDoulle, Anthea ?, Elizabeth Coxhead, Susan Perry.*

Left: *'Thinking Day', 1970.*

Opposite page: *Cullompton Guides, c.1946. Left to right, back: Margaret Heard, Edith Partridge, ?, Marion Force, Margery Gillard, ?, Margaret Manley; middle: Sheila Heard (holding flag), Margaret Broom (Captain), Marion Ford (Brownie Leader), Brenda Rainey, Valerie North, Doreen Govier, Mary Stone, Jennifer Reynolds, ?, ?, Margery Heard (Lieutenant), Theresa Marks; front: Dr Audrey Baker (founder Ranger Captain), ?, ?, Lorna Baker (Divisional Commissioner, Founder Captain), Lady Amory, Thelma Lowry (District Commissioner), Mrs Ford, Mrs Chas Carew, Mrs Muriel Whitton.*

1ST CULLOMPTON GUIDES AND BROWNIES

by Joyce Owens

'I promise on my honour that I will do my best; to do my duty to God and the Queen; to help other people at all times; and to obey the Guide law.'

This promise is made by every Girl Guide and Brownie at their enrolment ceremony and would have been made at the first gathering of Guides which was held on the Vicarage lawn on 18 September 1920 by invitation from Mrs Chas Carew. The 1st Cullompton Guide Company was formed by Miss Lorna Baker with her sister Dr Audrey Baker who was the Founder Ranger Guider. The meetings were held weekly, at first in Shortlands House and later in the Guide Hut, which was erected in Station Road on land owned by the Labdon family. The hut was officially opened by Mrs Carew in 1928.

During the Second World War the hut was taken over by the Army who used it as a billet for soldiers. Meetings were then held in the stable block at Court House. After a short break in 1964/5 the Guide Company was re-opened in 1966 and has continued ever since. To mark the 40th anniversary Miss Baker presented the 'New Queen's Colours' at a service of dedication in St Andrew's Church on 18 September 1960. At a later date it was decided to 'lay up' the original colours in the church for safe-keeping.

In 1967 Lady Baden-Powell, the World Chief Guide, visited a Girl Guide rally in Torquay and five Guides and one leader from Cullompton were privileged to meet her. When the Queen and Prince Philip came to Exeter in 1976, a party of Guides and Brownies from the Culm Valley were able to see them on their visit to County Hall.

Many girls in Cullompton have been members of the Guide movement and it is hoped that they have many happy memories of friendships and fun. The following poem was written by a former Assistant Girl Guide, Ann Board, after a visit with the Culm Valley Ranger Guides to Bowerman, a house on Dartmoor which is owned by the Devon Girl Guides. It sums up the true meaning of being a member of the 'Guide Family':

We journeyed from our valley
For a weekend on the moors.
We arrived at Bowerman safely
And settled to our chores.

We walked to Widdecombe on Saturday,
Had lunch on the village green,
Collected items for a collage
And discussed what we had seen.

We passed the medieval village,
And Jay's grave on the way,
Arrived back tired and weary
After a very enjoyable day.

It's nice to have this cottage,
Where one and all can come
To do some work for Guiding,
But also have some fun...

Boy Scouts

Below: *Cullompton Scout Troop, c.1910. Left to right, back: ? Tracey, Leslie Peters, Percy Labdon, Fred Martin, Claude Dunn, Lawrence Sansom, Alec Hillier, C. Nex; middle: B. Labdon, Arthur Jones, Frank Glanville, Wilfred James, Herbert Alleyne, Ray Baker, Harold Butt; front: Arthur Mitchell, Jamie Foster, Claude Church, Arthur Vodden, Sid Dymond, Harold West, Harold Dyer; on ground: Reg Frost, Frank Sweet.*

Above: *Opening of the new Scout Hut in Tiverton Road by Viscount Lord Amory in 1966. Revd Vodden, founder of the Cullompton Scouts, in the foreground.*

Left: *Groups gather to mark 75 years of scouting in Cullompton, November 1982.*

Opposite page: *Cubs leaving the Higher Bullring for a trip to Gilwell, Scout Headquarters, 1966.*

Cullompton Scouts

by Dawn Stevens

In 1907 the scouting movement in Britain began with Baden Powell as its leader. In Cullompton a few years later the 1st Cullompton Scout Troop was formed with Mr Vodden as Scoutmaster. Later in 1915 a second troop was formed under the leadership of Mr L. Salter.

Can you remember bob-a-job week? Each Cub and Scout was expected to raise money doing odd jobs. The money was sent to main headquarters for national funds. In 1959 each boy was expected to raise a minimum of one shilling.

In 1951 new Scout headquarters were built at the end of New Street, formerly an orchard. The hut came from Silverton and the troop had to raise £200 to cover the costs of moving and erecting the building. The site was purchased for £80 and placed in a town trust. Many local companies helped the troop out including Labdon & Sons, Mr Radford and Theodore Lawrence. Scoutmaster Mr Mears and assistant Mr Staddon could be seen most nights creosoting, painting, etc. A flag and flagpole for the new headquarters were given by Mr Bob Hooper and the new hut was opened by the County Commissioner Lt General Sir Edmond Schreiber on 15 September 1951.

In 1953 in a newspaper article an urgent appeal was put out for a scoutmaster to take over the Cullompton troop – nothing much changes!

On 3 March 1954 over 100 Scouts, Guides, Cubs and Brownies joined together for an 'Open Night' in the Parish Rooms. Demonstrations were given to the parents and the evening ended with a camp fire.

In 1965 three Scouts were awarded the Queen's Scout Honour: Chas Reed, Graham Foan and Michael Phillips.

In 1968 the Scout troop, and by then a Wolf Cub pack, moved to the present hut located in Tiverton Road as the troop had outgrown the one in New Street. With Mr Les Burrows as Group Scout Leader and Mrs Marian Dummett as Chairman of the Committee, fund-raising started in earnest and on Sunday 27 April 1969, in the diamond jubilee year, the Rt Hon. Viscount Amory officially opened the new headquarters. The hut had previously belonged to the Young Conservative Club and previous to that had been part of the local electricity company.

In 1973 the Cub Scouts in Cullompton, under the leadership of Mr Tony Goffey, celebrated their silver jubilee.

November 1982 saw the Cubs and Scouts joining together to celebrate 75 years of scouting; the current Scout hut was decked out with rope bridges and many activities depicting the Scouting movement.

In 1988 three Scouts were awarded the Chief Scouts Award: Steven Manning, Sam Thomas and Andrew Temple. In March 1992 Andrew Bowers also earned this award.

And what of the year 2001? Scouts and Cubs continue to thrive in Cullompton. The headquarters are still in Tiverton Road, although the time has now come when we may need to look for alternative accommodation. We are still in the situation of being on the lookout for leaders. The boys are still enjoying activities that first began back in 1907: camping, friendship, values and outdoor activities.

In looking back briefly on the history of the group many names have been mentioned, among them leaders, assistants, parent supporters, Group Scout Leaders, etc. There were just too many to name, but it is through all their hard work, time and support of the troop that the work with the boys continues today. To all of them we are extremely grateful.

The Girls' Friendly Society Choir, 1949.
Left to right, back: Patsy Dimond, Jean Shoosmith, Margaret Steer, Mrs Downward, Jean Atkins, Betty Manfield, Cynthia Copp, Barbara May, ?, Jean Manfield, Mavis Baker, Ann Talbot; front: Marian Brooks, Cicely Gooe, June Grandfield, Sheila Ford, Janet Phillips, Janet Spurway, Margaret Mitchell, Mrs Tinley, ?.

Girls' Friendly Society

by Mrs Jean Manfield

The Girls' Friendly Society was run by the vicar's wife, Mrs Downward. They met once a week in the St Andrew's Church Rooms for the usual club activities. One year a group went to the Isle of Wight for a week, staying in a Church Hostel situated on cliffs between Shanklin and Sandown.

In 1949 a choir was formed and they took part in a competition in Newton Abbot. The following year, after winning this competition, they went to sing at the Royal Albert Hall in celebration of 75 years of the GFS. Here they were joined by choirs from all over the UK and represented the South-West. While they sang songs such as 'London Street Cries' and 'Linden Tree', other groups performed a pageant. This all took place before the Queen in the afternoon and in the evening the Princess Royal was present. Although they all enjoyed this weekend the accommodation was not too comfortable. They slept in bunks in the tunnels below the underground railway and could hear the trains running overhead. There were soldiers on guard at the end of each tunnel!

The John Tallack Centre

When the Cullompton Community Association owned what is now known as Community House, George Mills, Elizabeth Bullivant and others started a Youth Club. This was very popular with the young people but it was clear that an upstairs room in the centre of town was an inadequate base for such a venture. In the early 1980s George Mills and his wife Veronica were inspired to try to create a purpose-built facility for the Youth Club which would also cater for the disabled. There was no other similar facility in the town and it took many years of hard work and persuasion on the part of a small group to bring the idea to fruition.

They were supported in the venture by a few local businessmen and George persuaded various local people to guarantee a small sum of money each to enable the project to go ahead. Eventually work started on the building in 1987 with the help of various grants. To save money it was decided to use a timber-frame construction but before the building was clad it was blown over during a terrible storm in March 1987. Undeterred, George continued with the project, named after a local and widely-respected doctor, which eventually opened in January 1988.

Since then the building has been used for a variety of functions. First and foremost it is the base for numerous youth activities organised by the local Youth Worker who is employed by Devon County Council. For over 20 years this was Paul Hague who was a devoted supporter of the Centre. Disabled groups used the Centre for meetings and it is rented out to various organisations and families for parties, etc. The present Youth Worker, Lisa Rutter, is keen to expand the use of the Centre to a drop-in for young people where they will be able to obtain advice on many relevant topics such as health, jobs, etc. Grants have been obtained from the District Council and further funds are being sought. The Management Committee is working towards a better future for the centre and the young people it serves.

Childhood Memories, 1930s

by Marian Dummett

I was born at Growen... and was always known as a country child. At five I started to attend school where the Magistrates Court now is. Our teacher was Miss Gunn and her class contained a huge rocking horse. We were taught to write on slates using a pencil also made of slate. Living in the country one had to take a packed lunch as school dinners did not start until later. My mother was delighted when this happened as we were able to have something hot to eat at midday. The dinners cost 1d. and we were given a third pint of milk free. At five I had to walk two miles to school in all weathers.

The toilets were at the top of the playground and on fine days one of the older girls, Betty Wright, would get us smaller children to sit by the wall and she would sing and entertain us during the dinner time – she sang 'Old John Bradlam'.

We had visits from the school doctor and the 'bug nurse' and I can remember having lots of colds and coughs. Mother used to rub my chest with camphorated oil and give me cod liver oil and malt to eat and syrup of figs on Friday. Oh, and chilblains – goose grease was the remedy for them.

At playtimes, mothers of the children who lived in town would bring cocoa and something to eat to the school railings. Sometimes Mr Vigar, whose shop was at the bottom of New Street, would bring a tray of buns, but they were only for the rich children...

In 1937 we transferred to St Andrew's School. This was brand new and we thought it was wonderful. Mr Robert Ashford was the headmaster and he rode a bike to school each day. We were allowed to go home early in bad weather so that we would be home by nightfall. There were only the lights of two or three houses between school and home for us; and the cemetery, which could be frightening, or fields and a muddy lane with water running through the middle. I think I enjoyed school. I remember Mr Ashford's teeth fell out once when he was teaching us Cherry Ripe – Francis Perry picked them up!

At home I saw very little of my father during the week. He was a thatcher and would have left for work by the time I got up and I would be in bed again when he came home. He would cycle to work wherever there was thatching to be done. [Our] food was plain and mostly home-grown. Father grew all our potatoes and vegetables and we used to pick watercress from the streams and mushrooms from the fields for special treats. We never had bought cake or anything tinned. Mother made all our cake and puddings and bottled all the fruit and made jam with the fruit from the garden; gooseberries, plums, blackcurrants – this for when we had colds and coughs. One of the daily jobs for the children was to fetch the milk from the farmer in a can and on Saturday fetch Father's jar of cider also from the farm.

From a very early age, our Sundays consisted of church and Sunday School, three times a day. We walked into church from Growen, leaving our muddy shoes at the end of the lane and changing into our best shoes. In Sunday School we were expected to learn a text from the Bible each week, for this we received a little paper text with flowers printed on it. During school time and on Sundays, there was very little time for leisure, but school holidays were different. We had four weeks a year in the summer and this is when the happy memories begin.

Many of the children in Cullompton would spend the time rabbiting in cornfields. Everyone had a stick with a knob on the end, with which to kill the rabbits as we chased them out of the corn. If the farmer in whose field you were gave you a rabbit to take home, that was a couple of days' dinner. In fact, in the summer time we lived on rabbit stew, rabbit pie and roast rabbit. We were not allowed in the hay field as Mother said that one of the farm men would make 'sweet hay' with the little girls. I have yet to find out what that entailed!

As we became older we were given little jobs on Saturdays; picking sticks was one. There was no electricity or gas in the country and all the cooking and hot water had to come from the coal range which had to be lit every day before we could have a cup of tea or hot water to wash. We broke up sticks for kindling and in the holidays went out to the woods, usually Hillersdon, with an old pram to pick up bigger sticks or chips of wood if any trees had been cut down.

Our toilet at that time was a bucket in the lavatory round the back of the house. The contents would be buried in the garden when necessary. Another job for children was to tear up newspaper, the *Daily Herald*, into little squares and thread them onto string for toilet paper! Baths were in the shed in the summer and by the living room fire on a Saturday night in the winter. We had to get the water from the well in the field next to the house and later from a pump at the back of the house – this pump would freeze in winter and then straw was burnt around it so that it could be defrosted. Once a week, mother would take me to town to do her shopping or pay for her meat and bread which had been delivered. My only treat was a 99 ice-cream from Mr Brown's and this cost 3d. When we went out shopping with mother, we were 'got ready' with our best clothes. We only had school clothes (not uniform), play clothes and 'best'. Most of my clothes were made by my mother.

Our later primary education was very strict and repetitive. We were taught our tables backwards and forwards along with multiplication and division. Sums had to be done until one could get six right at one time. We had scripture exams given by an examiner and had to stand up in class to read. I cannot remember PE, but then when one has had to walk over a mile to school that was all the exercise one needed.

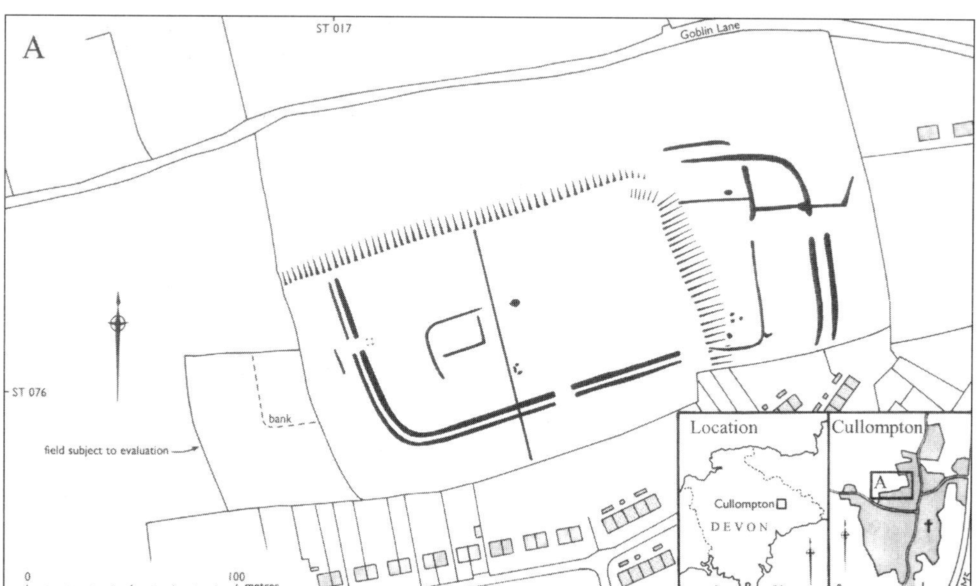

Above: *Aerial reconnaissance showing the outline of the fort on St Andrew's Hill.*

Left: *Site location and plot of cropmark features recorded in 1984 and 1989.*

Chapter Two

LAND & BUILDINGS

THE ROMAN FORT

From Simpson, S., and Griffith, F., Trial Excavations at the Roman Fort on St Andrew's Hill, Cullompton, 1993

The Roman Fort complex is situated on St Andrew's Hill immediately to the north-west of Cullompton. It was first recognised during aerial reconnaissance by Francis Griffith for Devon County Council during the summer of 1984. The whole site was scheduled as an Ancient Monument in 1986 and includes two Roman camps and two Roman forts. The former lie to the eastern side of the monument and are defined by double defensive ditches; one camp appears to overlie and thus post-date the other. Over the western side, a fort was constructed which is defined on its southern and western sides by double defensive ditches, each containing an entrance.

The northern and eastern sides appear to coincide with a second fort and partly underlie the northern and eastern defences. There are two lengths of ditch outside the west gate of the first fort, thought to represent a titulum and perhaps the site of a six-post gate-way. The second fort overlies the first and is also larger. To the north and east low banks indicate the ramparts but to the west and south they have been integrated in the existing field pattern and are still 1.5 metres high.

A partial excavation in 1992 revealed the extent of the outer ditch on the western side of the fort and indicated that it had been completely backfilled before post-medieval times. Finds from excavation and field walking have revealed pottery assemblages which confirm a date of AD50–70, although the exact abandonment date of the fort remains unclear.

Roman forts are rare nationally, particularly south of the Severn Trent line. As one of a small group of Roman military monuments, which are important in representing army strategy and therefore government policy, forts are of particular significance to our understanding of the period. The two forts at Cullompton have survived comparatively well. A great deal more information still remains conserved within the contexts of the forts and camps relating to construction and use of different structures, as well as evidence relating to the local environment.

LANDS: OLD HILL & THE UPCOTT FIELD

Prior to the motorway, among the most well-known landmarks in Cullompton were the five Scots Pines on Old Hill, which stood as a sign to drovers of livestock that the farmer on whose land they were would give them a night's lodgings and feed for their animals. These trees, with the exception of one, died when the earth was removed to build the motorway. However, in the year 2000 members of the Town Council planted five more similar trees for future Cullomptonians to enjoy.

The Upcott Field is situated in Tiverton Road adjacent to St Andrew's Primary School. It was given to the inhabitants of the town by Sir Frederick Upcott and his family in 1914. An official opening ceremony took place on 23 July 1914 after the service for the Laying of the Colour in St Andrew's Church. Following the service, the Territorials, preceded by their band and followed by a large number of the town's inhabitants, marched to the field.

Mr F. Sellwood presided over a large assembly at the ceremony and Colonel Acland Troyte declared the field open. Unfortunately it rained heavily on the day but many people still stayed on to enjoy the tea which was served on the field and in the Victoria Hall. Later in the evening, when the rain stopped, sports were held for the children and members of the Parish Council distinguished themselves in a friendly tug-of-war competition. The Territorial Band played during the afternoon and the Town Band in the evening.

BUILDINGS OF NOTE

There are two Grade I listed buildings in Cullompton: St Andrew's Church and The Walronds on Fore Street. Sited next door to The Walronds is the Manor House Hotel, a Grade II* timber-framed listed building which dates from 1603. There are seven Grade II* listed buildings and 90 Grade II listed buildings within the parish. The medieval street pattern in the centre has remained virtually intact although the 'great fire' of 1839 destroyed many houses of note on the west side of the town.

The Old Police Station

The 'Sessions House', better known locally as the Old Police Station, was transformed about 1846–50 by public subscription into a Town Hall at a cost of £400 and included a lock-up. It was used for concerts, lectures, etc. and as a Police court. The clock was an after-thought, and was placed there some time after the building was converted.

After a while the police business grew and Quarter Sessions notified the owners that they must have full control of the building, or remove the sessions elsewhere. The town sold the building to the county in 1870, using the money to purchase some old premises a few doors away; these were part of the Half Moon where judges stopped in coaching days on their way to the Assizes.

The clock was not sold but allowed to remain as the overseers had no place to put it. To celebrate Queen Victoria's Golden Jubilee in 1887 a public dinner was held in Higher Bullring and it was suggested that the old clock be restored to working order for the occasion. Police Superintendent R.G. Collins gave permission for the work to be undertaken. About a bucketful of old cob and decayed woodwork was removed and after cleaning and oiling it worked, to the great delight of everyone, and struck the hours throughout that Jubilee day.

When the building was altered in 1898 and a new front built, no provision was made for the clock. The designers did not want it put back, although they were eventually persuaded to alter their plans to make room for it. Before the alterations, the inside dial could be seen in the Court Room, but the large centre window would not allow the clock to be placed anywhere but in the gable under the roof.

There is an inscription around the clock face of 1898 and it is possible that the original was at that time replaced with a new clock. In a book of *Devon Clocks and Clockmakers* by C. Ponsford, the maker is said to be John Henry Baker of Cullompton (1889–1902). Bakers are understood to have taken over Mayne's watchmakers business when their shop was located in Fore Street, Cullompton, next to the White Hart.

Land on the north side was purchased from Mr Alfred Thomas Batten in 1914 for erection of a yard and garage. This was to accommodate a police patrol vehicle, or the resident sergeant's car. According to the deeds a Sergeant Dawe was the last officer to occupy the purpose-built accommodation behind the Police Station, but other constables followed.

Ron Browning of Cullompton was able to say that Fred Stephens, jeweller of Fore Street, wound Cullompton's clock for many years for £2.10s.0d. per annum. This was paid to him by Devon County Council from the Police Authority's budget. Ron took over from Fred and his remuneration, subject to negotiation, increased to £3.50 per annum. Ron Browning has said that there was evidence inside the clock doors that a considerable number of individuals must have climbed into the attic and written their names, so numerous were the entries.

When the building was sold in 1978 to Alfie Dolbear, the police retained ownership of the clock and Constable David Head demonstrated an avid interest in it and wound it for many years. This was much to the delight of the locals who complained vociferously to Mid Devon District Council when it had stopped or showed the incorrect time.

After being home to Alfie's Bargains for about 20 years, the building then became an estate agency in 2000 and the two-storey building has reverted to once again being the most prominent in Cullompton. The clock is still proudly exhibited, although it no longer shows the correct time.

Cullompton in the snow showing the Police Station (now Thorne & Carter) for sale, c.1970.

Manor House in Fore Street, formerly a merchant's house, built in 1603 for the clothier Thomas Trock.

THE MANOR OF HILLERSDON

The Manor of Hillersdon was held in the reign of Edward the Confessor by Sirwold and by Rainald under Odo Fitz Gamelin when the Survey of Domesday was taken. The ancient property was the seat of the Hillersdons, who were at some time lords of the manor of Cullompton who removed Memland in Holbeton in the reign of Henry VI, apparently becoming extinct with the death of Richard Hillersdon Esq. during the 17th century. The property was subsequently in the possession of the Cockeram family, four descendants of which are described in the Visitation of 1620, and afterwards in that of Cruwys.

By the late-18th century Hillersdon was owned and occupied by Francis Colman, the youngest son of William Colman of Gornhay in Tiverton and the last male heir of his family who died in 1820, then by David Sweet, John Laxon Sweet and, in 1847, by W.C. Grant, all of whom were lords of the manor of Cullompton. The lord of the manor had the right of appointing the Town Crier and he also exercised some manorial rights over the fishing. Formerly he held the power of life and death.

Mr Grant, on buying the estate, pulled down the existing mansion, which had become much dilapidated, and erected a new house to the design of the distinguished architect and playwright Samuel Beazley (1786–1851). These plans were exhibited at the Royal Academy of Arts in 1848. The new house was sited slightly in front of the original and was built over a period of four years by Messrs Kensole of Heavitree at a cost of about £10000.

Mr Grant died in 1877 and was succeeded by his son W.J.A. Grant Esq., a noted explorer, after whom Cape Grant in the Antarctic is named. Upon his death in 1935 the estate was bequeathed to Sir Mark Sturgis KCB, Sir Mark adopting the additional surname of Grant. During the Second World War the house was requisitioned by the military and afterwards for a short time was used as an hotel. Sir Mark died in 1949 leaving the estate for the benefit of his widow and descendants. They lived at Hillersdon, part of which at this time contained flats until, in 1982, it was sold to the present owner G.D.V. Glynn Esq.

THE MANOR HOUSE

The Manor House Hotel was formerly a merchant's house, built in 1603 for the clothier Thomas Trock. It was named 'Manor House' by Mr J.S. Upcott in 1850. The Veryards, originally a private dwelling, was incorporated into the Manor House Hotel in the 1980s. A four-gabled building of Elizabethan style, it is built of stone on the sides and of stone, woodwork and cob in the front. The back shows alterations of various dates; it is thought the chief reconstruction of the original house was carried out in 1718 and that, owing to the style, it seems likely that the original house comprised the present front portion. Past occupants include: Thomas Trock, Henry Skinner, John Kerslake, William Sellocke, Bernard Wright (surgeon), John Garrett (clerk, 1785), William Tanner (1791), Robert Baker (1791), William Upcott (1828) and John Samuel Upcott (1842).

It has changed hands many times and played host to many wounded American troops who were sent there to recover. During the Second World War it was commandeered and became the officers' mess for the various military units stationed in the town.

THE VICTORIA HALL

The Victoria Hall was erected in about 1830–1 and was the outcome of a community of religious people called Independents. Apparently it did not last long; in a matter of about 20 years they found that Independentism was failing. The Independent Chapel was bought by a syndicate for about £300 and inaugurated as the Assembly Rooms in March 1882. A newspaper article dated 12 March 1882 read:

For once in the history of its existence the quiet little town of Cullompton was all astir on the occasion of the inauguration of the new Assembly Rooms situated in the Tiverton Road. The event seemed to draw forth all the energy and enthusiasm of the inhabitants who assembled in large numbers to celebrate the opening of the building, the want of which has long been felt in Cullompton.

Hitherto there has been no large hall or meeting place in the town and this led to the acquisition by five enterprising townsmen of the structure formerly known as the Independent Chapel.

It was donated to the town by Frederick Burrows and was renamed the Victoria Hall on the Diamond Jubilee in 1897. It has been used for pantomimes, as a cinema and also as a toy factory. The firm once manufactured 'The Panda of Peace' – 'D.J. Bear', the mascot of the Football League in 1989.

The *Devon and Somerset News* of 21 April 1938 included the following note:

Mr W.J. Thorne disposed of the Victoria Hall, the property of the Parish Council on Wednesday. Owing to the graves around the building no alterations are allowed. Mr Thorne mentioned that he did not think that there has been any burials for 100 years. Bidding was started at £100, and the hall was sold to Mr W. Hill for £310.

The building was then put to use as Glanherne School. During the Second World War it was used by John Heathcoat of Tiverton who used it as part of the lace factory. At the end of this occupancy Mr W. Frost became the owner and R.B. Toys produced soft toys there for many years. It became Young Ones Day Nursery in 1999.

Fireplaces at The Walronds. Above is the fireplace in the room downstairs showing negro figures which were very unusual at that time. Left is that from the upstairs parlour, also dated 1605.

The Walronds

by Miss June Severn

Most of the older guidebooks on Devon state that The Walronds at Cullompton was built by Sir John Petre, 1st Petre of Rittle. The Petres were a very large family, the main branch of which descended from a tanner who was working at Tor Newton (which is still a farm in that very interesting triangle between Torbay, Newton Abbot and Totnes) in the reign of Edward IV. He had six or seven sons each of which in his own way was absolutely brilliant. The eldest, William Petre, afterwards Sir William, was Secretary of State through all five Tudor reigns and still managed to keep his head on his shoulders. It was his son John, who afterwards became the 1st Baron Petre of Rittle, who built Ingotston Hall in Essex which was the seat of the main branch of the Petre family for several centuries and now houses the Essex Record Office.

When we came here in 1954 we realised at once, having been to Ingotston Hall, that the coats of arms over the two fireplaces in the house were not those of Sir John Petre and his wife. Sir John Petre, the 1st Baron, married a Waldegrave, a very ancient family with one of those early, very simple coats of arms, purple azure and sable, whereas the wife's side of the shields over the fireplaces in The Walronds showed four lions rampant between a saltire. We had no idea of colours in those early days because both fireplaces had been smothered in paint; the downstairs one with layers of butter-coloured paint and whitewash, the upstairs with bright blue. When we had managed to wash and scrape a lot of this paint away and come to some colour we were able to more clearly define the family of the wife who had married the Petre who built The Walronds. She turned out to be a member of the Paris family, several members of whom had come down from East Anglia where they had borne arms since the 14th century in the unexplained migration of merchants and younger sons to the West Country early in the 16th century. They are recorded as buying and selling burgage strips during the 1500s in Chard, Chardstock, Thorverton, Silverton, Cullompton and Crediton.

Henry Paris, who settled in Cullompton, was a merchant with quarrying interests in Burlescombe and shipping interests in Exeter, but there is no mention either in his business papers or in those of his descendants of any connection with the wool trade. We first know of him when he was had up for taking currency unlawfully out of the realm in 1551 during the reign of Phillip and Mary. He was pardoned and promptly did it again! He died in 1566 and in his will he makes no mention of a house although I think we may assume that he probably lived on the site of the present Walronds. He left one of these funny old wills when people left their belongings. He left his gown furred with fox to his friend Edward Butt, mourning rings all round to his female relatives and £5 for a feast for the poor of Cullompton at his funeral.

His son Humphrey mentions his 'mansion house in Cullompton' in his will of 1594. By this time there was quite a lot of land, almost 250 acres in all, most of it on the east side of the town down the Honiton road, Newlands, Bathill, Upton and some fields which are now the site of Rivermead and the Community Fields. He had one daughter, named Emline, and by the time her father died she was quite an heiress. Some ten years before her father's death, she married the John Petre who built The Walronds.

You may ask how we know all this. About the time we were trying to identify the shield we became friendly with a Miss Joan Synar who had come to Devon to set up a County Record Office in Exeter. She was an enormous help to us and pointed us in the direction of 12 volumes of Petre papers which had been abstracted by an archivist named Olive Moger in 1927 who had been commissioned by an American Petre who had come over looking for ancestors. These volumes gave us all the information we needed about the Petre and Paris families during the early period of The Walronds' history. Emline's husband as it turned out was John Petre of Compton Pool. There were many branches of the Petre family living in the Torbay area and the South Hams and, as they were very fond of the name John, they were a little difficult to sort out. For those who know the area, Compton Pool lies on the road behind the village of Marldon at the back of Torbay on the right-hand side of the road just past Compton Castle. John Petre had been educated at Bishop Stapleton's

Foundation, Exeter College, Oxford, and he was a lawyer. He held a number of positions in the county. He was steward to the Pembroke estates in Paignton, trustee to the Careys of Cockington and also to the Blunts of Blagdon. The latter two families adhered to the old religion as did the Parises, and of course the main branch of the Petres, who lived at Ingotston Hall, were one of the leading Catholic families in the country and still are.

However, John Petre seems to have been, like so many men of his generation, an occasional conformer; all of his family marriages, christenings and burials took place in the parish churches.

John and Emline's marriage gave them quite a little empire. When Humphrey died in 1594 it is interesting to note that he left his widow Christian a house and land for her lifetime if her daughter and son-in-law should disturb her. John and Emline had business interests stretching from the East Devon border almost down to Plymouth. The Walronds was the most easterly house, Compton Pool was John's old home and there was another house at Dolbeer near Ashburton. They had quarrying interests both at Burlescombe and at Dolbeer. As quarries were held on lease from the Crown, when the head of the family died, there had to be an inquisition post mortem and this is why this period of the history of the house is so well documented.

John and Emline had a son and six daughters. Emline died in childbirth when her youngest daughter was born and Susan died also – she is buried in Cullompton and her mother was buried at Mardon. John continued a widower for a number of years and in 1615 married the widow of his great friend Simon Worth of Staverton. One of the daughters married Henry Worth of Worth which is an estate the other side of Tiverton. Now it has always been a bit of a mystery why John Petre built such a very smart house in a little town where he appeared to have no particular interest after the death of his first wife. Certainly, he was probably able to get hold of his wife's marriage settlement after her death, but even so, it is a house on which he must have spent an enormous amount of money and yet he doesn't seem to have lived in it. The son Abraham inherited a very encumbered estate, his father having spent such a lot of money on building and with five daughters to provide marriage settlements for. John died in 1626 and he was buried in Marldon Parish Church in his wife's grave. One can see their ledger stone on the floor of the tower which is also the ringing chamber and it bears the same coat of arms as appears over the two fireplaces in The Walronds.

When Abraham died in 1632 he was buried in the chancel of Marldon Church. His ledger stone in the chancel also bears the same coat of arms. John's second wife Susan died some years later and is buried in Staverton with her first husband. One might have supposed that Abraham, knowing how Tudor families went up in the world, would have married into a county family, but possibly because of his debts he could not afford to marry somebody who would have had a property tied up in a marriage settlement. Possibly he had already had financial dealings with his future father-in-law. In any case, he married Christian, the daughter of John Grose, who is described as a common money lender of Mamhead. Christian had already been married before. She was the widow of Richard Lee sometime Mayor of Totnes. Abraham's marriage does not seem to have helped him out of his difficulties. When he died as a comparatively young man in 1632 he too was heavily in debt. He had three children: John, Abraham and a little girl called Alice. Successive inquisitions post mortem show that John died at the age of ten and Abraham at the age of seven, but I have never been able to discover what happened to Alice.

After Abraham's death Christian returned to Marldon where she lived to be a very old woman. She was constantly engaged in law suits. She had property belonging to her first husband in Pinhoe which seems to have given her a good deal of trouble. There is a beautiful map in Taunton, a Wyndham Map of about 1638 or '39, which shows that the fields at the bottom of the town in Cullompton were still in the ownership of Mrs Christian Petre.

We do not know precisely when the Petre-Paris connection with Cullompton came to an end. It would seem to be about the time of the Civil War. In 1660 the Hearth Tax Returns and the Church Rates show the house in the ownership of Sir William Portman. It was then known as Sir William Portman's, previously having been known as 'Mr John Petre his house' and 'Mr John Petre his gatehouse'. We think that the house may have come into the Portman ownership through a Wyndham connection; during and after the Civil War the Wyndhams were buying up a great deal of land in the Culm Valley and the Wyndhams and Portmans, both West Somerset families, were very closely interconnected (see also *The Book of Silverton* and *The Book of Williton*).

After we had investigated the Petre-Paris ownership we rather ran out of steam. We were very busy, the Portman papers had not been abstracted, the Walrond papers had not been deposited, the Taunton Record Office had not really got off the ground and our friend Miss Synar had gone off to Derbyshire to set up another County Record Office; so I know very little about the following century or century and a half. Suffice to say that The Walronds became just another property on the Portman rent roll and in 1690 the tenant was officially Henry Walrond of Bradfield. We do not know exactly who lived in the house during the 99 years or three fives' lease which The Walronds held from the Portmans. There is some mention in my deeds of an Edmund Walrond of

Dufford but I don't know who he was. Mr Lionel Walrond, who is a member of the Ilminster branch of the Walrond family and who is the curator of Stroud museum, has told me that because The Walronds were such a political family they were always renting smallish houses in parishes all over East Devon and putting in relatives or close friends so that they could keep an ear to the ground and find out what was going on. This may very well be true because they do seem to crop up all over the place in this area.

The Portmans had very bad luck. They were always failing in the male line and all sorts of male relatives had to take over the succession. In 1785 the heir to the Portman estates was a Henry William Portman and at that time he was sorting out the estates. He it was who sold land in London on the site of which Portman Square, Bryanstone Square and Dorset Square were built and at the same time sold other property including The Walronds. The Walronds was sold to Robert Baker who was a lawyer from Tiverton and a member of the Carew family. He also bought and lived in what is now The Manor Hotel and he let The Walronds to his friend the Reverend John Sydenham.

John Sydenham and Robert Baker married two sisters, Frances and Alice Cross, daughters of James Cross of Knowle, who had a brother named Richard Cross – the very celebrated deaf-and-dumb miniature painter. There are two beautiful large oval miniatures of Robert Baker and his wife in the Victoria and Albert Museum by this gentleman as well as a number of other miniatures. Anybody interested in the Richard Cross story (and it is well worth exploring) can find a number of papers and letters in the *Walpole Society Proceedings* for 1923.

On Robert Baker's death his son Henry Blackmore Baker decided that he did not wish to live in Cullompton and he went off to Brighton or Brighthelmstone as it was then called and sold The Walronds to his father's friend John Sydenham who had been the tenant there for many years.

When the Reverend John Sydenham bought The Walronds for £800 from Henry Blackmore Baker there began an era of Sydenham ownership which was to last three generations; all of the owners being clergymen until 1889. We know very little about the first John Sydenham other than his connection with the Cross family. His son, John Philip Sydenham, seems to have been a much more colourful character. He was sometime Rector of Willand and during that time he had of course to live in the rectory. *White's Directory* of the time shows the property was let to various tenants but most of the time it is thought that he lived here at The Walronds. He seems to have been an extravagant man. He married twice and he managed to get through both his wives' marriage settlements and still died in debt. He was also, like so many Victorians, a bit of a snob. There is a marvellously interesting privately-printed book on the Sydenham family in the Devon Collection at the County Library which shows that the Sydenhams who lived at The Walronds were not of the main branch who were very well known in the 17th century at Winford Eagle in Dorset. Their immediate forbear was a Phillip Sydenham who was a publisher and bookseller in Barnstaple. John Phillip Sydenham nevertheless had one of these slightly suspect Victorian pedigrees in which he claimed to have 16 quarterings of the blood royal so I rather suspect that loving a lord he may have been the first one to say that the house was built by Sir John Petre the 1st Baron Petre of Rittle instead of the equally interesting Mr John Petre of Compton Pool.

John Phillip Sydenham had a favourite son, Phillip Wadham Sydenham, who was married and living in London. In his father's will he was left quite a substantial legacy but unfortunately there was not the money available to pay the bequest. There was another son, John George Sydenham, who had been disinherited by his father and who at the time was a poor curate in Bedfordshire. He had always been passionately fond of The Walronds and he too was able to break his wife's marriage settlement and use the money to repurchase his old home and pay his brother's legacy. We may imagine his satisfaction and joy at being able to return to The Walronds as he has scratched his name with a diamond in several of the window panes – in full on one pane in the downstairs room in the south wing (which reads: John George Sydenham 1876) and on one or two others with just his initials, J.G.S.

Unfortunately John George appears to have been no better with money than his father and by 1888 he had mortgaged the property to a local solicitor named Frederick Burrow. In 1889 he died and Frederick Burrow foreclosed on the mortgage and acquired the house. Mrs Sydenham and her youngest daughter Dora went to Exmouth where they kept a small school. Dora married a naval officer and went to America. In 1924 her daughter returned to visit Cullompton and scenes of her mother's early life.

Frederick Burrow was a man of parts and one about whom much more will be known in 2007, a century after his death when his papers will be allowed to be released. He was a prominent Baptist and a very successful solicitor. He was involved in local government at a time when the Vestry was giving place to the modern system of local councils. He was trustee to several turnpike trusts and chairman trustee of a number of charities. He started with nothing and died a very rich man having acquired much property by the then perfectly legal practice of foreclosing on mortgages. He invested a great deal of his property in a trust in his wife's name and my deeds include detailed references to the Charlotte Beale Burrow Trust in which one can read a catalogue of most of the prominent houses in this area.

By the time Frederick Burrow acquired the property it was in a pretty run-down condition because the Sydenhams had never had any money to spend on it. I do not think there would be a Walronds today had it not been for Frederick Burrow. He re-roofed the main block of the house using the main timbers but re-slating the roof with Welsh blue slates in place of the small kidney-shaped slates which were there before. Of the many repairs and alterations which he completed, one of the most notable was the addition of a picture gallery cutting off what are now the three rooms at the back of the house from the street which has made the house very much more liveable for modern use. He also 'Victorianised' the downstairs room in the south wing which had formerly been part of the service area and had been a big storeroom. In the dining room he had a pipe organ and a medieval red sandstone font. His wife had a relative who was a vicar in one of the Exeter churches and he was busy 'improving' his church and threw out the font which his brother-in-law retrieved. I think that the little quatrefoil window outside the garden door came from the same source as it does not seem quite right for the house.

Interior of The Walronds, 1999.

Frederick Burrow died in 1907 leaving the house to his son Alfred who had worked with his father as a solicitor for many years. Alfred did not want to live at The Walronds and lived instead at Upton – another of his father's acquisitions. He married a Mrs Barr, the widow of a former owner of Upton, and her son Raymond Barr was still alive when we came to Cullompton. He died a very old man in his nineties.

Alfred Burrow let The Walronds, first of all to a Major Holden and his family. Major Holden is shown in an early photograph standing in uniform outside the garden door. I met someone whose mother was a nanny to the family and they appear to have been an exceptionally nice family. Major Holden left at the start of the First World War and the house was let again to Commander and Mrs Plumpton. Cdr Plumpton was a member of a very well-known Cullompton business family who were sanitary engineers and you can see the name on manhole covers throughout the area. Cdr Plumpton was often away in the South Seas dredging up wrecks and looking for treasure and his wife was left at The Walronds. She was a Catholic and during the First World War brought down a party of nuns from London to escape from the zeppelin raids. There was no Catholic church in Cullompton at that time but there was a red-brick building, part of which is now two garages, at the rear of The Walronds, which the Burrow father and son had built as an extra office and which Mrs Plumpton and her friend Mrs de Las Casas, who lived at Bolealler, fitted out as a Catholic chapel. Mrs de Las Casas, who came from a wealthy family, always planned to build, or help build, a Catholic church in Cullompton, but it was not until the 1920s that St Boniface was built and dedicated.

When Mrs Plumpton left Cullompton in about 1930 the chapel at The Walronds became redundant but it was of use again when members of the Sisters of the Order of the Sisters of Mercy with their Reverend Mother came from Swanage to set up a school here. The main school was at Heyford House in the Bullring. The nuns themselves lived in The Walronds and they had a number of parlour boarders and several boarding pupils. The other pupils came to classes here. The period when the Sisters of Mercy were here was a very happy and fruitful time for Cullompton. Many women of my age went to school here and have stories to tell about their education.

After we arrived here, when the nuns had returned to Swanage, I used to have visits from several of them who had been young novices who had been professed here and they would tell me about their happy memories. The Reverend Mother was very highly thought of in Cullompton and is still remembered here, as of course is the Catholic priest Father Boucher who saw active service and was very badly injured in the First World War. He later set up the branch of the British Legion here and worked very hard for that organisation. The Reverend Mother died in 1942. It was a very difficult period of the war and the replacement head of the school was not able to manage either the school or the upkeep of The Walronds so it was once again empty.

Alfred Burrow was very anxious that the house should not be damaged. He did not want troops in here. The Americans had taken over the Manor and the first thing they did was to take out all the leaded light windows because they said they could not see to work with such small window panes.

Alfred Burrow did not want anything like that to happen to The Walronds so he installed his niece Miss Burrow and her friends Miss Blake and Miss Blake's father. The three of them worked the ground as a market garden. They kept geese and poultry and Miss Burrow, who was the county bee organiser, looked after the apiary. She only died recently, at 95, having lived in Sidmouth for several years.

Alfred Burrow died in the 1940s leaving the property to his sisters. They did not live many years after him. The Blakes and Burrows went to live at Honiton and once again the house was empty. On the death of Alfred Burrow's last sister, Mrs Jane Ellery, the house passed to her daughter, a Mrs Castle, who lived in London. Mr and Mrs Castle had no connection with this area and the house was sold to Mr and Mrs Nigel Neatby. Mr Neatby, an Army man, was a Cheshire man who had a mother and sisters living at Chissleborough in West Somerset. He loved old property and antiques and he had a great deal of knowledge. He wanted to run this house as an antiques business but I do not think he was much of a businessman. His wife told me that she had told him that unless she had a modern bathroom and modern kitchen she was not coming to live here. The house was at that time pretty primitive. Cullompton had only just gone on to mains water.

Mr Neatby set to work and made a very nice bathroom, still the main bathroom of the house on the first floor, and a little kitchen on the left-hand side of the front door as you come in. This was originally the buttery and later known as the justice room. That remained my kitchen until 1990. He also took all the paint off the main staircase leaving it looking like driftwood on the beach and it has taken many years of oiling and feeding the wood to bring it back to its present standard. What he did, he did very well, but it was very difficult to get materials and he was not able to do all he wished or to continue here. In 1954 he first of all sold the south wing to Mrs Helen Brocklebank and for some years it was known as Little Walronds. Later in the year he sold the main part of the property to my aunt the late Miss Yeoman. It is nice to know that Mr Neatby had a very successful later career as the first administrator at Saltram House near Plymouth for the National Trust. His wife ran the restaurant very successfully and they were responsible for the restoration of the ill-fated Dunsford House near Germansweek which was unfortunately burnt down.

My aunt and I fell in love with the house. I think we must have been quite mad. We did not even bother to have a surveyor; my aunt said the roof was all right and that if a house has a good hat and the drains work one need not bother about the rest! We always wanted to buy Little Walronds if the opportunity arose – not that we wanted to live in it but it soon became obvious to us it would be better managed, as far as the fabric was concerned, in one ownership. Mrs Brocklebank sold Little Walronds to Mr and Mrs Bullgaz in 1958. We were not at that time able to purchase it but we were able to purchase it four years later on the death of Mr Bullgaz. We did some essential repairs but my aunt's health began to fail and she died in 1969.

When I inherited the house I very much wanted to stay here but I had very little working capital. I decided that the house would have to at least in part pay for its keep. Rather unwillingly I sold an orchard plot fronting on to Shortlands Lane. That part of the orchard we had already turned into a vegetable garden and there were not many of the old trees left. The old orchard was coming to the end of its natural life. I had permission from the Council to move the rear entrance 80 feet down the lane and refurbish the back drive which was really only a cart track through the orchard by that time. I used the money from the sale of the orchard plot to refurbish the cob and stone kitchen block at the rear of the house and let a large granny flat on the first floor in the south wing for about 15 years to various families. In those days people were moving about a good deal, changing jobs and house-hunting. At first I mostly let to families who stayed for between three and six months. Later, when the landlord and tenant regulations were relaxed a little, I let to two families who stayed much longer – one three and a half years and one five years. Mr John Collins, who stayed for three and a half years, bought a second orchard plot and built a bungalow on it and he and his family lived there for five years before moving to Sampford Peverell. He asked me if he might name the bungalow Little Walronds as that name was no longer used for the south wing of the house and the bungalow is still known by that name today.

I continued until about 1989 when I was beginning to feel that I did not want the responsibility of so much property and I felt that I could not afford the really radical repairs that needed to be done – like the total rewiring of the property. I therefore decided to sell the South Wing on a 999-year lease, which is an effective freehold, to my friends Misses Daphne and Beatrice Reeves. I retained the ownership of the front drive. Their part of the house included two garages and two enclosed gardens, one for each of their flats. The smaller garden had been the former stable yard, the larger was the old tennis court. I do not think that I could really have managed this stage of the house without the help and patience of the Misses Reeves. We have worked together very successfully for the last five years but we all feel that it is now time to think about the future ownership and guardianship of this lovely property. I am always reminded of my first coming here when I was in a state of euphoria at having been so fortunate and so privileged. I already realised I was really only a link in the chain but perhaps I was at that stage a little possessive. A Mrs Rawlins, whose husband had an old family grocery business in the town, said to me with a twinkle in her eye: 'You're picking apples other folks have planted, make sure you plant apples for other folks to pick.'

A Brief History of Langford

by Mike Hines

After the Conquest a Norman called Rainer, the house steward of Baldwin the Sheriff of Devon, held the Manor of Langeforde along with seven other manors. After his death his descendants took the name of Langeforde, after the manor, and this was to remain with the family for the next 452 years.

In 1333 King Edward III granted the second John Langeforde a grace and favour Charter to hold a market once a week and a fair for three days in July each year; this was unusual as Charters were normally granted only to market towns or large villages like Bradninch. The fair was held on Langford Village Green.

The following year John de Langeforde became King's Constable and Keeper of Carisbrooke Castle on the Isle of Wight and so he remained until his death in 1343. A further six generations of male heirs of the Langeforde family owned the Manor of Langeforde and references in Exeter and Cullompton libraries state that the last of the male line, Sir John Langford, gave the holding to Corpus Christi College, Oxford. This appears, however, not to have been the case; indeed nobody gave land away – it was the basis of their wealth. A document at the college shows that it was Anne, his daughter and heiress through a clause in his will, who in 1518 sold the manor to Bishop Richard Fox of Winchester for £483. When the Bishop founded Corpus Christi College he gave the manor at Langford to the college, providing them with a regular income. Included in the sale was Sanguishayes Farm in Plymtree, which had come into the possession of the Langeforde family in 1241 (see *The Book of Plymtree*). Why they acquired this farm some distance from their manor is unclear, but it remained in the ownership of the college until the 1700s.

From the 16th to the mid-19th century there were 13 tenements in Langford village, but only 5 remain – 4 on the lane and 1 over the hill next to where the mill once stood; the other 9 tenements disappeared between 1864 and 1892 through neglect, and the surveyor to the college advised them to let the buildings fall down as it would have been too expensive to repair them. About the same time, four blocks of semi-detached houses were built on the old Village Green for farmworkers at Langford Court.

The Hitt family arrived in Langford in 1815, when George Hitt and his brother Thomas each rented half of Langford Court. After 450 years Corpus Christi College sold the manor at Langford to their tenant farmers, Mr Persey in Langford Court (South) and Mr Chattey in Langford Court (North). Newcourt Barton Farm and Langford Mill tenement were sold to Mr Michael and Mrs Sheila Hitt. In 1997 Michael Hitt, who farmed at Newcourt Barton and is the great-great-grandson of George, handed over the farm to his son Andrew, continuing the Hitt family's 185 years unbroken record of farming in Langford. Some other families having long ties with the settlement include the Wrights, Reads and Gyles, all of whom farmed for over 100 years. In the 19th century the family names of Chilcott, Ellicott, Radford, Pring, Veysey, Fair, Arberry and Salter appear in the records.

Langford has not changed greatly over the last century; five modern houses and a new church hall have appeared and increased traffic has damaged the roads, but what the future holds for small places such as Langford is difficult to judge; only time will tell.

Langford Court, c.1988.

Mutterton

by Mrs Thelma Shere

A small hamlet lying about two miles east of Cullompton, Mutterton boasted 60 inhabitants in June 2001, three of which were born in February and April of that year. The latest addition in April brings the fourth generation to Mutterton Dairy.

Mains water came to Mutterton in 1948 followed by electricity ten years later in 1958. Before that every household had their own well and used oil lamps for lighting. Some farms had a generator fitted for light and energy for their milking machines. Some of these wells are still visible in the yards and gardens today.

Many properties in Mutterton were once owned by the Burrow Estate, among them Sloughpool Farm, Higher Shutelake, Mutterton Dairy, Peverstone, Hackland and Wheatcroft Farm.

Apple picking in an orchard near Cullompton, c.1900.

In years gone by there were a dozen working farms in Mutterton, but now only five remain – all of them mixed farms producing milk, beef, chicken, pigs, sheep, turkeys and some cereals. Two of these holdings, Chaldon Farm and Mutterton Dairy, are producing organic produce, and Weeks Farm produces free-range pigs and turkeys as well as a pedigree herd of South Devon cattle.

Milk used to be left in churns at farm entrances for collection by lorry and taken to the local factories for distribution. Now, however, large milk tankers come to the farms and collect milk from large milk vats and it is taken for distribution around the country. Likewise cattle, pigs and sheep were taken to the local markets at Cullompton, Tiverton Junction or perhaps Honiton, but since the foot and mouth outbreak (February 2001) cattle can only be taken to a collection point or abattoir under licence, and sheep and pigs for slaughter at an approved abattoir.

Most of the farms in the area had their own orchards (*see above*). During the autumn all hands helped to pick the apples which would be put into sacks and transported to the well-known cider makers Whiteways of Whimple. The depot for this area was at Hele. During the 1960s and '70s most of the orchards were scrubbed out but at Weeks Farm an orchard is planted at the time of writing. The apples are now collected in bulk and sent further afield.

Mutterton Dairy was burnt down in the 1890s and rebuilt by Frederick Burrow in 1893, and a plaque on the house wall serves as a reminder of this. Mullion windows and stone walls are a feature of Nos 1 and 2 Dairy Cottages and Mutterton Cottage.

Mutterton Arms was the name of the public house in Mutterton which is now Weeks Farm. The name was revealed on the wall when the plaster was removed. Some 75 years ago Mutterton had its own football team and a gymkhana was held each year in the field opposite the pub. A postbox is now the only amenity left in Mutterton.

It has been said that Peverstone Cottage, now Dairy Cottages, was once the local school. The two front entrances, now leading to each cottage, were said to be one side for the girls and the other for the boys.

There follows a list of the early names of properties in Mutterton, some of which have now been renamed: Middle Shutelake, Higher Shutelake, Mutterton Cottage, Mutterton Dairy, Peverstone Cottages (now Nos 1 and 2 Dairy Cottages), Weeks Farm (which was once the Mutterton Arms), Sloughpool Farm (now Woodend), Chaldon Farm, Chaldon Lane Cottage, Wheatcroft Cottage, Five Cross Way Cottage, Hackland Cottage, Wheatcroft Farm, Hackland Farm (now Hackland Manor), Upton Farm and Peverstone.

Additional properties have been built within Mutterton in more recent years. These include Shutelake Orchard, Madelaine Springs, Waters Edge, Sherwoods and Little Always. A barn conversion from farm buildings at Sloughpool Farm is now known as Oak Tree House and Mutterton Barn, and at the time of writing another barn conversion is nearing completion at Mutterton Dairy.

Mutterton has recently become a thriving community for small businesses. Apart from the few working farms, there is now a dog breeder, a riding school, a chiropodist, fish pond hatcheries and, until recently, Peverstone Cheese Company.

Until recently, if one walked or drove through these quiet lanes it was hard to get one's bearings, so in 1994 the residents decided to have the 'Mutterton' signs erected. Now if you visit this part of Devon, Mutterton is a name recognised on the map.

Chapter Three

CHURCHES

In 1665 the Five Mile Act was introduced. This prohibited clergy who would not take the oath of allegiance (normally Nonconformists) from holding services within five miles of a corporate town. The penalty was £40, a vast sum at that time, so it was not unheard of for people to travel many miles to attend Sunday worship.

'Petty Toleration' (introduced in 1688) meant that Nonconformists could apply for licences to set up a meeting house. The first in Cullompton was 1690 but there is no record of the denomination. In the early years of the 18th century, Cullompton was a stronghold of dissenters. In 1736 the vicar reported to his bishops in Exeter that the population of his parish was 3558 souls, of which 728 were dissenters; made up of 508 Presbyterians, 133 Anabaptists and 87 Quakers.

There are several denominations in the parish. John Wesley's journal entry of 9 September 1748 records preaching 'in a meadow near the town' and a year later he preached at the end of New Street when he is reported as saying that 'he found the people of Cullompton to be a very dower congregation'. The Baptists were probably established in about 1700 and the Quakers had a meeting house in 1837. The Brethren met in Higher Street for six years and then moved to a meeting house in Fore Street in 1870. The Roman Catholics formerly met in a chapel at the rear of The Walronds. The present church was built in 1929, the gift of the de Las Casas family who lived in Bolealler.

ST ANDREW'S CHURCH

by Revd John Mapson (vicar 1977–89)

Coming from Exeter up the old A38 (now the B3181), down the hill from Bradninch, or from almost any other direction, you cannot avoid seeing the tower of St Andrew's Church watching proudly over the town. It has done so for 400 years since being added to the rest of the building. It still stands in spite of erosion – the result of weather and air pollution. Inevitably, many tens of thousands of pounds have had to be found to keep it in good order in recent years.

When we see the tower and hear the wonderful ten bells, we may think of the church building. The New Testament would suggest we think differently: there Church means the people, those called to follow Jesus and his teaching. So we need to think both about them (arguably the more important), and the buildings they used, and still use, for learning and worship.

Sadly, as a result of conflicts in history and human weaknesses, people now congregate in various places, but the oldest of them by far is this Parish Church. It is now St Andrew's, but was once dedicated to the Virgin Mary. It is one of the finest buildings in Devon, well over 500 years old, dating from the early-15th century (around 1430) and built in what was then the lofty and fashionable Perpendicular Gothic style.

It took many years to build, with Lane's Aisle (on the south side) a late addition a century on in 1525–6. John Lane built it partly to rival the Greenway Chapel in St Peter's, Tiverton, but most of all so that prayers could be said for him after he died, hence the Latin carving on the outside 'Say an Our Father and a Hail Mary for me.' The 12 stone tierce vaults of his south aisle are rare in parish churches. There is another chapel area, inside the beautiful rood-screen, on the other (north) side, for the Moorhayes family (the last being George Moore who died in 1711). The rood was a huge crucifix (Jesus nailed to the cross) which once stood high above the screen, and the iron fixings are still there. It was set into the middle of the one remaining Golgotha in Britain. This is a gruesomely carved tree trunk, which also has sockets for the statues of Mary and John on either side. All the figures have long since gone, and the Golgotha nearly went, having been heaved out into the churchyard. Mercifully it was recovered, its two halves put back together, and it is now on display at the back of the church (unless being shown elsewhere, such as a gallery in London).

Most of what you see now is the original building, including the long barrel-vaulted roof and some of its colouring; but not the pews. They date only from rebuilding in 1849 and later. The walls, window and floor level at the east end of the chancel (inside the

Above: *St Andrew's from a postcard dated 1917;* right: *the interior with 'flowers for a spring wedding', c.1976;* below: *St Andrew's Church Vicarage (now a nursing home) looking across the Mill Leat, c.1900.*

screen) have been altered. The entire floor was probably a little lower than now, with more steps leading down from the entrance under the tower, from what, by the time it was built, had become ground level. So what we have now is the work of half a millennium ago, replacing an earlier building – probably on the same or a nearby site. We know nothing about it except that there was one. In AD872, long before the Norman Conquest, Alfred the Great, King of Wessex, gave Cullompton to his son Ethelward. After 1066 the church belonged to Battle Abbey, with a college of clergy here. The medieval houses in Gravel Walk and Pye Corner are suggestive of a monastic close, with 1 Gravel Walk thought to have been the Abbot's house. (Little Rull and Gravel Walk houses would have been built at much the same time as the body of the church; The Walronds at the same time as Lane's Aisle; and Thomas Trock's merchant's house, later 'Wright's', now the Manor House Hotel, in the same era as the tower.)

Although St Columba came hereabouts in AD549, and some (like the vicar, Watkins Grubb, in his history) argue that the name comes from Columba's tun, or farmstead, the more likely source is 'The Town on the Culm' (see Professor David Pugsley's books*). The truth is that we do not know that much of the 1000 years before the present church. Some were 'dark ages' indeed, through first Saxon, then Viking, and finally Norman invasions. The church and its clergy served the local community long before 1181, when the list of vicars in the tower begins.

What is certain, is that Christian people have valued their places of worship, and have changed them to suit their evolving needs. For example, they put in seats when it became the custom to sit down rather than stand for the services; they used, abandoned, and then again adopted music from instrumentalists and an organ, and so on. The gallery, where the organ is housed now, is a fine Jacobean afterthought! So, although the building looks solid enough, neither the outside nor the inside have been unchanging.

The ideas of the people (and the clergy) have changed too. Not their essential beliefs, but much of the wrappings. Marriage has been seen as 'a good thing', but so, once, was celibacy for the clergy. Over a space of a few centuries the clergy progressed from living in a one- or two-room house with a beaten earth floor, and on very little money beyond what they could raise from farming their glebe land, to the mid-19th-century parsonage with its vast wine cellar and remaining nine bedrooms (others were demolished earlier in the 20th century) which served draughtily enough until being sold in 1982. Patronage, and money from the enclosure of common land, provided money for such 'improvements'. Clergy moved from being 'ordinary' people to being thought of as 'gentry' in the time of Jane Austen.** The rich became richer, and the poor (losing their common grazing rights) poorer. One vicar, William Sykes, who began here in 1830 as a popular curate, disgraced himself when he became vicar in 1834 by insisting on collecting tithes at a time of very poor harvests. He was followed in 1857 by Robert Pinkney, unpopular because he was suspected of Catholic beliefs and the civil action he brought about the smell from the nearby fellmongers. On the vicar's side was his gardener, who lived in a cottage just inside the carriageway gate to the vicarage grounds (extending to four acres) in Pye Corner.

Those days of ill feeling have gone, but memories in Devon can be long. I was once told how wealthy the vicar of Cullompton was, a century after it was true! Now, clergy have better relationships with people, more sensible provision of a house from which to work, and no tithes to collect. Among them there have been many notable preachers and pastors, including in recent times Jack Mardon, still well remembered for his smile, and sincere evangelical enthusiasm. Once a missionary in the Sudan, he became a Prebendary of Wells and their diocesan missioner on leaving Cullompton.

NOTES

* *The Town on the Culm*, *Our Vicars* (Lewis Upcott reprint), *Old Cullompton*, etc.

** *Jane Austen and the Clergy* by Irene Collins, 1994.

The Golgotha. The explanatory note inside the church reads: 'The Golgotha, carved from a single tree trunk, is a remnant of the medieval Rood and originally supporting cross in its central mortise hole, and had figures, possibly Mary and John, on the two adjacent platforms.
It was positioned on top of the Screen and signified the need of passage only by way of the Cross into the Church sanctuary and God's presence. At the Reformation it survived destruction, was divided into two parts and remained for many years on either side of the porch within the church.
We believe this artefact is the only one of its kind, and that it helped to illustrate the unique sacrifice of Jesus Christ to enable mankind, through forgiveness, to have access and fellowship with God.'

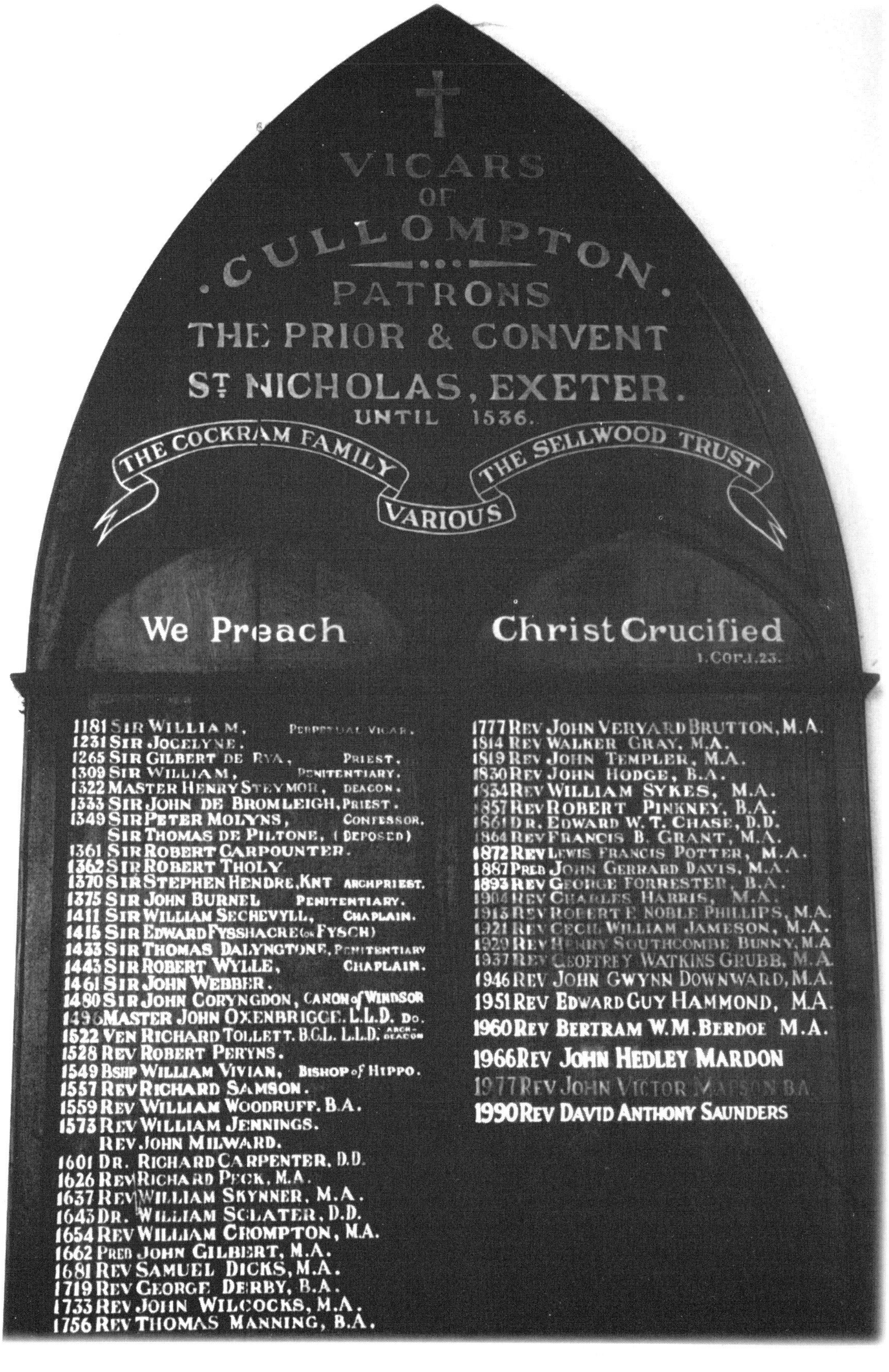

Clergy from 1181–1900. The present vicar is Revd Philip Stourbut.

Bells and Bell-ringers

St Andrew's Church has always been noted for its wonderful bells and is one of few churches in Devonshire with a peal of ten. The tower is 126 feet high and was begun in 1545 and completed before 1549, a landmark from near and far from which the bells have pealed on almost every occasion of national thanksgiving and English victory. An inventory of church goods and ornaments made in 1552, during the reign of King Edward VI, records that of all of the churches in Devonshire there were only three to possess more than six bells; Cullompton, Wolborough and Highweek all possessed eight.

Until the Reformation, and for many years after it, the parish clerk rang the bell for communion and other services, and items for payment for the ringing of the morning and curfew bell occur frequently in the church accounts. The curfew bell was rung at eight o'clock in the evening, when every person had to extinguish fire and light in his house; hence it was called the 'Ignitegium'. When all the houses were built of wood, this was a wise precaution, and the enforcement of the curfew dates to the reign of William the Conqueror and prevailed for many centuries; at Cullompton until the reign of Queen Anne.

In the early 1900s it became evident that there was a need for the bells to be recast and that the oak cage, in which they were housed, required replacing. The time was thought convenient to replace the eight bells with ten, appeals for funds were made and just over £1100 was collected. Two new bells, one in commemoration of peace and the other in memory of those who had fallen in the First World War, were given by the Revd R.N.F. Phillips and Mr A. Burrow. Cullompton is now the only parish in Devon, outside Exeter and Plymouth, to have a peal of ten.

On 3 July 1920 the peal at St Andrew's Church was dedicated. Many people travelled to Cullompton from neighbouring towns and villages and flags and bunting decorated the street near the church. The peace bell bears the inscription 'Thanks be to God for Victory and Peace, 1918' and on the memorial bell are the words 'To the glory of God and in memory of the men of Cullompton who died for their country in the Great War 1914–1918.'

In subsequent years teams of ringers from all over the British Isles have come to ring at St Andrew's. Many have been Cullompton men who have given their time and energy to ring. It was quite usual to ring at midnight on Christmas Eve, likewise New Year's Eve. The bells were always rung at 6.00a.m. and 7.00a.m. on Easter Sunday. During the Second World War people feared hearing the bells as it was in this way that the townsfolk would be warned of an invasion. The bells remained silent for the duration of the conflict.

After the Second World War there were bell-ringers' outings. The wives of the ringers would meet the evening prior to an outing at the home of Cliff and Mabel Hodge to prepare food. Mabel would make pickled eggs and onions and hundreds of sandwiches were cut. These were packed into boxes together with various bottles! Lunch was eaten on the moors or similar. The ringers' outing was a very important one on Cullompton's calendar.

At the same time as the ten bells were dedicated a peal of hand bells with tones similar to the large bells was purchased for the town. These are now kept in the bell tower and until a few years ago were played around the town regularly to raise money for charity.

In 1998 the bells stopped ringing because the tower's stonework was unsafe; the pinnacles were removed and over £230000 raised for repairs. Access to the tower was denied for some months following the repairs to enable the mortar to set adequately to resist the movement of the tower which is occasioned by the ringing of so many large bells in such a confined space. What a joy it was to hear the bells again in the town, after being silent for about two years whilst the tower was repaired.

St Andrew's Church bells, June 1920.

Church Community

Right: *Bell-ringers, 1962. Left to right, back: Ian Cummings, Trevor Jones, Boxer Salter, Len Wheller, Bill Bond, Sid May, Roy Hawkins; front: Basil Snow, Mr Ford, Joan Broom, June Saunders, Bill Norrish, Hedley Radford.*

Left: *St Andrew's Bell-ringers, 1946. Left to right, back: A.J. Mingo, W.H. Bond, E.W. Watts, R.A. Shove, A.H. Radford, W.A. Cording, J. Dew, S. May, L.H. Wheller, F.E. Kerslake; front: R. Norrish, F.G. Sellwood, Revd J.G. Downward, W. Brooks, A.G. Ford.*

Right: *Cullompton Church Choir, c.1939. Left to right, back: Eric Dummett, Peter Heard, John Sharland, Norman Thomas, Ron Skinner, Walker Brooks, Francis Venner, Derek Vigar, Arthur Hamilton, Ron Puke, Les Broom, Francis Dummett; middle: Joan Tancock, Muriel Brooks, Ron Greenslade, Robert Talbot, Reginald Reynolds, Donald Goss, Phylis Heard, Gladys Miller, Louie Rowland; front: Florence Milford, Olive Blackmore, Joan King, Bill Brooks (organist), Revd Grubb, Arthur Hammett, Betty Milford, Margery Smith, Lucy Milford; cross-legged: Leslie Stiling and George Manfield (these two were seated in the front because they were wearing ties).*

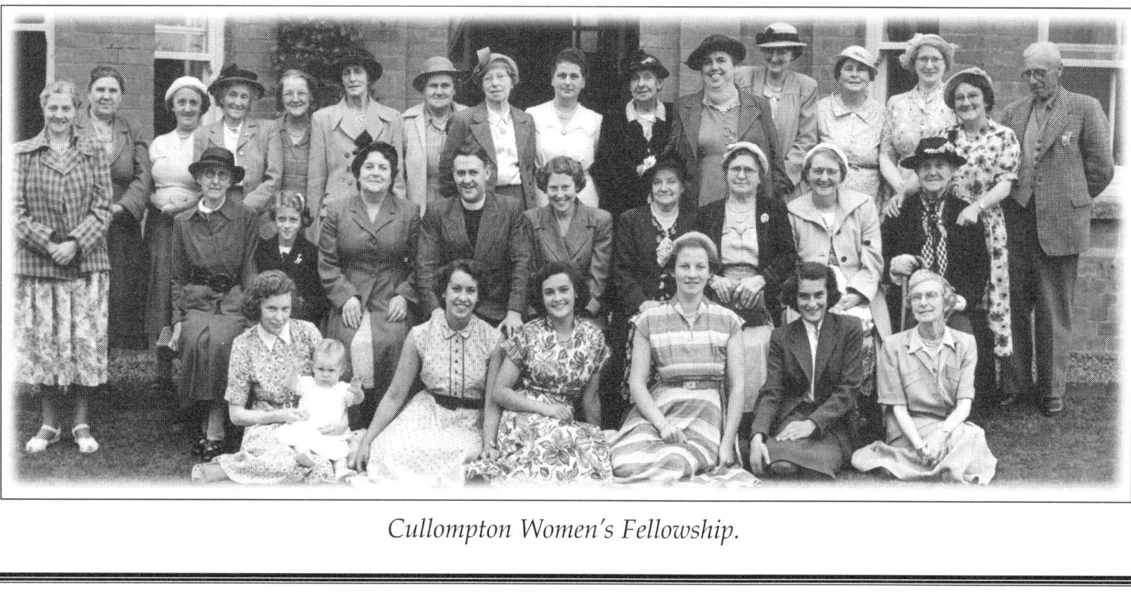

Cullompton Women's Fellowship.

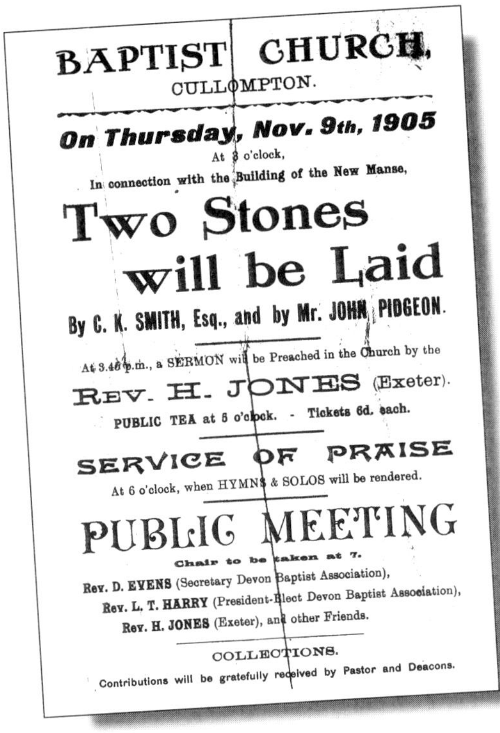

BAPTIST CHURCH,
CULLOMPTON.

On Thursday, Nov. 9th, 1905
At 3 o'clock,
In connection with the Building of the New Manse,

Two Stones
will be Laid

By C. K. SMITH, Esq., and by Mr. JOHN PIDGEON.

At 3.45 p.m., a SERMON will be Preached in the Church by the
REV. H. JONES (Exeter).
PUBLIC TEA at 5 o'clock. - Tickets 6d. each.

SERVICE OF PRAISE
At 6 o'clock, when HYMNS & SOLOS will be rendered.

PUBLIC MEETING
Chair to be taken at 7.
Rev. D. EVENS (Secretary Devon Baptist Association),
Rev. L. T. HARRY (President-Elect Devon Baptist Association),
Rev. H. JONES (Exeter), and other Friends.

COLLECTIONS.
Contributions will be gratefully received by Pastor and Deacons.

Flyer for Service of Praise in connection with laying of first stones of the new Manse to be built next to the Cullompton Baptist Church, 9 November 1905.

Cullompton Baptist Church

In 1700 Baptists in Cullompton met in a dwelling house in Cullompton, a branch of the church at Upottery, and continued to assemble in houses around the town for the next 40 years. By 1743 a meeting house had been erected where the present church now stands; it is thought that it was built through voluntary subscriptions. There is little information about this chapel but it is known that there was a small burial ground on one side.

In 1807 Revd Robert Humphrey of Stogumber was invited to the pulpit at Cullompton and, after preaching for 15 months, he was asked to take pastoral charge. He also preached at villages around Cullompton, including Sainthill, Bradninch, Thorverton, Kerswell and Honiton. Unfortunately the church could not afford to pay him an adequate stipend and he and his wife opened a drapery shop in the town to supplement their income. He finally left Cullompton in 1831. His successor was Revd Elliott, followed by Revd Amery and then Revd Uriah Foot in 1842 who retired due to failing health in 1869. He was succeeded by Revd Forth and then Revd Benjamin Miller in 1872.

During the 1870s the church decided to expand to cope with the growing Sunday School, and a new schoolroom was completed in 1883. In 1887 local solicitor and philanthropist Frederick Burrows conveyed two adjoining gardens to the church. These were used to establish the Burrows Trust which is still providing funds for the church today. The rent from the ground was used to make improvements to the building. In 1892 a new minister, Revd John Horne, arrived to replace Revd Miller and in 1901 he was succeeded by Revd Joseph Butler.

In 1904 Revd Joseph Beaupre arrived and the first Manse was built next to the church on part of the land given by Mr Burrows; it was completed in 1906 at a cost of £453. The 1920s saw a period of church growth as membership began to increase and improvements were made to the building. The church minute-book of 1946 records an 'outbreak of bad behaviour' as police were asked for help to combat rowdy youths outside the church during services.

The church organised regular outings for the children. At first it was walks to the fields for games and tea but after the First World War outings were started to the seaside, and for many children this was their one visit to the coast. A popular destination was Teignmouth. The outings were usually joint with the Wesleyans and always went by train. These treats or outings still continue and in recent years they often visit Forest Glade at the kind invitation of Freda and Norman Wellard.

In response to changing times in the 'swinging sixties' the church provided a youth club under the control of Ken Edwards and young people became far more active within the church. In 1977 a new manse was built in Manitoba Gardens and in 1989 Revd John Alvis was invited to take up the ministry. It was under his guidance, with the support of his wife, that the church opened a playgroup, now known as Noah's Ark, which is very popular.

The church has embarked on a major programme of rebuilding, involving the construction of a new modern kitchen, a new vestry and toilets, all the result of much fund-raising. Other activities are gradually being rekindled including the formation of a choir, a church bookstall and they have a new minister, Revd David Evans, who came to Cullompton with his wife from Bath in 1998. The church is now looking at ways of encouraging people moving to the area, and of course existing residents, to join them.

Cullompton Baptist Church, High Street.

Above: *Cullompton Methodist Church Nativity Play, 1936.*

Right: *Cullompton Methodist Church, Sunday School Anniversary, 1950.*

Cullompton Methodist Church Youth Club Party, 1959.

Cullompton Methodist Church

by Revd Alan Taylor

Cullompton Methodist Church may be found at the head of a courtyard in the New Cut off Fore Street. Methodists have worshipped on this site since the 18th century. John Wesley, the founder of Methodism, experienced a conversion on 24 May 1738. Just ten years later his first visit to Cullompton is recorded. Little is known of the early Methodists in the town other than the 'Minutes of Conference 1749' which record a Methodist society in Cullompton. In 1750 Wesley wrote: 'I came to Cullompton. I preached in a little meadow near the town.' A year later he recorded:

> *... reached Cullompton, preached in a little meadow at the end of New Cut. I observed one circumstance which I had not observed elsewhere; the people did not come close to me, but stood in a half circle some yards off... and the children behaved with remarkable seriousness! Here I rested on the sabbath and attended the church service in the evening.*

By 1764 the local Methodists had both the number and strength to have the confidence to build their own preaching house. A property was sold to the Methodist Trustees described as 'a house and two plots of ground at the upper end of Paul Dunkley's Court'. In 1806 the old chapel was rebuilt and survived until 1872 when a fire did considerable damage. The building had to be renewed and records show that by 1885 £1100 had been spent on the work. Thus the present building is the third on the same site spanning almost the entire history of the modern Methodist movement.

Members of the present congregation are active in the life of the town and are looking forward to continuing the contribution that Methodism has made to the community of Cullompton for many generations.

St Boniface Roman Catholic Church

by Mrs Alice Harris

The parish of Cullompton is squeezed between its larger neighbours of Tiverton and Honiton and runs from north of Exeter up the Culm Valley to the river's source by the Somerset border. It includes at least 11 medieval parishes and some 16000 people. In 1939 a Catholic church was built in Hemyock and proved very helpful to the American forces at Dunkeswell Air Base during the Second World War. However, the church of the parish is the one built in Cullompton in 1929. Until recently parishioners knew little except that it was built by a Spaniard and that the father of a present-day parishioner put up the roof.

The parish priest until 1946 was Father Aloysius Boucher who won the Victoria Cross in the First World War and was continually suffering back pains due to injury. He was succeeded by Father Biggs, Father McNamee (who had the presbytery built in the 1960s), followed by Fathers Donagher, Rossiter, Dolan, McGee, Pack, O'Donovan, Perkins, Cawley, Courtney, Julio and Father William Kiely.

Marriage records date back to 1938 and there is mention of nuns living at The Walronds in Fore Street during and after the Second World War. Recently Mrs Teresa Richardson of Cirencester, the last surviving daughter of Manuel de Las Casas (born 1868) who provided the church, visited us.

The de Las Casas family had moved from France to Spain at the time of the expulsion of the Moors and had settled in Seville. Two members of the family accompanied Columbus on his second voyage. One of those two brothers, Pedro, was the father of the first American priest, Bartolome de Las Casas, who was to champion the Indians and to speak for them before the King of Spain. The other brother was the ancestor of the Cullompton de Las Casas.

Four centuries later in the 1860s our church's builder came to Liverpool as Venezuelan Consul. When he was dying in 1872 he asked his wife to bring up his four sons in England, she purchased North House at Washfield, near Tiverton, and lived there with her sons until she died in 1922. The Washfield Village Hall was built in her memory. Manuel married an English woman and lived with her and their six children at Bolealler House near Cullompton.

In 1929 the Catholics had no church nearer than that at Tiverton and they met at The Walronds instead. Manuel and his wife decided to build a church and purchase some land around it so that eventually a presbytery for the priest could be built. St Boniface today is very vibrant and continues to grow. Its history should not be forgotten by its parishioners for so much is owed to the de Las Casas family who were its inspiration.

St Boniface Church, Crow Green.

Above: *The Unitarian Chapel in 1911 immediately following its collapse.*

Right: *The Unitarian Chapel after rebuilding.*

UNITARIAN CHAPEL, POUND SQUARE

by Mrs Muriel Coxhead

The Unitarian Chapel is the oldest Nonconformist congregation in Cullompton. It owes its origins to the ejection of the Vicar of Cullompton, Revd William Crompton, from the established Church in 1662. He continued to preach in the area and the Protestant Dissenters Meeting House was built in 1698. This was replaced by a much larger building in 1815 on the site of the present chapel. This building was constructed of cob and in 1911 a large congregation had just vacated the building when it collapsed. No-one was injured and under the guidance of Revd Jeffery Worthington a new chapel was erected and opened in 1913.

During its long history a staunch Nonconformity has been maintained at Pound Square which has gradually widened into modern liberal Christianity.

HEBRON EVANGELICAL CHURCH

The name of the fellowship, formerly the Gospel Hall, was updated in the 1980s. The original members formed the Assembly in the early 1930s and proceeded to erect a temporary building. This was used until 1962 when the present building was constructed by Mr Charles Callard and later extended to provide additional space for increasing youth activities. Records show that there was a chapel built on the same site in 1695.

Chapter Four

Shops & Businesses

The local retail tradesmen are certainly the chief rate-payers in the average town. Today many of them find their task a hard one, owing to the fact that residents are in the habit of ordering their goods from the great cities. This is a mistaken policy, remember empty shops pay no rates. Both residents and visitors should support the local trader. It is surely better to be one of a few score of valued customers than one of thousands in a big Department store.

From The Cullompton Town Guide, *1928.*

The Market

The market was originally granted in 1278 to Baldwin de Insula, Earl of Devon. It was to be held on Thursdays, together with a fair for three days at the festival of St John the Baptist. In 1317 the Abbot and Convent of Buckland had the grant of a market to be held on Tuesday, together with a fair of three days at the feast of St George.

The market was initially held in the Shambles, a long, narrow wooden structure roofed over and standing on the east side of Fore Street. The corn-market was also held in the same place and a bell in the little turret on the top of the Shambles used to summon the farmers every Saturday for barter. This was also used as an alarm in case of fire. It was here that the farmers brought butter, cheese, vegetables, eggs and various other commodities for the towns-people to purchase. There were no shops in those days and the market stalls were the housewife's only means of stocking up her larder, apart from food which she produced herself. The market was held weekly.

In 1810 the inhabitants decided to do away with the Shambles as it was considered a public nuisance. The Market House was built and used as a meat market until the declining prosperity of the town caused butchers to sell from their own houses. It was then used as a dwelling house and ordinary shop; the yard was used for storing the hurdles for the cattle market.

Sheep and cattle continued to be sold in the Higher Bullring on the first Wednesday in each month until 1917, when a field was acquired near the station and the market was moved. Hurdles would be brought from the Market House Inn, where they were stored, and set up in the wide cobbled streets, ready to pen the sheep and cattle when they were brought in for sale by the local farmers. Other traders would set up their stalls to be patronised by the many folk who came to market on horseback, in pony and trap or even on foot; people thought nothing of walking ten or twelve miles.

The following appeared in a local publication on 1 December 1837:

It is a matter of regret to many who feel an interest in the prosperity of this Town, that the Market is fallen into so neglected a condition. There are those now living among us who remember it under better circumstances, when the usual market commodities were amply supplied on a Saturday, and a good stroke of business done in the Corn Trade, around the lower end of the Old Shambles, and the balcony of the Salutation (now the Globe) Inn.

That a good Market is a great benefit to a Town is universally allowed. The collection of numbers of people to transact business is a considerable advantage to Tradesmen and the inhabitants generally; every rightly constructed mind derives pleasure from the promotion of his own and his neighbour's welfare; it is hoped united efforts will be made to secure it.

This Town is most happily and healthily situated. An eminent Physician of Exeter, very recently, whilst noticing our beautiful stream of Town Water, bore his testimony to the salubrity of the air, and the healthiness of the place.

In this and ten immediately adjoining Parishes is a body of agriculturists as respectable and living upon rich and productive a soil as any district in the West of England. Here is an extensive Woollen Manufactory, where an immense quantity of Wool is used; here a Wool Fair or Market may be established, with every promise of success, being in the centre of Manufacturing Towns of Wellington, Wiveliscombe, Exeter, Chagford, Crediton, Morchard, &c.

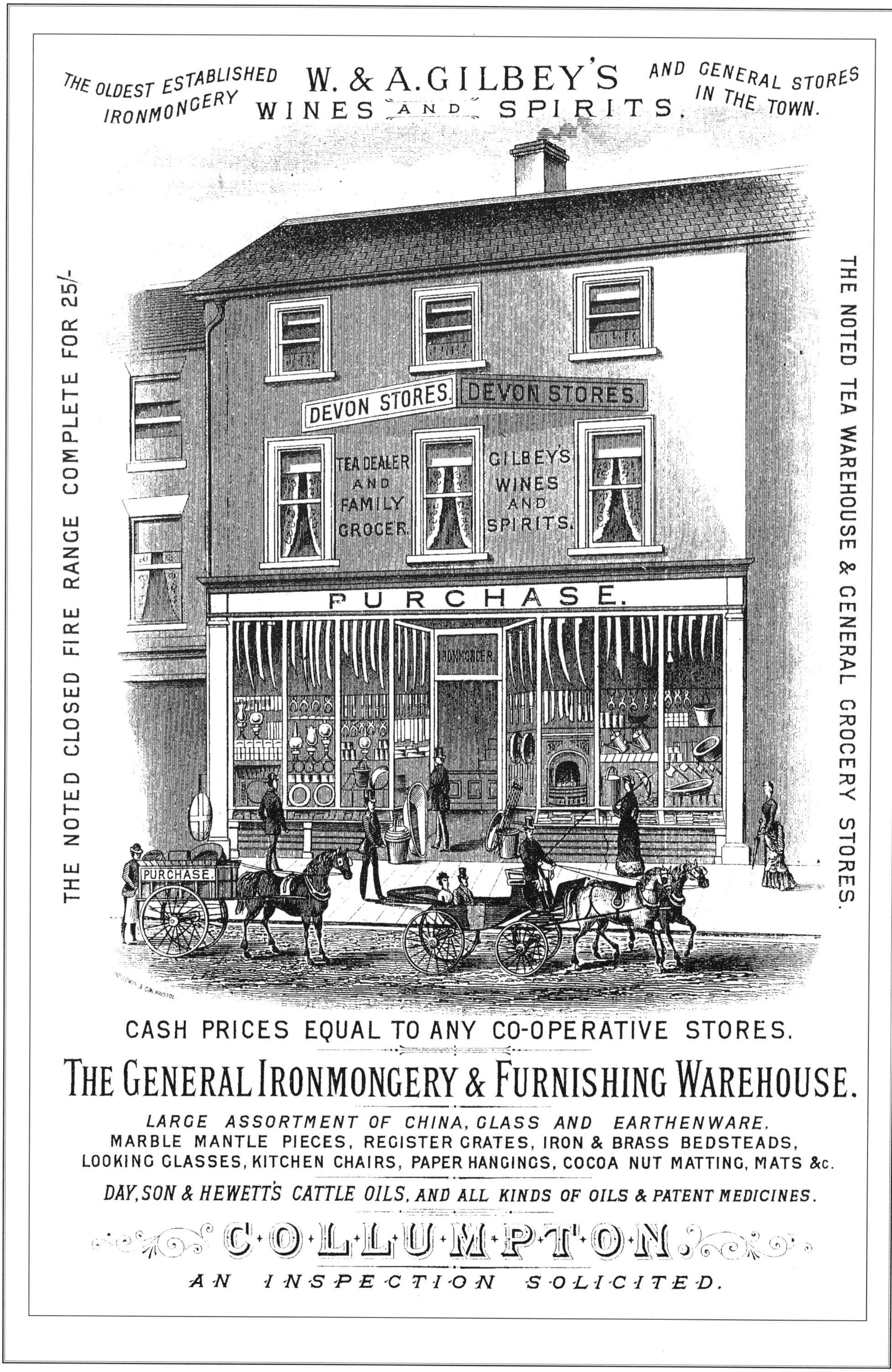
THE OLDEST ESTABLISHED IRONMONGERY
W. & A. GILBEY'S WINES AND SPIRITS.
AND GENERAL STORES IN THE TOWN.
THE NOTED CLOSED FIRE RANGE COMPLETE FOR 25/-
THE NOTED TEA WAREHOUSE & GENERAL GROCERY STORES.
DEVON STORES.
DEVON STORES.
TEA DEALER AND FAMILY GROCER.
GILBEY'S WINES AND SPIRITS.
PURCHASE.
IRONMONGER
PURCHASE.
CASH PRICES EQUAL TO ANY CO-OPERATIVE STORES.
THE GENERAL IRONMONGERY & FURNISHING WAREHOUSE.
LARGE ASSORTMENT OF CHINA, GLASS AND EARTHENWARE,
MARBLE MANTLE PIECES, REGISTER GRATES, IRON & BRASS BEDSTEADS,
LOOKING GLASSES, KITCHEN CHAIRS, PAPER HANGINGS, COCOA NUT MATTING, MATS &c.
DAY, SON & HEWETT'S CATTLE OILS, AND ALL KINDS OF OILS & PATENT MEDICINES.
COLLUMPTON.
AN INSPECTION SOLICITED.

Collumpton has a population of about 4000 inhabitants, among whom the consumption of Butcher's Meat, Poultry, Fish, Corn, Malt, Vegetables, and other products must necessarily be considerable.

In the great and increasing thoroughfare of the Town, perhaps 60 or 70 horses are employed in the run of 5 daily coaches and posting: of course the consumption of fodder is great. In addition to these, and many other advantages already possessed by the Town, others may be reasonably calculated upon as being by no means remote.

In the course of a year or two the Great Western Railway from Bristol to London will be opened, then 8 or 10 Coaches may run upon this line of road. Travelling, Passengers, and Visitors will still further increase, and with these the business activity, prosperity of the Town will increase also.

The very extensive Union of Parishes here under the New Poor Law (of which Union this Parish is one) may ere long render a division necessary; in such case COLLUMPTON would be the centre, and its Tradesmen derive corresponding advantage.

There appears to be a prevailing feeling against small constituencies sending two Members to Parliament: from this it is not impossible that one of those sent by the town of Honiton may some time hence be returned by the more numerous inhabitants of Collumpton... the usual benefits would accrue.

Still further advantage may be calculated upon when the Town shall be well lighted and paved, by an influx of respectable persons as residents here.

The Noble Lessors of this Market have large estates in the neighbourhood; a proper application may secure their favourable notice, together with the assistance of their tenantry in carrying out a measure which could enhance the value of their own property. With such materials in possession and prospect, it is submitted a good Market may be established by the cordial and hearty co-operation of 'One and All'.

As a commencement it may be suggested –

That the Bakers of the Town request their Four Factors and the Millers of the neighbourhood to call upon them for transaction of business on Saturdays only.

That the Millers and Maltsters deal principally with those who brought their Samples, or Wheat and Barley to Market on that day.

That the Post Horse Masters, and the other keepers of Horses, act upon the same plan in the purchase of Oats, Beans, Hay, &c. Dealers so respectable would never be deprived of the pleasure of meeting those on the Market Day who have such commodities to sell. Thus Farmers and other having expectation of selling Wheat to the Miller, Barley to the Maltster, Oats &c. to the Post Horse Master, Wool to the Manufacturer, and other produce to persons generally, would have the strongest inducements to attend.

The inhabitants individually should use every endeavour, and give their best support to those Bakers and others whose steadfast efforts were made to carry this important point.

It seems that the subject of trade, business and local prosperity has often been the subject of deliberation. The Revd G. Forrester provided this comment for *St Andrew's Parochial Magazine* in February 1898:

My Dear Friends

The social dinner, at which our farmers and tradesmen recently met, marks, I hope, an onward step in the progress of our Parish. Anything that tends to bridge the gulf that separates the several sections of the community from each other, and links them together by bonds of mutual interest, cannot but be for the general weal. We were glad to gather from the speeches both of farmers and tradesmen that the gloomy views of the markets and trade of the town, which we had occasionally heard expressed, were not warranted by the facts of the case. The speakers recalled vastly worst times, and saw no reason for despondency. The upspringing of new markets in the neighbourhood had, it was admitted, diverted some of the trade to other places. But these new markets were not inaccessible to our local agriculturists, nor had they materially affected the business done in Cullompton...

It is obvious that the increased facilities for travelling and conveyance of goods possessed in the present day must bring the more distant markets within easier reach, lessen the loss of time and cost of carriage. And the vast addition of merchandise brought to our town in these days, as compared with the records of earlier years, is practical proof of steady improvement in trade.

It would be well if some fresh industries could be located among us. But the enterprising capitalist does not seem to see such special advantages in Cullompton as to make it the scene of his venture.

So we must trust, I suppose to... console ourselves with the reflection that we seem at least as well off as our neighbours, if not better, and are not that moribund body which the pessimists would have painted us.

Cullompton Cattle Market in Higher Bullring before 1917 when it was moved to a field in Station Road close to the railway station.

E.A. Fry Butchers, Fore Street (at the top of Middle Mill Lane), c.1920. There was a slaughterhouse behind – where Dairy Cottage is now.

E.H. Ellicott, baker and confectioner. The Campbell family who worked there still have the scales which were used to weigh out snuff in quarter ounces and tobacco in ounces.

Batten Bros. Garage, High Street, c.1930. It later became Clark's Motors.

F. Batten's Cycle Shop, c.1904 (now Crossley & Son Funeral Directors).

Above: *Staff at the first Post Office, Fore Street (now Pickwicks).*

Right: *Cherry Tree Stores, 1957, at 112 Exeter Road. Local people were not the only customers; coaches would stop for ice-creams and cream teas and proprietor Ron also sold groceries on a local country round. He introduced chocolate flakes on top of the ice-creams (called 99s) and also raspberry syrup as well as clotted cream.*

Left: *This shop was opened in 1964 following the demolition of the cottages where the Cherry Tree Stores had been. The new store was named Dennings after its owner, Harold Denning. Until he sold the shop in 1972, the only ice-cream flavour he stocked was vanilla – like Mr Dyer before him.*

The Post Office

White's History, Gazetteer and Directory of the County of Devon for 1878 records the following:

> *Post, money orders, telegraphs and government annuity and insurance office and savings bank at Mr Samuel Mitchell's jun. Letters are delivered at 7am, 8.50am and 5.50pm and despatched at 7.15am, 8.50am, 12noon, 1.50pm and 4.50pm and 9.10pm. On Sunday there is only one delivery at 7am.*

The Post Office was originally situated where Pickwicks now trades and the late Mrs W.H. Terry remembered that as a child of eight, on her way to school, she saw a telegram in the right hand window saying 'Mafeking has been relieved'. She had no idea what this meant except that she was delighted to learn a half-day holiday from school had been granted.

The Post Office and Sorting Rooms moved to the present site of the Sorting Office in the early 1930s and Mr Les Rowe was the postmaster for many years. As well as working for the Post Office, Mr Rowe was a well-known member of the community who served for many years as town clerk and later as Chairman of the then Parish Council. The Post Office and Sorting Office separated in the mid 1980s and the Post Office moved to the site of the former Plymouth Brethren Meeting Room where it is today.

Cullompton Library

Permanent library facilities were first opened in Cullompton in 1938 on Exeter Hill. This was the 14th branch library in the county and opened for six hours a week with Miss Harding as the first librarian. It moved to premises situated next to the King's Head in High Street in the 1950s before being transferred to the present site on Exeter Hill in the 1980s. There would appear to have been some controversy over the opening of the original library because of the cost to local ratepayers and some members of the Parish Council refused to attend the opening ceremony.

Cherry Tree Stores

by Mrs M.R. Broucke (granddaughter of Joe Dyer)

Cherry Tree Stores was started by Joe Dyer in his front room, between 1913 and 1914, and so named after the tree in the garden. It opened seven days a week, until 10p.m. There were strict rules about what could and could not be sold on a Sunday and fines were heavy if the law was not upheld. Joe started selling vanilla ice-cream, which became well known for its quality. He died in 1944 and his son Ron took over in 1945. In 1957 Harold Denning, Ron's first cousin, bought the shop and called it The Cherry Tree. In 1963 the top two cottages were pulled down and a new store, Dennings, was built.

Easterbrooks

by Mrs Jane Campbell

My grandmother was married to a Mr Rogers who was a plumber working for Mr Plumpton. In 1906 he died very suddenly of pneumonia leaving her with three children and expecting a fourth. They had contracted to buy a house in New Street so she moved in with her young family and survived by taking in lodgers. (The garden and orchard later became Vicary Close.) She later married a Mr Easterbrook who had been in the Indian Army and they had two sons. The family moved to 60 Fore Street and opened a sweet shop (now the hairdressers).

The Easterbrooks were the first tenants and I remember my grandmother saying that when they lit a fire on the first evening they were horrified because smoke poured out of the walls of the living room above the shop. This was because the property had been built to burn and the walls were lined with chaff from the mill, also owned by the landlord. He was later convicted of arson following two fires in properties he owned, one of which was in Exeter from which the tenants narrowly escaped death. During her time in the property my grandmother was careful never to leave any embers burning at night.

One of her daughters, Alice, married Sidney Salter and they had a butchers shop on the corner of Church Street, now the opticians. Another daughter, Edith, married Don Steer. The Steers kept an outfitters and also sold high-quality household linen, etc. (now Londis). One son joined Liptons, the grocers, and moved away to work in London, and another son, my father Leonard Rogers, started work with 'Tourney Burrows' when he was 14. Fred Easterbrook worked for Devon General Bus Company in Exeter and Harry Easterbrook became the District Valuer in Anglesey. Leonard married my mother, Beatrice Dummett, in 1936. They started married life in the flat above the outfitters shop where I was born.

When she left school my mother went to work for Ellicotts, the bakers. Although the hours were long she was very happy there, partly because she was delighted to be treated as one of the family with Dulcie, Norman and their sister. Her own brother was 19 when she was born and her sister 14 so she really appreciated working with young people of a similar age to herself. My father took over the sweet shop when my grandmother retired, I think in 1949. The sweet shop closed in the early 1980s. During the war years sweets were rationed and the shelves were bare. Following the war supplies gradually improved and the walls were lined with glass jars, but rationing continued for some time. Almost everything had to be weighed out; very little was pre-packed. I remember sitting around the dining room table at home helping to count the sweet coupons and tie them into bundles following which they were delivered to the Ministry Office in Exeter.

HIGH STREET & FORE STREET IN THE 1930S AND '40S

by Mick Lawrence

Each time I walk through the town on my periodic visits to Cullompton I find myself looking at the shops and other buildings and trying to compare what is there now with how I recall things as a young lad in the latter part of the 1930s and early 1940s. I must stress that the recollections are mine and mine alone and if there are any glaring mistakes I apologise in advance.

AT THE TOP OF STATION ROAD

Today	**The same site in the 1930s–'40s**
Open area and Shelter	Cocker's sweet shop
Opposite side of road	Miss Graves' (?) sweet shop then the Lands' house with steps down from the pavement. The low roof can still be seen from the end wall of Ian's Fish Bar.

HIGH STREET EAST

Today	**The same site in the 1930s–'40s**
Ian's Fish Bar	International Stores
King's Head Pub	King's Head Pub with landlord Mr Peters. The part on the corner of Higher Mill Lane was Mrs Graves' game, rabbit and poultry shop.
Hairdressers	Flo Paul's general store
Cullompton Chiropody, etc.	Private house
Private house	Private house of Mr and Mrs Ford
The Bays Dental Practice	Private house (The Bays) of Miss Cole
Market House Pub	Market House Pub
Small's Pet & Garden Supplies	Small's corn and seed shop
Baptist Chapel	Baptist Chapel
Private house	Baptist Chapel Manse
Clark's Motors	Isaac's Garage
Thorne & Carter	Police Station and Magistrates' Court
Bike Zone	Private house belonging to Mr Trevenen (?)
Accountants	Mr and Mrs Hallet
Vacant property	Brown's sweet shop
Probert's Bakery	Fare's grocery shop
Cullompton Town Hall	The Parish Rooms

FORE STREET EAST

Today	**The same site in the 1930s–'40s**
Bakers Dolphin	Labdon's
Londis store	Steer's outfitters shop. Donald Steer was a fine musician and was Conductor of Cullompton Male Voice Choir.
Lloyds TSB	Lloyds Bank with Manager Mr Jago
NatWest Bank	National Provincial Bank with Manager Mr Cox
Dalzell Distributors	Fry's outfitters shop
Fresh 'n' Fruity	London Central Meat Co. with Manager Mr Ellis
Leisure Shop	Eric Batten's shoe shop. All the repairs were done in a big hut behind the shop in Mathew's Court which had a wonderful smell of new leather and wax. The cobbler was Ernie Watts whose mouth was lower on one side than the other due to a lifetime of holding bunches of tacks there.
Bubbles	Frank Stevens' radio shop
White Hart Hotel	White Hart Hotel with landlord Mr Hanney

FORE STREET EAST (CONT.)

Today	**The same site in the 1930s–'40s**
Vranch House shop	Lawrence's paper and stationery shop. Having been born 'over the shop', literally, and spent so much time folding and delivering papers, I find the smell of newsprint most evocative. I can also recall the running battles with dogs while delivering papers – two of the most cunning ones who waited for callers to get well inside before showing themselves belonged to Mr Rawlings up Willand Road and Mr Canniford in Belle Vue. I understand that way, way back when stagecoaches became the first organised means of public transport on wheels this property was part of the White Hart which was an important posting house for travellers on the main route between Bristol, Exeter and points west. Nearly all the buildings to the rear were stables and beside the main side entrance there's a big granite stone which travellers on horseback could stand on to get up into the saddle. The last time I can recall the stables being used for their original purpose would be around the end of the 1930s. A gentleman called 'General' Ellicott used to drive to town in his pony and trap each Market Day and always 'parked' at the White Hart. When I wasn't in school he paid me a penny (less than $^1/_2$p) to unhitch the pony from the trap, take off the harness and put her in a stable with some hay to eat. Around mid afternoon when he got back from market the process was reversed and he set off home and my everlasting impression is that it was a good job the pony knew the way back up over Old Hill because her driver certainly wasn't too clear about it after a day out with his friends!
Balfour News	Reynolds' ironmongers shop
Imperial Cancer Research	Tiny Hellier's general store
Fulfords Estate Agents	Rawlings' grocery shop. My late brother-in-law, Bill Heard, was threatened with instant dismissal from his after-school job of delivery boy on a carrier bicycle just like Granville's in 'Open All Hours' if he ever again ate the cheese from any of the orders entrusted to him – an allegation which he strenuously denied.
Instep Footwear	Wakefield's outfitters shop with Managers Mr Ball then Bob Beale
Let's Go Travel	Denner's sweet shop
Steven Ash	Phyllis Osmond's hairdressing salon. Short back and sides for small boys cost 4d.
Vacant property	Fred Stevens' jewellers shop
Moonlight Pizzas	Paul's bakers shop which had a chewing gum machine outside which used to swallow my collection money, and that of my sister if I could get it off her, on the way to Sunday School.
Cullompton Photographic	Frisby's shoe shop with Manager Mr Marlow. My father used to tell the story, not apocryphal I was assured, of how during the war Mr Marlow was walking home across the fields in the dark after a night shift at the Royal Observer Corps Post up on Ganders Hill when he fell over a sleeping cow and got the strap of his gas mask caught around its horns. The resulting noise led the new watchkeepers to believe that he was being attacked by the enemy but by the time they got to him the strap had broken and the only injuries sustained were to the nervous systems of man and beast. But German bombers or not, Mr Marlow always used a torch from then on.
Pickwicks	Post Office and Telephone Exchange. This was the original site before everything was moved to a new purpose-built complex on the opposite side of the street. The postmaster was Mr King and the telephone operator was Miss West who presided over a switchboard which had a mass of wires with plugs on the end that had to be manually pushed into sockets to make the connection between two telephones. Long-distance post was carried on the Mail Train and the transfer point was beside the railway a few hundred yards the Exeter side of Cullompton Station.

Brooks ironmongers in 1895 (now First Studio Hairdressers) owned by George Brooks who was also the Fire Chief. Standing outside is his daughter Muriel who later became Mrs Whitton.

Cockers, demolished in order to widen the Station Road/Higher Street junction.

FORE STREET EAST (CONT.)

Today	**The same site in the 1930s–'40s**
Pickwicks cont.	The actual transfer was primitive but effective and involved a postman carrying the mail in a very thick leather pouch from the Post Office, down Middle Mill Lane, along the footpath beside the Mill Leat as far as Parson's Bridge then turning sharp left across the fields to the railway. The pouch was then hung on a swivelling cantilevered arm beside the track to be scooped up in a net sticking out from the side of the train which had to be pulled back in pretty quickly to avoid hitting the road bridge by the station. An exact reversal of this procedure was used for incoming mail, i.e. the arm stuck out of the train and the net was beside the track.
1st Studio	Cullompton Gas Company shop. Manager Mr Brooks. This was where bills were paid and appliances sold and repaired but the gas was produced in furnaces and stored in a huge gasometer at the Gasworks which was sited on parts of the land adjacent to Labdons and a garage in Station Road.
Culm Meat Supply	Culm Meat Supply with Manager Mr Hill
The Golden Eagle	George Cross' photography shop
Mark Hellier's	Joe Simmonds' barbers shop
Community House	YMCA
Bill and Taylor and Henry's Hair Salon	Sid Salter's butchers shop
Post Office	Plymouth Brethren Chapel
Mortgage Services	Private house of Mrs Staddon
Mid Devon District Council	Private house of Superintendent Johnson (Devon Constabulary)
Private house of Mrs Heard	Private house of Miss Catford

LOWER BULLRING

Today	**The same site in the 1930s–'40s**
Lower Bullring	Before traffic levels reached anything like their present intensity – in fact when there was hardly any traffic at all – this used to be the focal point for kids of all ages to gather to spin tops, roll hoops and play conkers, and the stone monument in the middle of the road was the recognised start and finishing point for all roller-skate races. What a pity that those who drew up the plans for the 'improvement' of this area didn't have sufficient foresight to design something a bit special to serve as a focal point for the lower end of the main street – still, they were probably the same mob who decided under the guise of highway improvements to do away with the rare system of gutters that carried the free water supply which was given to the town way back in the early 1600s. This water originated at Combe Farm way up past Knowle and then flowed below Ponsford and Heathaller to run roughly parallel to Tiverton Lane, across what is now the Shortlands Estate and down through the gardens of The Walronds to join the gutters in Fore Street.

FORE STREET WEST

Today	**The same site in the 1930s–'40s**
Present Time	Private house of Mrs Potter
Oddbins	Miss Batten's butchers shop. She had a large black Labrador dog who always seemed to be chewing on a huge marrow bone.
Nikkis	Rossiter's chemists shop
Crossley & Son	Francis Batten's cycle shop
Haircraft	Easterbrook's sweet shop

Fore Street West (Cont.)

Today	**The same site in the 1930s–'40s**
Culm Florist	Culm Weavers
	Culm Florist. Mr Hellier
Furry Friends and Sue Ryder	Globe Inn
Culm Vale Bakery	Bailey's bakers shop
Alfies	Kelly Luxton's furniture shop
Options	Len Murray's hairdressing salon
Dave Edwards & The Jumping Frog	Ellicott's bakers shop
Cullompton Delivery Office	Bowerman's general store
Gone Bananas	Sharland's dairy
Veysey's butchers	Veysey's butchers
Cullompton General Store	Later Joe Tancock's ironmongery shop
Nationwide Building Society	Terry's electrical shop
Tavy Textiles	Half Moon Hotel with landlord Mr Persey
MDE Communications	Phyll Sweet's toy and china shop
Ye Olde Tea Shoppe	Bill Broom's furniture shop
Prescotts	Wellington's sweet shop
Moss Pharmacy	Foster's chemists shop. As well as running a pharmacy like we now only see in period films, with large bottles of medicinal compounds all labelled with gold leaf titles, Murray T. Foster was a keen botanist with many exotic plants in his heated greenhouses, a local historian of some note who was convinced that the proper spelling for the town's name was 'Collumpton' and the keeper of the meteorological records for the area. Whenever he was away from home it was my job every evening to climb up to the little platform on the highest part of the roof over the shop to change the card in the sunshine recorder and to make a note of any rainfall.
Early Days & Cullompton Cleaners	David Martin's outfitters shop
The Merchant's House (vacant)	Alfred ('Tourney') Burrows' solicitors office
The Walronds	The Walronds. Before becoming a private house this was the living quarters for the nuns in the religious order connected with the Convent in High Street. There was a story that originally it had been inhabited by monks connected with St Andrew's and that there had been an underground passage from the building to the church which passed through my father's garden at the bottom of the yard between his shop and the White Hart. When he was digging the foundations for his new house in the garden he excavated a trench to see if any trace of this passage could be found and while there was certainly evidence of some man-made structure uncovered, it was not possible to positively identify it as a tunnel – but he still went ahead and called the new house 'Monks' Walk'.
Manor House Hotel	The section of the hotel right next door to The Walronds was a private house called 'Veryards' with the remainder being the original hotel building.

High Street West

HSBC	Midland Bank
Carpet Centre	Private house (of Mr and Mrs Copp) and the Regal Cinema where we would go to the Saturday afternoon matinee for the near bankrupting sum of threepence. On entering, Mr Kerslake, the commissionaire/ticket collector, would check that we weren't carrying any lemonade bottles as these, when released at the top of the sloping floor, made a horrendous noise as they rolled downhill towards the front and an even worse one when they hit the metal tray filled with sand underneath the screen.

High Street West (Cont.)

Today	The same site in the 1930s–'40s
	(Regal cont.) This tray was part of the required Air Raid Precautions during the war and its contents were to be liberally scattered on any incendiary bombs which Hitler saw fit to drop through the roof, but all I ever saw it used for was stubbing out cigarette ends. Also at this performance the very back row of seats was out of bounds as it had been known for the lightest person available to be lifted up so that he could hold his hat over the hole from the projection room thereby blanking out the screen completely. In later years when girls turned out not to be so bad after all and it became imperative to sit in the back row, we had to change our habits and go to the early-evening performances when all seats were available – but pleasures didn't come any cheaper then than they do now because admission went up to one and threepence, and twice that if you couldn't avoid paying for whoever you were with. All in all pretty awful behaviour, but we didn't do drugs and none of us ever knocked over an old lady to steal her pension book.
Seddons Estate Agents	Good Companions fruit and flower shop
Denners	Culm Weavers
Bradleys Estate Agents & Harris Fowler Solicitors	Convent School
Chic Hair Salon	Private house
Hippotek	Private house
Junction 28 Gallery	Drs Murphy and Gidley's surgery
Private house	Miss Dolly Grant
Private house	Mrs Grant
Golds Place (Vacant)	Bill Woolcott's dental practice
Barclays Bank	Culm Vale Electricity Company with Manager Mr Tincknell. This was the Headquarters and Showroom of the Company but power was generated by turbines sited beside the river at a location roughly between Little Copse and Bradninch.
Manchester Building Society	Private houses
	Mr and Mrs Evans and Phyllis Potter's hairdressing salon
The Vale Veterinary Practice	Private house of Mr and Mrs Bill Hill
Hamiltons	Private house of Mr Martin (?)
Dunn & Baker	Unitarian Church Manse of Revd Pocock
Conservative Club	Conservative Club
Private house	Private house of Mr and Mrs Snow
Barber's Shop	Private house of Mr and Mrs Cottrell (?)

The Silent Cinema

Muriel Coxhead

The first cinema was run by my father, Mr Bill Terry. After he was demobbed from the Royal Flying Corps in 1918 he set up a cinema in the Victoria Hall. The films were silent and accompanied on the piano by Len Dyer who was only 14 at the time but a very competent pianist. Admission was 4d. and the seating was wooden benches. There was only one projector so there was an enforced interval while the reel was changed. He also used to tour the neighbouring villages in an old Model T Ford showing the latest silent Charlie Chaplin or Mary Pickford film.

The Regal Cinema

Eileen Andrews

The Regal Cinema was situated behind what is now the carpet shop. My earliest memories are of my father, Mr E. Kerslake, who was the commissionaire. He wore a very smart uniform plus a peaked hat and very well polished boots. Being an ex soldier he looked very much the part and certainly kept order. Anyone misbehaving would be escorted outside. My mother then joined the staff as cashier and I used to think my father looked most important and my mother looked very efficient. At the same time my sister became an usherette and I used to envy her

Local Business

Above: *The coal business at Exeter Hill of Mr Stanley Perryman and his father Francis. The names of the men in the photograph are unknown, 1930s.*

Left: *The building of Heyford House by Labdon & Sons, 1901–03. The house was built for Dr Gidley who is in the centre of the picture (next to the ladder) (now the premises of Harris Fowler Solicitors).*

Right: *The Half Moon, Fore Street.*

Below: *High Street, c.1910. Martin's is now HSBC.*

Looking down Fore Street towards Exeter Hill.

smart uniform and her opportunity to watch the films every night if she wished. After a couple of years, although I was really not old enough, I also became an usherette. Mr and Mrs Copp, who owned the cinema, would come in from their house which is now the carpet shop. They would check that everything was all right. I was told off for sitting down instead of standing up looking smart more times than I care to remember.

The seat prices started at 3d. old money for the first two rows, then 5d. for the next three, gradually rising to 9d. and 1s.3d. then 1s.9d. To sit on what was called 'the step' for the back three rows cost 2s.3d. and woe betide my sister and I if we let any of our friends sit in a more expensive seat than they had paid for.

In the post-war years there were frequent cuts in the electricity supply and the films would come to a halt. Sometimes the cuts lasted only minutes then the show would start again, but on other occasions the audience went home having seen only part of a film! The films were on more than one reel and there would be an interval while the projectionist changed over the reels. When cowboy films were being shown, certain people would come to the pictures wearing a cowboy hat, and the cheers would echo around the cinema when the bad cowboys were killed. I can remember when there were long queues to see a good film. It was one of my jobs to go along the queue and say how many seats at a certain price were left. Very often people went away disappointed but they would reserve a seat for the next night. My father would carefully look at the seating plan to make sure the correct seats were reserved.

The Regal was a place where many a youngster smoked their first cigarette but if my father happened to see someone smoking in the threepennies or the sevenpennies then he would confiscate the cigarette. While pretending to look for empty seats I used to shine my powerful torch at the courting couples – much to their embarrassment.

In the half-time interval we would always carry around a tray full of ice-cream, sweets and cigarettes. Very often I would visit the projection room and try my skill. Mr Chilcott was a very patient man.

As well as the main film, there was always a 'small film' and the newsreels. Sometimes there were cartoons. The seats were very comfortable but if you stood up your seat would fly up behind you.

I believe that parts of the old cinema are still recognisable behind the shop. It would be wonderful if it could be restored and the town could have its Regal back.

REGAL CINEMA, CULLOMPTON

Complimentary Ticket

To admit M

Holidays Excepted). To be shown at door also to Excise authorities when asked for.

DATED

Signed Directors

Three Mariners, Fore Street (which later became the Half Moon), now Tavy Textiles.

The Rising Sun (now Community House) and the Angel Inn
(now the site of Culm Meat Supplies and the Golden Eagle Chinese take-away), Fore Street.

Chapter Five

Inns of the Parish

In 1965 Cullompton had 19 fully licensed premises including ten public houses: the Bell Inn, the Commercial Hotel, the Cullompton Hotel, the Half Moon, the King's Head, the Manor House Hotel, the Market House, the Merry Harriers, the Railway Inn and the White Hart. It also had seven registered clubs including: Cullompton and District Conservative Club, the Royal Antedeluvian Order of Buffaloes, Culm Valley Bowling Club, the British Legion Club, Cullompton Rugby Supporters Club and St Andrew's Masonic Club.

Cullompton Cricket Club's first licence was granted on 10 March 1969. The Crow's Nest Café in Exeter Road, later renamed the Inglenook Restaurant, had their first licence granted on 19 June 1967 and the Georgian Café in Higher Bullring, later renamed the Bullring Restaurant, was first licensed in December 1969.

Cullompton has always had a good number of licensed premises and the *Church Parochial Magazine* of April 1903 records that a deputation had been sent to the 'Brewster Session' explaining that the number of licensed houses was too large for the population of the parish. A petition was presented, signed by 450 adult parishioners. At those 'Brewsters Sessions' the solicitor acting for the police said that the main street in Cullompton was practically honeycombed with public houses and he objected to the renewal of all licences. The Revd Forrester stated in his article that when people were asked to sign the petition:

One or two eccentric individuals, indeed, expressed a wish that the number were 'doubled'. I trust their reason was, that they thought that by such multiplication the 'Houses' would kill each other.

He continued:

I do not expect that the withdrawal of the few Licences, thus far abolished, will have any very great immediate effect upon the use of intoxicants. But it will have some; and the effects will be more apparent, as time goes on... We all know right well – and none better than our Magistrates – how much of the crime, poverty, and misery of our land is due to the 'drink'.

The public houses in Cullompton have included:

Admiral Hawke In 1830 its address was recorded in a trade directory as being in New Street and the landlord as William Teed. However, in 1844 it was listed at Exeter Road. William Teed was still the landlord. There is a thought that it may have eventually changed its name to the Commercial Inn, which later became the Pony and Trap.

The Angel This pub was sited in Fore Street, now Culm Meat Supplies and the Golden Eagle Chinese take-away. One of the objections raised to these premises in 1903 was that there was no accommodation for horses and traps. The licence was not renewed and the following December it was reported in the *Licensing World* and the *Licensing World Review* that:

William Heatman had for many years carried on 'The Angel' at Cullompton in a manner which gave perfect satisfaction to the public and to the police. He had invested his capital in the house and reasonably looked forward to remaining in undisturbed possession thereof, as long as he conformed to the law of the land. But at the last Licensing Session the renewal of his licence was refused, not through any fault of his own, but because of the Magistrates – who had previously licensed the house in the interests of the public – came to the conclusion that 'there were too many licences in Cullompton'. So poor Heathman had been driven to the Bankruptcy Court.

However, this report may be incorrect, as the licence was only transferred to him in 1901 and, although he had received no convictions, he had been warned by the police on many occasions about keeping a disorderly house. The house was also described as 'dirty' and 'a small and very badly arranged house within 65 yards of four other fully licensed houses.'

Bell Inn At one time there were two Bell Inns, the Old Bell Inn, near the church, and the New Bell Inn, in Exeter Road. Both were listed in 1830, but by 1856 only the New Bell Inn was listed and by 1888 it was referred to merely as the Bell Inn.

Globe Hotel Darts Team, 1950–51. Left to right, back: M. Palfrey, J. Sharland, A. Emery, D. Sanders, G. Perry, P. Fowler; front: W. Palfrey, E. Sanders, S. Morgan, J. Lake, L. Broom.

Outing from the Crown and Thistle (now a fish and chip shop), Cockpit Hill, 1913.

Bishop Blaize This inn in the High Street was listed in 1830 and in 1870 but not in 1889. The compilers have been unable to determine its exact location.

Boot Inn Some reports of the great fire of 1839 state that it started at the Boot Inn in New Street, others that it started at a small house in Exeter Street, the home of John Walters, a shoe maker. John Walters was listed as beer retailer and shoemaker at this address. It is thought that the pub was in Exeter Hill opposite the entrance to New Street and horses were taken in through a passage at the side.

Commercial There was a Commercial in Fore Street listed in 1830 and we know that there was also a Commercial Inn in Exeter Hill in 1878 – it may be that this was originally the Admiral Hawke. In 1976 it was renamed the Pony and Trap. No-one could think of an appropriate sign for the Commercial and Mrs Dorothy Prigg, wife of the landlord Mr Alan Prigg, suggested a change of name as a reminder of Mr Oburn (Obie) Luxton and his horse Snowball. Mr Luxton lived close to the pub and Snowball was stabled underneath the skittle alley for many years.

The pub sign shows Mr Luxton and Snowball who walked the streets of Cullompton for 39 years. Mr Luxton first drove one of his father's cabs to and from the railway station and later he had his own courier's business with a horse and cart in Cullompton. At one time Obie would drive up through the town ringing a bell to let everyone know he was going to Exeter, to which town he would deliver parcels and letters.

Crown and Thistle Now a fish and chip shop, the Crown and Thistle on Cockpit Hill was formerly called the Crown Fish and Chip Shop. The licence was objected to in 1903 as the landlord had supplied a constable on duty with liquor, but it was renewed.

Cullompton Hotel Opened in 1930, this establishment was funded by a group of local entrepreneurs. The original Board of Directors included Messrs J.E. Bamsey (Chairman), Plumpton, R.F. Miller and A.W. Salter (Secretary). It was erected as a purpose-built hotel and gentlemen's drinking club and included what is now the Culm Valley Bowling Club. It changed its name to Toad Hall in 1988 when it was sold to Mr Peter Radford and two partners, an apt though entirely coincidental alteration as the field opposite, on which Knightswood is built, was once known as Frogpool Meadow. The reason for the change of name given by the new owners was that it reminded them of Toad Hall as you walk in through the main entrance. It was later sold to the Bampton Project and became a residential home.

Devonshire Inn In 1878 William Walters was listed as town crier and victualler at this address. It is thought that the inn was located where the present-day cottages run off Queen's Square towards Cockpit Hill. It was listed in the 1891 census but the licence was not renewed in 1903, as the police complained that there were too many entrances to the house. At that time it was stated that 'the landlord, Mr Benjamin Elston, was a respectable man. He had been landlord for 8 years and had no other occupation, getting crippled up a bit.'

Dolphin: Situated in Fore Street, the Dolphin is now Cullompton General Stores. In 1903 it belonged to Messrs Starkey, Knight and Ford, and the licensee told magistrates that he did not allow women to drink at the inn and did not encourage loose characters. It later became a fish and chip shop and then an ironmongers.

Fountain Inn Situated in Fore Street, the Fountain Inn is now Moss Chemist. In 1903 it was the only free house in the town. A chemist's business was carried on in the premises. The licence had been held by Mr Foster since 1859 and before that by his father for 30 years. There is a side window which overlooks Fore Street and the landlord would watch for the congregation coming out of church on Sunday morning and have the pints of beer lined up on the bar by the time his regulars arrived from church.

Globe Hotel Listed (in Fore Street) in 1830, the Globe Hotel occupied the site which became Cullompton Rugby Club and later Animal Fayre and the Sue Ryder Shop. The downstairs was the Labour Exchange and during the 1930s this was where people 'signed on'.

Half Moon This pub was listed in 1830 as a posting house, the address given being High Street. In 1845 the premises were for sale by auction and included the inn, with the yard, stables and two gardens. It is thought it may have originally been named the Green Dragon. It is also thought that the inn included land from the Town Hall to Middle Mill Lane down to the Mill Leat. Cottages in Middle Mill Lane were originally quarters for the ostlers and servants working in the inn. In 1870 part of the Half Moon was sold to the town and the Town Hall was later built on the site. The Labdon family bought the land in about 1896.

Three Mariners (located where Tavy Textiles is now) later changed its name to the Half Moon, and in 1878 the address for the Half Moon was given as Fore Street and the Three Mariners was no longer mentioned.

King's Head Located at 35 High Street, this inn was named after Charles II. In 1903 an objection was received to the renewal of the licence because the landlord had been fined for keeping open his premises during prohibited hours. The then landlord, Mr Darch, told the court that he had been in the house for 15 years, it was always full on market days and sometimes he had 30 horses in the yard. He had 10 or 11 soldiers and horses billeted on him.

There is a story that the pub is haunted by a US airman who was stabbed in the public bar and has been back to haunt the pub on a number of occasions. At one time part of the pub was a public library.

London Inn This inn in Low Street (now Station Road) was listed in 1830 and was situated opposite Belle Vue Terrace. The licence was not renewed in 1903, the objections being that the premises had changed hands three times since 1896 and that there had been complaints of people loitering about there on Sunday mornings.

Manor House Hotel This hotel was originally a private house. On Christmas Eve 1981 a fire, thought to have been started when it spread through floorboards from a chimney breast, trapped Justin Tolcher, aged 16, son of Mrs Tricia Tolcher who ran the hotel. Justin was saved but the hotel was closed, to be reopened in May 1983 with new owners Mr and Mrs Ron Peters. Mr and Mrs Peters later bought the adjacent property, Veryards, and incorporated it into the hotel.

Market House Inn Listed in 1830 in Fore Street, this inn was once known as the Shambles, where meat was sold.

Merry Harriers Mr and Mrs Ron Splatt took over the pub at Westcott in 1960 and sold it in 1981. Mr Splatt's grandmother had been the first landlady 90 years previously. It was know locally as the Merry Dogs. After its sale the pub attracted much publicity in 1981 when its name was changed to the 'X' in an attempt to enter the *Guinness Book of Records* as the shortest pub name. It soon returned to its former name.

Mutterton Inn This inn was a beerhouse.

Railway Hotel In 1903 this hotel on Station Road was reported as an establishment with plenty of bedroom accommodation and stabling, and it served as a useful house for people who had to go by rail as it was only 300 yards from the station. It was later renamed the Showman in recognition of the fairground people who live near the pub during the winter. It eventually became the Weary Traveller in 1990 when it was refurbished, the reason for the change of name being that many tourists stop here.

Rising Sun This Fore Street pub is now Community House and was next door but one to the Angel Inn.

Three Mariners Elizabeth Serle was listed as landlord at this Fore Street establishment in 1830 and it was also in her possession when it was advertised as being 'to let by auction' in 1845. It was later renamed the Half Moon and was situated where Tavy Textiles is now.

White Hart The White Hart, also in Fore Street, was a posting house where James Tapscott was landlord in 1830. In its coaching days it was much bigger than it is now with its own ostler and stables at the rear. There was also a field so that horses could be grazed before going back into service. It is thought that General Buller stayed here whilst on his way to Plymouth.

Above: *The Half Moon Inn, c.1950s. Left to right: Reg Norris, George Ellis, Kath Norris and her mother Mrs James.*

Left: *White Hart Outing to Paris for England/France Rugby match, 1961.*

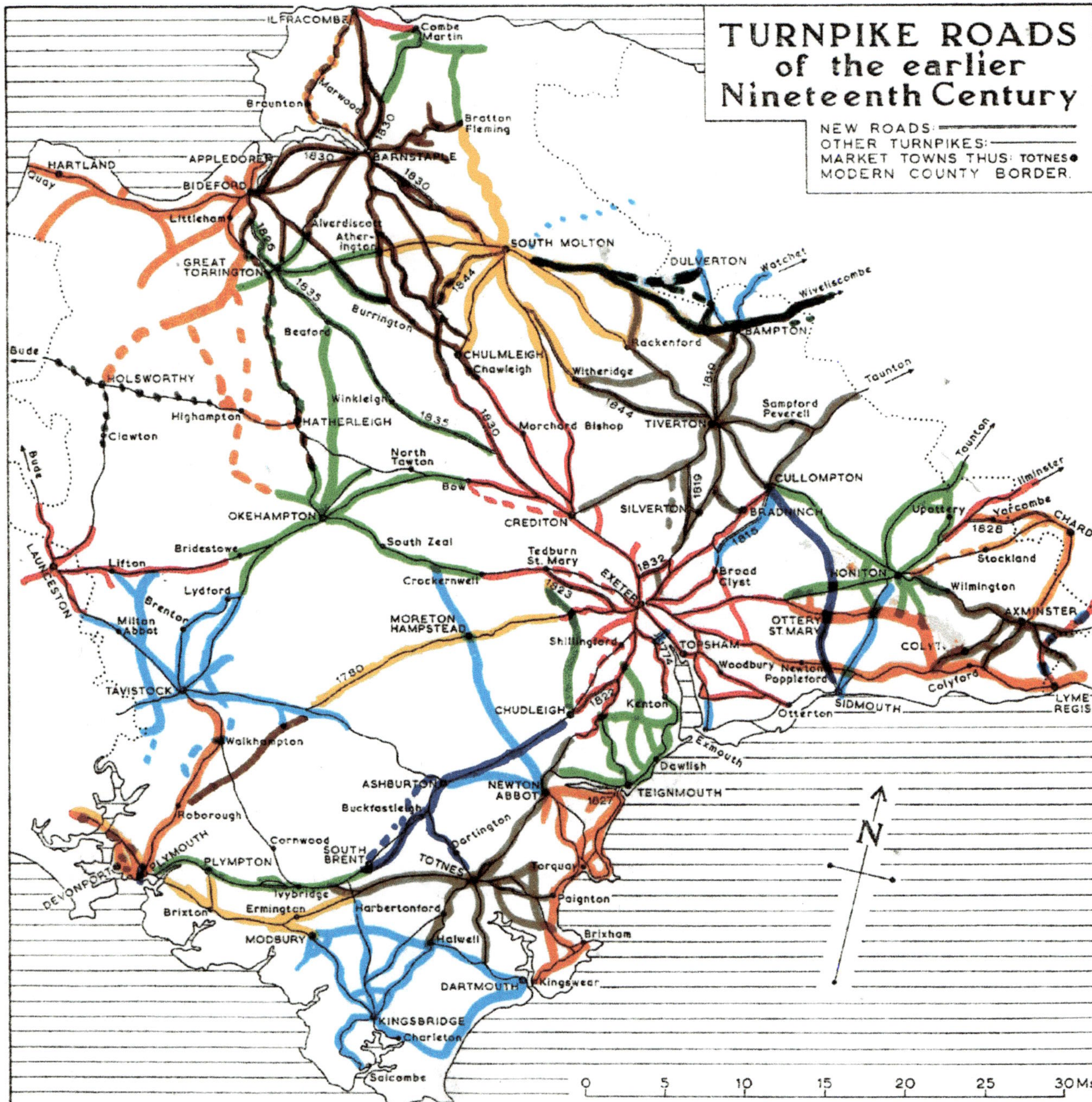

DEVON TURNPIKES

map based on Sellman (1962)

Created	Mileage	Turnpike Trust
1754	28	Ashburton (Ashburton & Totnes Consolid)
1763	104	Barnstaple
1764	42	Bideford
1829		Braunton
1838	21	Combe Martin
1866	5	Combe Martin and Ilfracombe
1769	2	Countess Wear Bridge
1813	6	Cullompton
1812	7	Dartmoor and Roborough
1765	38	Dartmouth, Torquay and Shaldon
1754	26	Devon and Dorset (Axminster)
1753	147	Exeter
1832	2	Exmouth
1765	69	Great Torrington
1754	49	Honiton
1807	15	Honiton and Ilminster
1816	7	Honiton and Sidmouth
1824	56	Kingsbridge and Dartmouth
1758	39	Lyme Regis (Charmouth to Wimple)
1759	16	Modbury
1772	16	Moretonhampstead
1761	26	Newton Bushell
1760	38	Okehampton
1804	16	Plymouth and Tavistock (New Road)
1757	16	Plymouth, Eastern
1844	16	Sidmouth to Cullompton
1759	42	South Molton
1784	4	Stonehouse
1762	51	Tavistock
1831	9	Tedburn St Mary to Chudleigh
1823	27	Teignmouth and Dawlish
1758	88	Tiverton
1759	44	Totnes and Bridgetown-Pomeroy
		From Other Counties
1760		Launceston
1759		Chard
1765		Minehead Roads
1786		Wiveliscombe
		Holsworthy Highways Board
		Roads dis-Turnpiked early

Chapter Six

TRANSPORT

Due to its location Cullompton has always been a place that people pass through. At first it was on horseback, later by stagecoach and in recent years in their cars and lorries. The Pigot's trade directory of 1830 describes Cullompton as a 'thoroughfare town between Exeter, Bath and Bristol'. By the middle of the 19th century Cullompton parish had 38 miles of roads and under the Poor Law Act could impose a threepenny rate for maintenance. This raised £160, and one man, called the foreman of the roads, was employed full time. Farmers whose land flanked roads had to pay for their upkeep and consequently they were frequently in a very bad state.

Some of the roads were maintained by tolls and by 1854 there were ten miles of turnpike roads in the parish. These were divided into four trusts: one entered the town from the Exeter direction and ran to the top of Exeter Hill; the Tiverton turnpike entered the centre of town and ran to the end of Tiverton Road and by another branch to the college turnpike gate; the Honiton turnpike came into what is now Station Road; and the Cullompton trust started at Padbrook Bridge turnpike and included the rest of the road through town towards Willand.

Gatehouse, Tiverton Road. A gatehouse once stood at the entrance to Langlands Road, this little cottage was a toll-house and farmers bringing their animals into town had to pay a fee. At the same time sheep were taken to Sir George's Well to be dipped. They would be taken up Growen Lane and through Rull to evade the toll charge.

A great deal of traffic used to pass through the town in those days. Posting houses such as the White Hart and Half Moon were stopping places for stagecoaches which were very expensive and used solely by the rich. The poor used the slow stage wagons, great carts piled high with goods and pulled by six or eight horses.

The days of horses galloping over Cullompton's cobbles ended in the spring of 1844 when the Bristol and Exeter Company completed its railway line to Exeter. At that time first-class carriages were tolerable, the second moderate and third-class open tubs like cattle wagons, exposed to wind and weather.

With the passing of the old mail coaches Cullompton became the centre of a new postal district, east of Exeter to the Somerset border. No longer were cities and towns isolated from each other; for the first time there was a network of communications that could make news available in hours rather than days.

The construction of the railway, combined with the later introduction of the car meant that Cullompton's position as a stopping place gradually became less important. The railway enabled the growth of other large manufacturing towns, and local industry, particularly the woollen and weaving trades, gradually shifted from rural areas to large factories in these manufacturing towns. Gradually Cullompton's traditional industries declined and thus so did its wealth.

After the Second World War, as affluence gradually increased, more people were able to afford cars and holidays. Mrs Dummett explains:

People from up country decided they wanted to come down this way for holidays and through the summer it was horrendous along the main street. Friday night and Saturday the whole town was nose to tail all the time. It was all holiday people because you see that was the route they used to take to Cornwall and South Devon. The motorway wasn't out there and everything from the north had to come through us and you'd be standing there an hour – you know you just couldn't get across; it was chaos and that was until the motorway was built.

The toll-house on Exeter Road next to the Bell Inn.

Old Hill before the motorway was built. Mr Bill Wright and his horses Champion and Princess. The hay was taken to Mr Jack Force at Heron's Dairy, Colebrook Lane. This was before Meadow Lane and it had to be taken up Duke Street and through the tanyard.

To ease this problem a town bypass was completed in October 1969 and upgraded to become a section of the M5 motorway in 1974. Cullompton has now gone full circle; the building of the motorway attracted housing development which, together with an increase in car ownership and the amount of freight moved by road instead of rail, resulted in the main road through the town being busier than before the bypass was built.

The railway station was closed in 1964 as a result of the Beeching Report which questioned the economic viability of rural services and prompted a 29 per cent reduction in rural lines. The local authorities are now actively seeking to re-open Cullompton Station and there are many people who consider the building of a new town bypass to be the answer to Cullompton's traffic problems.

In 1990 Devon County Council sent a questionnaire to every home in the parish asking 'do you believe Cullompton's traffic problems can be solved by building a new road?'; approximately 50 per cent were returned, just over 85 per cent replied positively. Six options were given for a preferred route for such a road but, although a route was agreed, there is no intention in the year 2001 to build a road.

A Motorway Services Area (MSA) was opened in 1999 and Cullompton became the first town to have a McDonalds Restaurant on a Motorway Services Area. Unlike many MSAs it is close to housing development and within walking distance of the town. There was a lot of opposition to its construction particularly from owners of take-away restaurants and cafés in the town centre, as well as from people living on Culm Lea who were concerned that the roundabout would cut them off from the remainder of the town.

The decision to allow the development of the MSA was prompted by public opinion as many believed it would bring about the re-opening of the station. The construction of the MSA has provided the necessary road infrastructure and land has been set aside for a railway platform and car parking. However, since the proposal to re-open the station was first mooted the railways have been privatised and it is now the train operating companies that need to be convinced of the feasibility of a re-opened Cullompton Station.

Government policy, at the time of writing, is to encourage less reliance on the motorcar and promote the use of public transport. There is no funding available for the building of new roads and, although the possibility of constructing a motorway junction between Cullompton and Broadclyst has been investigated, for a variety of reasons, it is not a viable option at the time of writing.

THE STATION

by Marian Dummett

There are conflicting reports about where the name Nags Head came from. I have been told that Irish navvies were brought in to lay the lines and that a pub was built at Nags Head to accommodate them, hence the name. However, I have also been told that it was so called because the railway line at that location was the shape of a horse's head.

Furthermore, it has been suggested that whilst Brunel was building the railway he carried out some work in St Andrew's church. At this time there were said to be rods placed across the barrel roof in the main aisle to stop the roof from falling as a result of the vibrations caused by the trains passing through Cullompton.

My mother, who was born in 1889, used to tell how once when a very important engine went through Cullompton, people stood on the hills to watch, and likewise when the royal train was passing through everyone went out to the station to view the event. I can remember doing this, but we never saw any of the royals.

Having passed a scholarship I had to go to Tiverton to school each day by train. We caught the 8.03a.m. which would stop at Tiverton Junction. We would then catch the Tivvy Bumper (the nickname for the train which ran between Tiverton Junction and Tiverton). Cullompton Station, at that time, consisted of a goods office, the stationmaster's office,

Above and right: *The bypass being built in the 1960s.*

The Railway

Above: *The bridge at Cullompton Railway Station.*

Right: *Cullompton Railway Station in 1954 with GWR 4-6-0* Cornish Riviera.

Below: *Landscape view of Cullompton showing a steam train heading for the tunnel.*

Right: *Six traction engines, part of a collection of nine, lined up at Cullompton railway goods station, c.1952. They were to be broken up for scrap. Owned by Mr T. Manfield of Cullompton and Mr Bray of Plymtree, they were bought by Mr Jones of Taunton (in the light coat). With him are Mr J. Hawkes (stationmaster) and Mr S. Bending (foreman). Also present are Messrs J. and W. Jones (sons of Mr Jones), Mr J. Lock (uncle of Mr Jones senior) and Messrs J. Matthews and J. Stabb (employees).*

the ticket office, a general waiting room and a ladies' waiting room all on the north-bound platform. One then had to cross the bridge to the south-bound platform where there was also a general waiting room, a ladies' waiting room and a gents' toilet.

There were three railway lines running through the station; one up and one down and one in the middle for fast trains. There was a stationmaster, ticket collector and porters working on the station and I remember that all the furniture in the waiting rooms was made of leather and wood and was very highly polished, as was the floor. In the winter there was always a very large coal fire burning in the grate no matter what time you travelled.

As children, we were travelling during the war with blackout and troop trains. These trains, full of soldiers, would sometimes delay our local train and make us late for school! Stan Aldridge remembers that when he was called up for the Navy, he left home at 6.00a.m. and after about five changes of train arrived in North Wales 18 hours later. These 18-year-olds had no food, very little sleep and had probably never left Cullompton before. They were then marched one and a half miles to their barracks. This was a holiday camp, a naval training centre known as HMS Glendower. Stan's wife, Bet, told of a visit to Manchester that she made just after the war to visit a penfriend and she had to stand all the way.

Trains then were usually crowded. Betty Sanders has said that she would come off night duty in a munitions factory and when coming home would go to sleep standing up in a crowded train. This was from Bristol – home for the weekend if you were lucky.

After the war, the railway changed. Cheap day return tickets came into being. One has to remember that hardly anyone amongst the working population had a car and so at weekends in summer practically all the young families would head for the sea on the excursion train. We took prams and pushchairs and of course our food. These were steam trains and the children were repeatedly told to stop looking out of the windows as they could get 'smuts' in their eyes. The fare to Dawlish Warren was 1s.6d. increasing to 2s.3d. to Goodrington Halt. The further down the line one went the better the chance of getting a seat coming back. By the time the train got to Dawlish on the return journey, it would be standing room only and some in the guard's van.

Then there were the Sunday school treats. Once a year all the Sunday schools had an outing to the sea. Again the whole town took part. Usually the destination was Teignmouth. Often it rained and then we sat under the pier and ate cockles and winkles bought from a little stall. In many cases this was the only time children had seen the sea or travelled by train.

When at last we could afford holidays, usually a week in a caravan by the sea, again we travelled by train. The pram was loaded with luggage, in fact everything but the kitchen sink. One remembers walking to the station and again walking to our campsite the other end. If it rained we got wet.

After the war chocolate and cigarette machines were introduced on railway stations; 1d. for a bar of chocolate and 2d. for a packet of ship cigarettes. As there were still shortages the news spread like wildfire when the machines had been filled.

In addition to a passenger station, Cullompton Station was virtually the centre of trading. There was a coal yard and a goods yard. Coal was brought in open trucks, unloaded and then put into sacks to be delivered around town by Bill Irish with his horse and cart. The factories also obtained all their coal from the trains unloading at Cullompton. Then there was Jack Rugg who also had a horse and wagon. He delivered any parcels which had been sent by train, likewise he would collect. The wagons were kept in Higher Street, opposite Forge House, and the horses taken into a field at the bottom of Middle Mill Lane each evening. As well as small parcels, almost everything to be used in the factories and the town came by rail. Most of the raw materials came this way. Likewise animals, having been bought or sold, were transported in cattle trucks and then walked through the town to their farms. The milk train would stop to pick up churns left by farmers (before milk lorries), and the produce of the town was sent by rail to be sold – paper boxes of tomatoes, bales of skins; the station was our outlet to the rest of the world. The factories worked to a deadline according to when the trains were due.

Then in 1964 we had Dr Beeching and the town went into panic – what would happen without the trains? But of course by this time there were more lorries and cars about. Cullompton survived but the sound of goods trucks being shunted, the fog detonators going off in the winter and steam trains and later diesel were missed around the district for a very long time. As were the fires on the railway banks caused by sparks from the steam engines during, what seemed to us to be, continually hot summers.

Bus Travel

by Jane Campbell

In the immediate post-war years the availability of regular and frequent buses to Exeter from the Higher Bullring encouraged Cullompton's transformation into a commuter town. Several children went to school in Exeter, the boys to Mount Radford and the girls to Bishop Blackall and The Maynard. The student fare was 8d. return in 1947. The buses were more popular than the trains because of the distance between St David's Station and Exeter city centre. The buses drove through the city centre to the depot which, at that time, was in Queen Street which is now the Harlequin Shopping Centre. An increasing number of workers travelled with the children leaving the Bullring at 7.55a.m.

In the early years the buses were in such poor mechanical condition that it was not unusual for the passengers to have to get off the bus and walk up over Bradninch Hill and then get back on at the top. Later, the number of passengers grew to such an extent that two double-decker buses left Cullompton – one went via Bradninch and the other took the direct route along the A38 (now the B3181) and waited at Hele Cross so that the buses could make the rest of the journey together. By the time they reached Broadclyst one bus would be full and the rest of the seats and standing room would fill up at Pinhoe. For the return journey at 4.20p.m. and 5.20p.m. it was usual for two double-deckers and a single-decker bus to leave the depot, now in Paris Street, and for the passengers to transfer to one bus at Broadclyst to complete the final stage of the journey.

As the city grew it became more difficult for workers to complete their journeys by public transport. For example, when Devon County Council moved to Topsham Road, there were no buses from the depot to the offices and workers gradually changed to car sharing and eventually almost everyone travelled to work in their own car.

WHITTON'S

Whitton's of Cullompton was one of the biggest names in south-western haulage. It was founded by Mark Whitton who was originally a farmer who started in haulage almost as a sideline using a horse and cart for timber haulage in the early 1900s. After the First World War his eldest son Reg took over, carrying coal from the railway to the local gasworks and nearby paper mills. In 1923 they bought the first of many Sentinel steamers which carried paper products up to Bristol returning with loads from the feed mills for the Devon farmers. Paper from Culm Valley and Exeter mills became their staple traffic, horses being kept at work on the coal round until 1945.

During the Second World War long-distance vehicles ran under the Ministry of Transport and in 1945 two of the firm's Mammoth Major eight-leggers were sent to Holland for three months to ferry supplies from the coast to major Dutch cities. By the end of the '40s they had a fleet of over 40 lorries and, being an obvious candidate for nationalisation, the entire fleet and premises were acquired in 1949.

Brothers Reg and Harold, who were running the business, had differing feelings about this enforced sale (their brother Wilfred, who had also been part of the family firm, had left in the early '30s to start a dairy business). They both kept jobs with BRS but while Reg took to the large firm, Harold missed being his own boss. They decided to buy a local bus operator, Green and Cream Coaches, but the business never took off. Being more at ease in haulage they bought two S-Type Bedford artics, quickly followed by another 20 vehicles and Whitton's Green & Cream was created. Control of the company eventually passed to Martin Whitton, son of Harold, who took over as Chairman, and together they saw the fleet peak at around 80 vehicles. Unfortunately, in the 1970s the company found itself faced with cashflow problems and, after being run by the receivers for two years, it was sold to Wild Transport of Exeter in 1973.

Whitton & Sons, with driver Wilfred Whitton.

Chapter Seven

HEAT, LIGHT & WATER

LET THERE BE LIGHT

A public meeting was called in May 1920 to consider an electricity supply for Cullompton. As a result a public company was formed with Mr E. Browning as secretary. Dr G. Gidley was extremely interested in the project and with Mr W.H. Terry worked out the details of a generating station in Tiverton Lane, on land belonging to the doctor. This was before the days of the 'Grid' and they decided on a scheme with the advice of Messrs Christy Bros of Chelmsford. It was a 430-volt, three-wire DC supply, giving domestic consumers a supply of approximately 210v. The power units (which stood in the building now occupied by the Scouts) were a single-cylinder Tangye, 45HP paraffin and an Allen twin two-stroke, 80HP heavy oil. These took the day load and a 460-volt 250-amp Hour battery carried the night load. The first premises supplied by the firm were Messrs Fare & Sons (now Proberts Bakery).

Owing to its limited power and capital the company was unable to extend to places such as Willand and in 1927 the bold step was taken to amalgamate with the Bradninch Electric Company and work under the name Culm Valley Electric Supply Co. Ltd. Starting at Broadclyst the new line was to extend to Hemyock with loop lines for places such as Halberton and Kentisbeare. It was promised that the cost per unit would be much less.

GAS

Cullompton gasworks in Station Road closed in 1956 after supplying gas for the town for 91 years. The gas was, in future, to come from Exeter. The retorts were installed by Messrs Willey and Co. in 1865 for the Cullompton Gas Light and Coke Co. With its three beds of coke chambers and 20 horizontal retorts, the works could supply a maximum of 150000 cubic feet of gas per day. At first only Cullompton was supplied but the service was later extended to Bradninch.

In 1929 the Cullompton Gas Company passed into the hands of the Devon Gas Association until it was nationalised in 1949. In 1956 it was 'integrated', a word coined by the South Western Gas Board to explain its policy of concentrating the supply of small towns in high-pressure mains in much the same way as electricity power is supplied from the grid system.

TOWN WATER

The year 1356 was an important one in the history of the parish. The inconvenience, dirt and disease occasioned by the lack of a proper water supply, magnified by the incidence and aftermath of the Black Death, led the people to petition the lord of the manor for leave to construct a watercourse of clear wholesome water from the hills on his estate to flow down through the town. The deed of gift of the Abbot of Buckland, the lord of the manor, granting and confirming this gift of running water, 'the greatest boon ever conferred upon the town', is preserved among the most valuable parish archives. It is quite legible, although the seal attached to it is somewhat clipped. A translation from the Latin is as follows:

Know all men, present and to come, that we Thomas Abbot of Bokelonde and of the Covent of the same place, have given, granted, and by this our present writing have confirmed to our whole Homage of Columpton, leave to have a watercourse of clear wholesome water between the ditch of Weremede, the land of my Lord the Earl of Devon, and the land of Thomas Vacie unto the High Street of Columpton, over all our domain, and the land of our tenants for ever, without the hindrance of our successors. In testimony whereof of our common seal is hung to these presents,

These being witnesses –

Thomas Gambon	*William Furneaux*
John Roke	*Thomas Facie*
William Whitemore	*Henry Chopyn*
(and many others)	

Given at Bokelonde, the sixth day of May, in the year of the reign of King Edward the Third, since the Conquest of England, the twenty ninth.

Cullompton's old water supply, known both as the Town Lake and the Watercourse, was given to the

Cullompton Sanitary Authority, c.1910.

Street scene showing the open watercourse, commonly referred to as 'The Gutter'.

town by the Abbot of Buckland or Bokelande on 6 May 1356; his generosity was commemorated in the naming of Bockland Close. From then on water was brought into the town via a stream which rises at Coombe Farm, about two and a half miles west of the town, and about a mile nearer the town it joins another stream from Hillersdon, running through several meadows and into a pond just outside Shortlands. After Shortlands it was divided into several different channels and distributed through various gardens and courts. It ran in open channels at the sides of the streets to all parts of the town – nearly every court had a little running stream.

There was considerable conflict as people either diverted or blocked the flow of the water. The Cullompton Watercourse Company was set up and Water Bailiffs were appointed to protect the interests of the town and prosecute offenders. The Company's minute-book records its activities until October 1878.

'Possessioning Day' was a ceremony which took place every seven years. The 'possessioning' took place rather in the manner of a beating of the bounds, to point out the proper channel to younger inhabitants and ensure the water wasn't being abused. The earliest 'possessioning' recorded is 13 August 1716 when numerous obstructions and diversions were found and their perpetrators threatened with legal action. Participants would assemble outside the White Hart at precisely 1.00p.m. and proceed up the stream to the Spring Head where a hogshead (a large cask contained approximately 50 gallons) of prime cider and cakes were served. There are records of drunken behaviour in the town following this ceremony, with people being drenched with water.

In 1861 a Nuisance Removal Committee was set up following the Public Health Act and a visit from a Board of Health inspector in 1854. At that time the watercourses were used for 'pot' purposes, i.e. boiling vegetables, for surface drainage and at night for emptying cesspools. Sewerage, drainage and the supply of water and sanitary conditions were investigated and the report came to the following, rather grisly, conclusion:

Typhus and other epidemic diseases are so prevalent here more so than in any other parish in the Union and the mortality of the parish is as high as 28.3 per 1000, about 23 per cent being due to contagious diseases.

The watercourses were eventually only used to keep the streets clean but people were very proud of them. In a radio interview for 'Have A Go' recorded in December 1961 the then Chairman of the Town Council Mr Stafford Hill, who was a farmer, made the comment that:

The people of Cullompton, I think, would fight for that more than anything else in the town; one time we had a public meeting when the county talked of taking it away from us to widen our main street and of all the 50 years I've lived in Cullompton it's the only open meeting that I can ever remember well filled; there were more people in the street than could get in the hall and it was overruled!

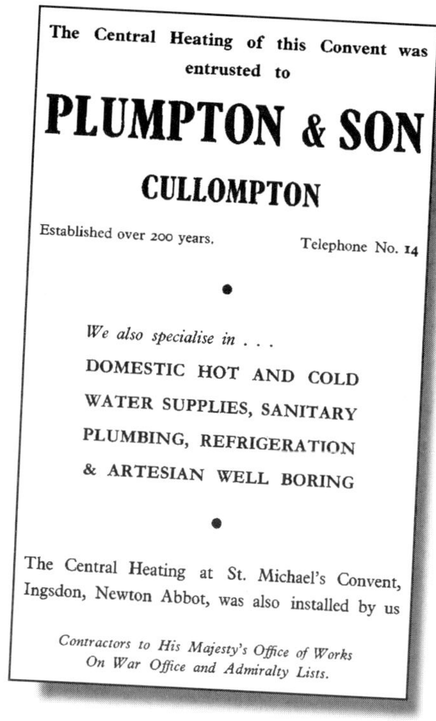

Unfortunately the water would flood some cellars and the Council and town elders decided that they would not take on the upkeep of the water from the Tiverton Rural District Council who wanted to hand it over. There was a public outcry but to no avail. The Council of the day decided that the watercourse should be closed and the flow of water through the streets stopped in 1962. One of the biggest moans amongst older Cullomptonians today is 'we should never have lost our water.'

The 1st Cullompton Scouts revised the tradition of 'possessioning'. This took place for three consecutive years in the early 1990s. Large numbers of people met in the Higher Bullring and walked the course of the water which took them through the meadows behind Langlands, on to Knowle and up into the hills below Bunnyford's Cross where cider and cakes were served.

REFUSE REMOVAL

At Cullompton Parish Council's Annual Parish Meeting in 1930 a Mr A.W. Clitsom protested that the present method of collecting refuse in an open vehicle was unhealthy. Refuse was blown all over the streets and sometimes into shops. He suggested that when the contract came up for renewal there should be a clause requiring the provision of a closed-in cart. There were concerns that this would increase the rates but the motion was carried.

Cloth Industry

Above: *Fox Brothers outing, 1960s.*

Below: *Heathcoats Factory, Tiverton Road (now Young Ones Day Nursery). The event is Mrs Drew's retirement, 1957. Left to right, back: Stella Young, Helen Simmonds, ?, Dora Talbot, Ada Whitton; front row includes: Dorothy Julian, Mo Clark, Mrs Ingersent, Annie Holway, Mrs Chubb, Mrs Drew, Violet Johns, Bert Reynolds, Margaret Rowe, Lil Hiscox, Elie Luxton.*

Above: *Lady weavers outside the factory, c.1920.*

Opposite page: *Fox Bros Textile Workers, 1912. During the First World War, when the company's whole output was devoted to khaki cloth and the famous 'Foxes Puttees', over 200 people were employed there.*

Chapter Eight

TRADE & INDUSTRY

BILBIE BELL FOUNDRY

In 1746 Thomas Bilbie established a bell foundry in Shortlands Lane. His relatives lived at Veryards which was next to the Manor House Hotel. The Bilbies were a Somerset family and famous bell-founders throughout the West Country. Between 1746 and 1815 over 400 bells were hanging in Devon church towers including a peal of eight at St Andrew's. The business continued until 1815 when Thomas Castleman Bilbie (Thomas' grandson) sold it to local tinman William Parnell who moved it to New Cut. His son Charles moved the business to Exeter in 1850. It is reputed that after his death Thomas Bilbie was buried in the church porch under the bells.

THE CLOTH TRADE

While plain coarse cloth would have been made on primitive handlooms from time immemorial, it was in the early-15th century that the weaving of fine kersies and later serges was introduced by weavers from the Continent. Cullompton, Tiverton and Crediton became well known in this trade.

Most of the weaving would have been done in cottages; a merchant would have premises in which the fleece was combed and sorted to be spun by hand, and the warps prepared. After the cottage weavers had done their work it would be sent to Exeter to be 'finished'. A great quantity was exported to Europe. There were several cloth merchants in Cullompton at that time, the best known being John Lane who gave the beautiful aisle to St Andrew's Church in 1526. The wool trade flourished in Cullompton and in 1816 Mr Upcott employed 60 weavers 'and many spinners' in a large building at Shortlands (now the site of Hammett Road).

Around 1910 Mrs Gustavus Gidley, the wife of a local doctor, revived the hand-weaving industry in the stables of Heyford House, now occupied by St John Ambulance. This evolved into machine-knitted garments and was known as 'The Weavers'.

On the mechanisation of the weaving industry, Messrs Fox Bros of Wellington built a branch factory at Cullompton (in 1900) which continued to make high-quality woollen and worsted cloth until 1977 when the branch closed down, putting an end to the long history of weaving in Cullompton.

The Weavers, on the site where St John Ambulance is now, c.1914.

Paper mill workers, early 1900s.

Paper Making

In the late 1800s paper making had changed from hand- to machine-made using the Fourdrinier system. Mr Reed of Reed & Smith came to the West Country and built modern mills at Buckfastleigh and later Higher Kings Mill. The original machine, used until the early 1970s, was marked 1892 on its cast framing.

Mr Reed had a backer, Mr Smith, and gradually built up the paper-making group Reed & Smith with the purchase of Silverton Paper Mill and Wansborough at Watchet. Mr Reed had four sons so they managed one each until the demise of Buckfastleigh in the 1930s. Higher Kings Mill continued with its 1892 machine until 1956 when a new, larger machine was built which produced the blue sugar-bag material and wallpaper base.

In the early 1980s St Regis bought Reed & Smith and Higher Kings Mill continued to thrive. The mill recycles over 30000 tonnes of waste paper into many paper grades, including coloured drawing paper for schools, hanging files, wallpaper base, core paper for the inside of toilet rolls, photograph album paper, etc.

Since the 1950s the mill has directly employed 100 plus people, and today there are 120 workers. Initially the mill was run intermittently to fit in with farming. Itinerant workers farmed in the summer and made paper in the winter. Now the mill produces 24 hours a day, seven days a week, 357 days each year and the employees work in shifts.

Paper making at Higher Kings Mill has been an important source of employment in Cullompton for over 100 years.

Top: *St Regis Paper Mill outing, c.1958. Left to right, back: Joyce Westcott, ?, ?, Mrs Sweet, ?, Mrs R. Clarke, Mrs Wotton, ?, ?, ?, ? ?, ?, ?, Mrs Land, Mrs L. Clarke; front: ?, Mrs Norman, Mrs Hoskins, Cynthia Stanbury.*

Above: *Workers of the Salle (where paper was sorted), July 1948. Left to right, standing: ?, Mrs Hunnings, Kath James, ?, Dulcie James, Evelyn Dodge, ?, Flo Chilcott, Mavis Carter, ?, Edue Perham, Olive Glanville, Albert Denner, Frank Burrows, Ted Gray; seated: Enid Clarke, Glen Wotton, Eileen Kerslake, Dorothy Wotton, Ian Hunnings.*

Leather & Jam

Left: *Machinists at Drevon and Brown, manufacturers of high-class leather gloves, c.1939. Left to right, back: May Jarvis, Betty Whitton and Decima Warren; middle: Pam Few, Marlene Chidgery, Verona Milford, Olive Pike, ?, ?, ? Stiling; front: Mary Greening, Kath Splatt, Joan Wilson, Marjorie Payne, Marion Mayne, ?, Pat Vinnicombe, ?.*

The jam factory was located where Ploudal Road is now, extending back to the present-day site of Roberts Close. Mr Copp was the manager during the 1930s and they produced Devon Dale Jam. The jam jars were kept in a wooden shed beside the factory where children often played. The workers' most vivid memories are of wasps and the smell!

Above, main: *Jam factory outing. Left to right, back: Manny Copp (obscured), ?, Mr and Mrs Pratt, Mr Nicholas, Mrs Copp, Mrs Dummett, Peggy Wilson, Mrs Richards, Mrs Nicholas, ?, Mrs and Mr West, Mrs Atkins, Win and Bill Brooks (Bill is obscured); front: Joyce Westcott, Alice Chilcot, Cynthia Copp, Betty Manfield, Marion Brooks.*

Above right: *Jam factory workers. Left to right, back: Ivy Atkins, Mrs Evis, Mrs Nicholas; front: Edie Mitchell, Angela Glass, Win Yendell, Betty Cross.*

Town Cabinet-Makers Since 1800

by Sid Russ

Luxtons was started in late 1800 in a loft at the rear of the 'Pony and Trap', Exeter Hill, Cullompton. Picture frames and small items of furniture were made, but the firm gradually progressed and employed more than 50 people as cabinet-makers, French polishers, upholsterers and women who sewed on facings, silk cords and gimps on upholstery. There were also carters who looked after the horses and on Monday mornings would tow wagon-loads of furniture bound for London, returning on Friday with timber, etc.

The workshops by then were at Cockpit Hill and Duke Street, with a large store near the church. All the work must have been done by hand, as there was no evidence of any machinery being used. Boys started work from about 12 years old and were trained until the age of 21 when they became journeymen (qualified) at their trades. During the last year of their apprenticeship they would make a small item of furniture from the waste pieces of wood, e.g. chests of drawers, writing desks or sideboards showing their skills in making the carcass, dovetailed drawers, mouldings and inlays. These were known as apprentice pieces and are now collectables.

Having finished their pieces, workmen would put their name on the back of the drawers, under tops of tables and in other out-of-sight places. One such name was Woolcott, a maker who had four sons and two daughters. One son became a RA, two became dentists, and the younger son Bill Woolcott became a well-known local dentist. A road in the town was later named 'Woolcott Way' in his memory.

The firm of George Luxton was at its greatest before the First World War, but inevitably it lost many of its workers to the conflict. One man, William Broom, who was unfit for military service, was sent to Bath Cabinet-Makers to make aeroplanes. Returning to Cullompton after the war to marry Elizabeth Woolcott, he started his own business in the town as a cabinet-maker.

When the war finished Luxtons returned to making furniture for the local trade and opened a retail shop in Fore Street. A wood called Satin Walnut was used quite extensively but it was popular with the furniture beetle and not many pieces of this material have survived.

During the 1930s a Ford Model T truck was used for deliveries. This survived until the Second World War and was later sold to an antique dealers. During the slump in the 1930s most firms reduced their workforce and just kept going. During the Second World War furniture was made under licence and was called 'utility'. It could only be purchased with dockets obtained from the Ministry offices. This furniture was well made and plain and is now also collectable.

Brothers Keith and Jack Luxton kept the firm going, retailing and doing repair work until it closed in the mid 1960s.

William Broom started his business in 1920 at a workshop in the New Cut with a retail shop in Fore Street. Trade was quite good to start with, and seven or eight workmen were employed, but in the slump of the 1930s the workforce was reduced. It was about this time that built-in furniture became popular and the firm did work for the Hon. Mrs Adams at Bradfield House.

Some made-to-order furniture was produced with repairs and alterations keeping the firm going up until the Second World War. By this time William Broom was the only workman and he made portable altars for Service Padres, also offering- and wafer-boxes. Church furniture repair work was also done for Wippels of Exeter, which gradually increased along with a steady flow of orders for memorial chairs and tables, etc. for churches and chapels. Meanwhile, the retail shop continued to sell 'utility' goods. Electricity was installed in the workshop and the first machinery was used.

In 1947 Sid Russ joined the firm and married Margaret, William's daughter. At this time, French polishing was on the decline owing to the high cost of the process and lacquers coming on the market. Re-upholstery of pre-war chairs and settees became a very successful part of the business. Formica then

Mr Sid Russ.

came onto the market and many tables and counter tops were covered with this new material. All the wartime restrictions had by now been removed leaving a healthy amount of timber and other materials open to be bought up. Mass production of furniture began, leaving small firms with little hope of competing. Thus repair work became the firm's main source of income.

With the death of William Broom, the firm was continued by M. and S. Russ and a decision was taken to build a new workshop in Shortlands Lane and to concentrate on antique restoring. Contact was made with a dealer in Somerset and a very successful partnership began, resulting in years of restoring for the export trade – a gypsy caravan being one of the many items taken on.

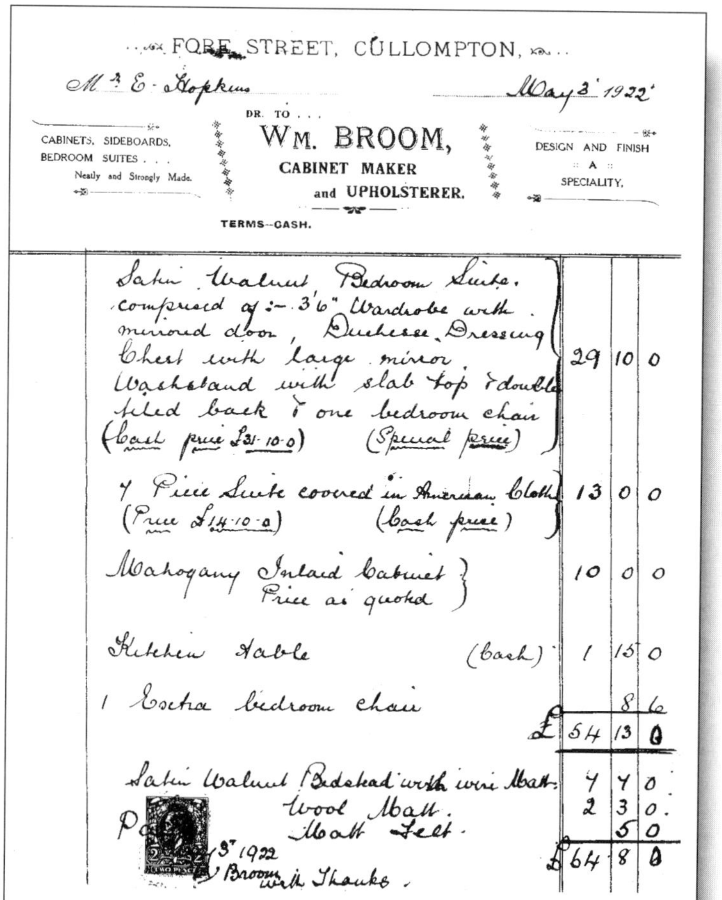
FORE STREET, CULLOMPTON,
Mr E. Hopkins — May 3rd 1922
DR. TO . . .
WM. BROOM,
CABINET MAKER and UPHOLSTERER.
CABINETS, SIDEBOARDS, BEDROOM SUITES . . . Neatly and Strongly Made.
DESIGN AND FINISH A SPECIALITY.
TERMS—CASH.

	£	s	d
Satin Walnut Bedroom Suite, comprised of :- 3'6" Wardrobe with mirrored door, Duchesse Dressing Chest with large mirror, Washstand with slab top & double tiled back & one bedroom chair (Cash price £31-10-0) (Special price)	29	10	0
7 Piece Suite covered in American Cloth (Price £14-10-0) (Cash price)	13	0	0
Mahogany Inlaid Cabinet, Price as quoted	10	0	0
Kitchen Table (Cash)	1	15	0
1 Extra bedroom chair		8	6
	£54	13	0
Satin Walnut Bedstead with wire Matt.	7	7	0
Wool Matt.	2	3	0
Matt Felt.		5	0
	£64	8	0

Pd 3rd 1922 Broom with Thanks.

Invoice from William Broom dated 1922.

With advanced training in London, Sid Russ became a registered restorer with Rural Industries. His great knowledge of decorative veneer work earnt him commissions to restore some very valuable pieces of furniture for members of the royal family, the National Trust and many large houses in the West Country. The company closed in 1990 with the retirement of Sid Russ.

KENNETH (KELLY) LUXTON

by Percy Cross

Kenneth Luxton, who was known to all as 'Kelly', was a 'real character' – a bit of an eccentric with a heart of gold. He would put on private movie shows at Sunday school prize-givings, etc. The films were always very old and kept breaking, but no-one seemed to mind. How he was cheered at the end and given a vote of thanks by the vicar!

He and his brother Jack continued their family's furniture business in Fore Street. They lived in St Andrew's House in Queen's Square which years before had extended down to the present Rivermead. The block of terraced houses, 3–9 Duke Street, had once stood in the grounds and been a furniture factory, where the Luxtons had once manufactured their own stock. This had all changed by the 1920s and the factory was converted into four residences.

In April 1943 Kelly, an ardent angler who shared his passion for fishing with George Cross and other prominent businessmen in the town, gave the surviving members of the group some good news – he had rented the fishing rights of the River Culm from Stoneyford Bridge to Last Bridge at the bottom of Old Hill. What was more he was awaiting a quote from the Fish Farm at Dulford to restock the river.

For several years after the war ended, Kelly organised an annual fireworks display. These events could not be classed as spectacular as the modern displays to which we have become accustomed, but there were always many very loud bangs and we enjoyed every flash and explosion.

CULM LEATHER DRESSING WORKS

Culm Leather Dressing Works near the railway station employed over 110 people treating and dying skins into fashionable colours. It was founded c.1921 by Leonard Vickery and Mr W. Stone who came from Yeovil and brought with them experienced leather workers. At first they tanned gloving leather from sheepskins and later made clothing leather also from sheepskins. Virtually all the men who worked there came from Cullompton. In the 1970s they were taken over by Strong and Fisher of Rushden who ran the factory, exporting a large percentage of their output. This continued until 1982 when they closed the factory putting 112 men and women out of work. At this time the tannery was run by Mr Ronald Vickery who was well known in the Scout movement and also a town and district councillor.

Chapter Nine

CARNIVALS, FESTIVALS & FÊTES

CARNIVALS

Until 1962 it is believed that Cullompton always had a night-time carnival during November which was lit up with hand-held torches. Daytime carnivals were held in 1935 for the Jubilee and in 1937 for the Coronation.

In May 1935, as the climax to Silver Jubilee week, a daylight carnival of 'extraordinary size and variety' was held in Cullompton, organised by Police Sergeant H.J.C. Wilshire. The *Devon & Somerset News* explained how, having conceived the idea only the previous Tuesday evening, he immediately approached a number of townsmen. A committee was formed and officers were appointed and Superintendent L.T. Gill and other members of the Cullompton Police Force also threw themselves wholeheartedly into the venture. Cullompton rallied around and the result was the staging of the largest and best spectacle ever seen in the Tiverton district, raising £70 for the Local Jubilee Fund.

Church parade passing the Rising Sun, date unknown.

The newspaper recorded feverish activity as people got themselves ready, and the final procession was estimated to be a mile in length including bands from Bradninch, Silverton (see *The Book of Silverton*) and Cullompton, decorated cars, costumed pedestrians and floats. The 'King and Queen' state coach was arranged by the police; the king was Police Constable S. Johns and the queen Miss Nancy Gill (daughter of Superintendent Gill). The floats included one entitled 'Waiting for Cullompton's swimming pool' on Mr Labdon's lorry. Children in costume paraded in the garden of the Cullompton Hotel (now Toad Hall) for judging.

The procession was followed by a confetti fête in the Higher Bullring where prizes were awarded to the costumed children. The proceedings wound up with a dance at the New Assembly Hall (now the Masonic Hall) which saw a crowded attendance. Music was by a band conducted by Mr Norman and the first to take the floor were the king and queen. MC duties were discharged by Messrs M.W. Woolcott and L. Endicott. When midnight struck all went home.

Some 50 years ago the carnival was in full swing. It was held in early November and each year there would be carnival fever at least two weeks before the event when many of the families of the town, as well as places of work, would be sworn to secrecy as to what would be featured on their carnival float. The procession was led by Obie Luxton on his horse, Snowball, followed by the Town Band. There would be as many as 25 lorries and many walkers, both children and adults.

There were frequent disasters with the lights on the floats. In the late 1940s and '50s the only lighting would be from a battery which seemed always to fail while judging was taking place. Everything, including costumes, was home-made, particularly on the floats entered by individual families. Many hours were spent over several days making paper flowers and on one particular float, hundreds of stars were made for 'Swinging on a Star' – a popular song of the time. Other memorable floats included a wedding cake and one entered by the paper mills portraying a huge windmill with hundreds of paper flowers. One float which swept the board was called 'A Gypsy Caravan' which had a real camp fire and was entered by the Kerslake family.

In recent years the route was from Meadow Lane to Station Road car park, and was organised by the Round Table for 15 years. In 1995 the carnival was discontinued as the organisers could not afford the £500 insurance cover.

Carnival Capers

Above: *The Royal Coach made a striking spectacle at the 'Jubilee Carnival' in May 1935.*

Left: *This carnival entry is from 1913. The girl on the left is Winnifred Spurway and the boy on the bike is Leonard Spurway. The pearly king on the right is William Spurway.*

Below: *The date is 24 November 1921. This carnival entry features costumes from all around the world including 'Uncle Sam', a cannibal on an elephant, several people holding spears, a very English lady and a nun.*

Top and above: *Carnival entries, 1920s (top photograph 1922).*

Above right: *Cullompton Festival pram races, 1980, with Julie Metcalf and Lynne Lane.*

Right: *Culm Vale Playgroup carnival float, 1985.*

✣ Coronation Street Party ✣

Below: *At the tea party, standing from the left: Mrs C. Tubb, Miss J. Chesterman, Mrs M. Hodge, Miss M. Woolcott, Mrs E. Broom, C. Gode, J. Gove, Mrs C. Gove, Mrs M. Terry, P. Miller, Mrs F. Batten; seated: A. Payne, M. Terry, C. Payne.*

Top left and bottom: *Coronation tea party in Higher Bullring, 1937.*

Above: *PE display in Higher Bullring.*

Right: *Included in this shot of the party are: Gladys and Audrey Miller, Phyllis, Olive, Jean, Joyce, Margaret, Margery and Peter Heard, Ida Heywood, Miss Batten, Phyllis Potter, Mrs Potter, Essie Stoneman, Josie and Eileen Kerslake and Marjorie Butt.*

OTHER REVELS

Murray T. Foster in his *Short History of Collumpton* explains that it was the custom to hold revels in different parts of the town and mentions those that took place in Duck Street (now Duke Street) and New Street. The Duck Street revel happened each Oak Apple Day (29 May) when the street was filled with stalls. In the latter part of the day children and adults joined together in the merry-making.

A seemingly more boisterous annual event emanated from New Street, which in the past was an area of the town predominantly occupied by the cobbling trade. Each Whit Monday a 'Mayor of Boot Quarter' was chosen and possibly paraded in the town. It is thought that the Boot Inn in New Street was the focal point of this revel. The proceedings were concluded by the giving of a tea to the old women in New Street.

Cullompton used to be a great centre for wrestling and the Championship of the West was once contested here. Bull-baiting and cock-fighting were popular sports until the beginning of the 19th century. The last bull-baiting took place in 1805/6 and it is probably from this sport that Higher and Lower Bullring got their names. The name Cockpit Hill also indicates that there was an area for cockfighting years ago.

In c.1922 Whiteleggs and Jones were advertising their usual Good Friday Fair to be held in the field near the station, with 'an increased variety of up-to-date amusements', including overhead aeroplanes, chairoplanes, roundabouts, swings and a massive new organ with all the 'latest songs'. The Railway Hotel would serve teas and refreshments, and late buses would run to get the customers home.

In 1863 the jovial parson, the Revd Dr E.W.T. Chave, who was said to be very fond of dancing, had an open-air dance in the Higher Bullring with 1300 other parishioners when the Prince of Wales was married. Tables were placed on each side of the street and the idea has since been repeated on days of national importance.

The Bullring has always been a focal point in the town. Over the years it has been used for bull-baiting, the livestock market and street parties. It is also the site of the War Memorial. When an excuse could be found, skittling in the Bullring would take place (lasting for a week), usually to raise money for the school or Scouts. The Bullring would be littered with straw bales. In the early days the prize for the highest score during the week would be a pig, but later it became the fashion to give money. Today it is the site of the weekly street market where the trees provide a welcome green canopy.

Right and below: *Celebrations on 22 June 1911 for the Coronation of George V, Higher Bullring.*

CULLOMPTON FESTIVAL
by Cullompton Festival Committee

In 1981 Paul Hague, the Youth Worker employed by Devon County Council, called a public meeting and established a small committee to organise a Town Festival. It was felt that there were many people moving into Cullompton who were unaware of the range of organisations and opportunities available to them. The original idea was to provide an opportunity for all the local groups to promote themselves. Local pubs, clubs, organisations and churches as well as individuals took part and thus the Cullompton Festival was started. They were encouraged to hold events, not only to raise money for themselves, but to advertise their group and make people aware of what Cullompton had to offer.

Jinette Mitchell was one of the founder members and says that the Committee co-ordinated events during the week. The week opened with a fête at the Community College at which all local groups and clubs had stalls. They donated 25 per cent of their takings to the Committee and the balance went to boost the funds of those groups participating. Any surplus funds were donated by the Committee to local charities and good causes. For example, medical practices received nebulisers and donations were made to the Scouts, Cubs and St John Ambulance. Seats were purchased for use by residents of Vicary Close. The Committee also organised a gala dance to mark the end of Festival week and possibly one event in the middle of the week, but their main role was to co-ordinate the programme of events.

Pubs and clubs organised events including skittles, pool, darts and quiz nights, which proved to be a lot of fun. Calling in at each of the pubs and clubs took its toll, especially on the way to the Football Club, when many a competitor fell in the river. It took hours as every pub, club and the Cullompton Hotel was visited.

This, the first Festival, proved to be a great success and it was decided to make it an annual event. Not all events were held in pubs. All kinds of competitions have taken place over the years: the pram race and the three-legged race always raised a laugh, along with the tug-of-war and the back-breaking lorry pull.

For many years a fête at the comprehensive school was well supported. Our local majorettes would give a dazzling display and at one time we were honoured by a visit from a Prince from far-off lands whom we later discovered to be an impostor! There were always a lot of side-shows and stalls. One particular year the Cullompton Disability Action Group manned their usual stall – it was a competition where the winner would win a slice of bacon and an egg – which health regulations would probably not allow nowadays – but they proudly showed off their brand-new ambulance van kindly given by the then popular 'Devon Air' radio station promoters. It has served them well and they were so grateful. Another popular part of the fête was the Baby Show. Of course every mum knows their baby is the best and we have lots of photos proving this. To think that many of those babies are now parents themselves! In addition to all of these attractions, cream teas were being served by a group of willing helpers.

In later years it was decided to hold a parade through the town. This was headed by a local Festival Princess, followed by Tiverton Town Band and parading behind would be Scouts, Cubs, Guides, Brownies, members of St John Ambulance, plus Badgers, and members of the Royal British Legion. Originally held in the afternoon, the parade was changed to Saturday morning and this disrupted the traffic flow quite a lot. The police were wonderful and the traffic was halted for the parade and people lined the streets. Again they were able to see what Cullompton had to offer.

One proud Festival memory was the year when the Cullompton Town Flag which had been made by

Top: *Silver Dolphin Majorettes at the 1985 Cullompton Festival.*

Above: *Pupils from Willowbank Primary School maypole dancing at the Festival, 1998.*

members of the local Craft Group, was presented to the Town and carried in the parade. It now hangs in St Andrew's Church. The Craft Group was also presented with a golden opportunity when they were offered the chance to put on a public display in The Walronds. Not only was some excellent craft-work seen, but many enjoyed the opportunity of seeing the inside of this wonderful building.

As the years went on, the Festival Committee hosted a series of new events, one being the Three Schools Prom. This was a time when children of all ages entertained with their musical talents. It never ceases to amaze the audience what exceptional talent we have in our schools.

The Committee has tried to keep traditions alive. The maypole dancing by children of Willowbank School on Wednesday – Market Day – and country dancing by children of St Andrew's School have become a tradition. It is good that traditions are upheld and encouraged.

For several years there has been a united Songs of Praise when all the town's religious denominations hold a united evening of prayer and praise.

Spot the Odd Object in the shop windows and a competition for the best window display have been popular regular features of Festival week.

For the past four years a street fayre has been held in the Higher Bullring bringing stall holders from near and far with a mixed array of goods to sell. An effort is always made to arrange to have all kinds of street entertainers in attendance. In the past we have had buskers, jugglers, clog dancers, stilt walkers, majorettes and in the year 2001 we were entertained by the Tiverton Town Band and the local Ring O' Bells Morris Dancers. The sun was shining and there was a lovely feeling that people were happy and enjoying themselves.

Another popular event which started many years ago was a tea party for all pensioners given by the local Young Farmers. This has now become a three-course high tea sponsored by the Festival Committee and Town Council. In the year 2001 well over 85 senior citizens of the town enjoyed a wonderful get-together in the Town Hall. Entertainment was not needed as everyone had so much to talk about.

Each year we hold a friendly competition to determine our oldest guest and for the past four years Mr Bob Clark has proved to be our winner at the age of 94 years. Local playgroups and pre-school groups take an active part in the Festival which ensures that all age groups are included in the Festival week.

The Festival Committee still encourages groups and organisations to promote themselves by arranging events and the week surely brings fun and enjoyment to a great many people. It also helps to boost the trade in the town by bringing more people to Cullompton. Thus the aims of the founders of Festival week are being upheld.

Church Fêtes

by Marian Dummett

In the interwar years, the church held afternoon teas and lunch parties beside the lake at Upton. These were very popular and included an opportunity to be rowed across to the island. In the time up to the 1970s the annual Church Fête was an important occasion for all local people. Held on a Thursday afternoon, to coincide with the early closing of the shops, it was later transferred to the first Saturday in July. The fête took place in the Vicarage garden with tea being made in the kitchen and carried a considerable distance over difficult lawns to the tea tent.

Many of the women in the congregation were involved in preparing rolls, sandwiches and cakes for afternoon tea. I remember the cream teas were made up with chudleys topped with clotted cream – made locally – and home-made jam. Later scones took the place of chudleys. It must be remembered that there was no sliced bread in the early days and that all the bread (usually about 20 loaves) had to be cut by hand. Mrs Palmer used to be the most accomplished at this and the cucumber sandwiches were her domain. She was a joy to behold, cutting bread wearing her best hat and pearls. It was quite in the order of things to cater for 600. Serving tea was one of the most tiring things you could do whereas eating the delicious home-made produce was a real pleasure.

There were all sorts of stalls, the usual white elephant stall, crafts such as hand-embroidered tablecloths and cushions, etc., pony rides, bowling for a pig, and stalls where you tried to pick your bacon-and-egg breakfast from eggs in sawdust, or win the prize of treasure hidden on a desert island by paying for a flag and putting it on a map. There were many years when a local band played background music and schoolchildren performed country dances on the lawns. The fête was not only an important social occasion, it was always regarded as a major fund-raising event. The most successful fêtes raised in the region of £4000. In the 1970s people found the fêtes less interesting as there were many other things to do and they no longer form any part of the life of the town. The fête was a lot of hard work for a few people but gave pleasure to very many townsfolk when travel was difficult and expensive and it was necessary to make our own entertainment.

Other Shows

Flower shows were always popular, as also were chrysanthemum shows where local gardeners showed massive blooms. There were also 'Fur and Feather' shows when rabbits, guinea pigs and all sorts of chickens, bantams and pigeons were exhibited. It seems that years ago everyone had an interest of sorts, but of course there was no TV and fewer opportunities to travel.

Cullompton Town Band, 1884. Mr W.H. Biss is in the front row with the small drum.

Cullompton Town Band on the occasion of the Coronation of George VI, 1937.

Above: *Cullompton Orchestra, c.1922. Left to right, back: Dr G. Gidley, ?, Harry Chubb, Bill Ayres, ?, ?, ?, ?; front: ?, Joan King, Len Dyer, Bandmaster Cox, Miss Morris, ?.*

Right: *Cullompton Band, c.1920, including Mr Sharland, Harry Chubb and Ron Tucker on the piano.*

Left: *Ron Harris Band, c.1950s. Left to right, standing: Jack LeRoy, ?; seated: Eddie Taverner, Douglas Nex, Ron Harris, Harry Chubb, 'Chalky' White.*

Above: *Dutch children on holiday in Cullompton, 1945. Top of stairs: Bill Norrish. On platform, from left to right: Clarise ?, George Heywood, Muriel Jago, Reg Whitton, Miss Gear, Ivy Heywood, Arthur Hammett.*

Below: *Empire Day Parade, 1943, including members of the Home Guard, Air Training Corps, Army Cadets and Civil Defence.*

Above: *Members of Cullompton Bible Class, 1950, including: Pat Galpin, Peter Vinnicombe, Clive Ford, Alan Turner, Ken Vigar, Derick Budd, Mick Lawrence, John Kemp, John Davis, Bill Heard, Peter Frost.*

Chapter Ten

WARTIME

SECOND WORLD WAR MEMORIES

by Derek Budd

I was just eight years old when the news came that England was at war with Germany. At that time I did not realise what war was about, but I was soon to find out. Menfolk of the town started to disappear and all the male teachers at school were replaced by ladies. My father joined the RAF; he had to walk almost into Exeter to sign on. Quite soon there were troops with guns in our town and they dug trenches all around St Andrew's recreation ground as well as several gun emplacements on the 'rec' which were manned night and day. When the siren sounded (it was mounted on top of the old Police Station in the Bullring) all the people who lived nearby were supposed to rush, with their gas masks, to these trenches for protection.

I remember the dark tape which we used to secure paper over the windows to stop the light getting out, and to stop them shattering if we were bombed. It was also used on the headlights of the few cars there were in the town. Everyone was aware of the blackout. The stock in the shops dwindled quickly and sweets were hard to find. We did manage a little chocolate sometimes. As there was a black market most things could be bought if you had enough money, but we didn't.

You must remember that there was no television so the only news came from the radio and was six or seven weeks late. We also saw newsreels at the Regal Cinema which was in the Bullring, where the carpet shop is now. At first the news was bad with the Germans pushing us back, but gradually the news changed in our favour. The Americans entered the war and soon we were enjoying their gum and sweets thrown from the back of their lorries as they passed through our town. The Durham Light Infantry were stationed at the Old Laundry, a long building demolished soon after the war. It was along the Tiverton Road just past the site of the present-day Fire Station. As D-Day approached Americans were stationed in the town.

The 'Yanks', as we called them, were stationed all over the place; some were in huts used by the Scouts, some were in the old Post Office, where 'Pickwick's Tearooms' is at the moment, and some were up the alley by Westward Counties Insurance. They had a cookhouse next to the building which is now the Royal British Legion Club. They were tucked away all over the town. The Americans had a base for their 'Liberator' bombers at Dunkeswell, the only American naval air station in this country. I remember seeing an enemy plane shot down over the hills at Dunkeswell. The 'Liberators' were designed for hunting and bombing German 'U' Boats in the Atlantic.

The bombing of Exeter still sticks in my mind; there was a squadron of spitfires stationed at Exeter airport, flown by the Poles. They were no match for the bombing onslaught from Germany and often I could see the glow of fire in the sky as Exeter burned during the constant bombing. I saw one bomb come down in Cullompton very close to the site of Willowbank School. When I moved to senior school, which was on the site of the present-day Magistrates Court, I was amazed at the number of tanks, guns and Army troop lorries that passed the school, often with the 'Yanks' throwing chewing gum and sweets to us kids, who would scramble to find it.

We did not think of the war as brutal or of people dying; we were kids caught up in a grown-up thing. How could we imagine that these men throwing sweets could possibly soon be dead on the battlefields of Europe? We were very naïve at that time. We were actually quite excited about the war but we did not like going without things like sweets. We didn't mind the absence of soap and we enjoyed the Americans' chewing gum. We had new friends from amongst those evacuated into the town. We saw prisoners of war working in the fields as there was a camp for them near Kentisbeare. Sometimes, during term time in the summer, we schoolchildren helped on the farms; we dug potatoes, picked rosehips for the jam factory and helped with hay-making.

As D-Day approached there seemed to be a never-ending stream of vehicles passing the school; big guns and armoured vehicles, tanks and troop carriers just seemed to keep on coming. When D-Day arrived the sky was full of planes and hundreds of aircraft flew overhead. They were mainly bombers but some were Dakotas pulling behind them a string of gliders. These were full of troops all ready for the big attack. I remember Exeter was still being bombed as were most of the major cities at the time of D-Day.

From this time on, things gradually improved. The air raids on Exeter suddenly stopped, more goods and food started to appear in the shops, our troops were pushing their way towards Germany. VE Day came; Victory in Europe sent most people crazy, dancing in the streets, sitting on top of lamp-posts, parties everywhere. Everyone felt elated and the relief was palpable. Cullompton had survived; the community was still intact. For years all the people had worked together, helping each other to keep the community alive – and they had succeeded!

VJ Day came with another round of street parties. Soldiers started to return home and it was not until then that I began to understand the price that Cullompton, and all the other towns and villages, had had to pay for the winning of the war and the freedom we now enjoy.

Mrs Marian Dummett's Memories

I was ten years old when war was declared. The vicar (Revd Grubb) announced it in the church and I could not understand why my older sisters, who sang in the choir, were crying. One by one our young men were called up and later the girls, some for the forces and some for the munitions factories. A few of the men, 18-year-olds, went as 'Bevan Boys', to work in the coal mines.

Just like everyone else, we were rationed. Mr Pring allowed everyone 1lb of sausages per week, but living in the country there were rabbits, old hens, eggs, extra milk and of course any vegetables that you could grow. Some people even kept a pig in the garden for meat (the chittlings were lovely), also when the lambs tails were cut off we had pie, and sweetbreads when the lambs were castrated. We would collect them from the farm in a bowl, blood and all.

With the war came the soldiers. Every large building in the town housed the troops. Large houses were taken over and nissen huts built in some gardens. At one time there was a Scottish regiment at Hillersdon who would play the bagpipes as they marched into town for the church parades. We also had the Durham Light Infantry REME, Somersets and the Americans. They gave us our first taste of chewing gum and later nylons. When the troops were in town the Regal Cinema was full each evening. It was situated where the carpet shop is now and if one was in the queue past the War Memorial you knew you would not get in.

There was a YMCA where the community house is and this was open every day for the soldiers as a café-come-drop-in centre. Several romances and marriages were the result of the war and there are still a few men with 'foreign' accents living in the town. The Americans stayed in Cullompton until the D-Day landings. One day the town was full of 'Yanks' and the next they were all gone.

With the coming of the evacuees, the schools became very crowded. Little children, some as young as four, came from London and Plymouth to stay with anyone who had room for them. They arrived by train with their teachers, little suitcases and gas masks. Later some of their mothers came to stay until the end of the war and many friendships were formed, some lasting to this day. Of course, everyone carried a gas mask and at one time the Upcott Field was dug into trenches so that the children from St Andrew's School had somewhere to go during an air raid.

Several bombs were dropped in Cullompton; one behind Trumps Barn and one around Knowle – the craters seemed enormous. The first time the air-raid siren sounded, I was in a cornfield at the bottom of Toms Hill with all the other children trying to catch rabbits. Mrs Dummett from St Andrew's Estate (later my mother-in-law), ran all the way up to the field and made us lie under the hedge until the all-clear sounded.

On VE night, everyone in the town congregated in the Higher Bullring and Mr Woolcott played dance music from his wireless through his window so that everyone could dance. What a thrill to have lights on again – no blackout! Someone even found a tub of confetti from somewhere and the boys had no end of fun chasing us. There was a lot of explaining to do to mother when we got home!

When the war was over, and the soldiers started to come home, there was a great amount of hard feeling in the town over housing. There was often over-crowding with five or six adults and children living in two-bedroomed houses. Everyone lived with their parents until houses were built.

It was a time of no sweets, no fruit like oranges or bananas and for many no Dad for four or five years. The soldiers had been promised a bright new world but rationing and shortages went on long after the war ended. Even if one wanted a pair of stockings one had to be on a waiting list. When and if our stockings laddered, we sent them away to be mended. As a town we were a lot luckier than most but there was, nevertheless, a lot of heartache in families.

The Home Guard parade outside Exon Buildings.

Memories of an Evacuee

by Mrs Joyce Owen

In May 1940 the British Government decided that as many children as possible should be evacuated from areas of danger. The school I attended was Trumpington Road, Forest Gate. We were taken by bus to Paddington Station, complete with our labels, gas masks and a small suitcase containing our worldly goods. Our destination was unknown even to our parents.

As an 11-year-old this seemed like a great adventure to my friend Jean Rennie and me as we boarded a train which eventually travelled to Tiverton. On arrival we were taken by bus to the market-place where we all had to have a medical examination and were then given refreshments. I presume we must have been found to be fit enough to be acceptable to continue our journey to Cullompton.

On our arrival we were placed in the old school and sat at desks to await our fate – inspection by the local townsfolk. Jean and I had decided before we left London to stay together whatever happened, this decision meant we were almost the last to be 'chosen' as most families only wanted to take one child and not a 'double act'.

However, we were extremely lucky to be taken home by 'Auntie Liza' (Mrs Osmond) and her daughters Margery and Phyllis. Our first home was at 35 Fore Street, where Phyllis ran a hairdressing business. We thought the living quarters were wonderful as we seemed to have so many rooms after our small London houses.

Later Auntie Liza, Margery, Jean and myself moved to Higher Mill Lane to live next door to Harry Drewe the local blacksmith. Phyllis had married Len Hillman by this time. We were quickly integrated into the local schools and made friends easily.

By September 1940 the London Blitz had started, Jean's mother decided to join us in Cullompton and soon after, my grandmother's house was hit and she was buried under the rubble so Auntie Liza suggested she should join us along with my young cousin who lived with her. By now we had a very full house. We only had an outside toilet and no running water, just a pump. Baths were taken in a tin tub in the 'linney' which had a boiler to heat the water and it had to be lit well in advance of bath time. We all agreed this was to be preferred to life in London during the Blitz.

During school holidays Mr Drewe would take Jean and I out on his rounds to the local farms in his pony and trap. He would shoe the horses and carry out repairs as required. This was great fun until one day the pony slipped on ice going up the hill towards the station and threw us out onto the road. We were never keen to go after that. Although I missed my parents, life for me in Cullompton was lovely.

We had a cinema with a change of programme twice weekly and when we were considered old enough we were allowed to go to the weekly dances in the Assembly Rooms. I remember sledging on 'Old Hill' when we had snow and also the excitement of viewing the bomb crater around Knowle. The bomb was dropped during a raid on Exeter.

In the summer we swam in the river at Head Weir, we cycled and left our bicycles in the hedge, no need to use chains in those days. Schools from Exeter and Plymouth were evacuated to Cullompton and had to be fitted into the schools somehow. Many troops were stationed here prior to their service overseas. I clearly remember a Highland regiment being billeted in the King's Head public house; the backyard being opposite our house we were often woken up by the pipes and drums practising.

I did return to London for a short time but returned in 1947 on my marriage to Bernard Owens. Our first home was with my in-laws in Belle Vue Terrace. After moving around due to my husband's job, we finally returned to Cullompton in 1964 where I have lived ever since.

Top: *Joyce Owens and Jean Rennie, August 1945.*

Above: *Wartime fête. Left to right, back: Hilary Hodge, Maureen Benson, Joyce Owens, Grace Hellier; middle: Clarence Bond, Margaret Galpin, ?, ?, Mrs North, Jean Atkins; front: ?, ?, Eve Valentine, Dick Mitchell, ?, ?.*

Lest We Forget: First World War

The following information (and that relating to the Second World War) was gathered by Bridget Hill as part of her research into the names on the Cullompton War Memorial.

BASTONE – William David: Private 1st/4th Battalion Devonshire Regiment. Son of Mr D. Bastone of The Bungalow, High Street, Cullompton. Killed in action 3 February 1917, aged 19. Buried Amara War Cemetery, Iraq.

BISS – James: Sergeant 2nd/6th Battalion Devonshire Regiment. Husband of Ellen E. Sprague (formerly Biss) of Mathew's Court, Cullompton. Died 27 February 1918, aged 37. Buried Amara War Cemetery, Iraq.

BLACKMORE – William H: Private 1st/5th Battalion Duke of Cornwall's Light Infantry. Died 24 July 1918 of illness contracted on active service. Buried Cullompton Cemetery.

BOWDEN – Ernest: Private 10th Battalion Worcestershire Regiment (not Devons as stated on memorials). Died of wounds 30 May 1918. Buried Terlincthun British Cemetery, France.

BOWLES – James: Pioneer Special Depot Brigade Royal Engineers. Killed in action 27 June 1916. Commemorated Ploegsteert Memorial, Belgium.

BRADBEER – Richard James Edwin: Able Seaman SS *Obuasi*, Royal Naval Volunteer Reserve. Son of James and Eugenie Bradbeer of High Street, Cullompton. Died 11 July 1917, aged 19. Commemorated Plymouth Naval Memorial.

BROOM – Sidney Charles: Private 24th Canadian Infantry (Quebec Regiment). Died 18 May 1917. Commemorated Vimy Memorial, France.

BROWN – Walter George: Thought to be Private 20th Battalion Durham Light Infantry. Killed in action 4 September 1918. Commemorated Tyne Cot Memorial, Belgium.

CARDEW – George Eric MC: Captain 4th Battalion Devonshire Regiment, attached 6th Battalion Durham Light Infantry. Son of Henry Masters and Beatrice Mary Cardew of 'The Birches', Churchdown, Gloucester. Won the Military Cross for the action in which he was killed on 9 April 1918, aged 31. Commemorated Ploegsteert Memorial, Belgium.

CHICK – Edward John: Sapper 5th Signal Company Royal Engineers. Killed in action 24 July 1916.

Cullomptonians in India, probably before the First World War.
Left to right, back: Pte Whitton, Pte Voisey, Pte Dyer, Pte Morgan, Pte Ingersent; sitting: Cpl Palk, Sgt Warren, Sgt Tidboro, Sgt Major Potter, Sgt Pratt, Cpl Davey.

Commemorated Thiepval Memorial, Somme, France.

COLEMAN – Joseph: Rifleman 2nd Battalion 3rd New Zealand Rifle Brigade. Brother of John George Coleman of Higher Street, Cullompton. Died 8 June 1917, aged 43. Commemorated Messines Ridge (NZ) Memorial, Belgium.

COLES – Albert John: Private 58th Battalion Canadian Infantry (Central Ontario Regiment). Son of Samuel and Harriet Coles of Station Road, Cullompton. Died 8 October 1916, aged 31. Commemorated Vimy Memorial, France. (Brother of Ernest and William Coles.)

COLES – Ernest: Private 50th Battalion Machine Gun Corps (Infantry). Son of Samuel and Harriet Coles. Died as a prisoner of war 9 October 1918. Buried Niederzwehren Cemetery, Germany. (Brother of Albert John and William Coles.)

COLES – William: Private 3rd Battalion Coldstream Guards. Son of Samuel and Harriet Coles of Station Road, Cullompton. Husband of Florence Coles. Died of wounds 13 November 1914, aged 33. Commemorated Ypres (Menin) Gate Memorial, Belgium. (Brother of Albert John and Ernest Coles.)

CONIBEER – Edward James: Private 14th Field Ambulance Royal Army Medical Corps. Killed in action 6 November 1917. Buried Menin Road Military Cemetery, Ypres, Belgium.

DANIELS – George: Private 1st Devonshire Regiment. Killed in action 31 October 1914 or 1915. Born Portsmouth and enlisted in Exeter, giving his residence as Cullompton. Cemetery/memorial unknown.

DAVEY – Ernest: Lance Corporal 1st/4th Devonshire Regiment. Died 17 June 1916. Buried Amara War Cemetery, Iraq.

DAVEY – Fred: Private 1st Devonshire Regiment. Killed in action 30 August 1918. Commemorated Vis-en-Artois Memorial, France.

DENNER – John: Private 9th Devonshire Regiment. Son of Mrs J. Denner of Station Road, Cullompton. Killed in action 1 July 1916, aged 23. Buried Devonshire Cemetery, Mametz, France.

EALES – John Harry Aldridge: Sergeant 1st/4th Battalion Devonshire Regiment. Son of Henry Eales of Exeter Road, Cullompton. Killed in action 3 February 1917, aged 33. Buried Amara War Cemetery, Iraq.

EVANS – Tom: Shown on memorials as having served as a Private in the RAF. Nothing more known.

EWENS – George: Private 43rd Battalion Canadian Infantry (Manitoba Regiment). Only son of the late Tom Francis Biddlecombe Ewens and Eleanor Maria Ewens of 'The Bungalow', Colyford. Died 21 September 1916, aged 26. Commemorated on Vimy Memorial, France. Also commemorated on brass plaque erected by his sister in St Andrew's church.

FORD – Reginald Richard MM: Sergeant 'Z' Special Company Royal Engineers. Son of Richard and Kate Ford of Coronation House, Crow Green, Cullompton. Killed in action 3 April 1917, aged 29. Commemorated Arras Memorial, France.

GIGG – George: Thought to be Private Charles James Gigg, HMS *Monmouth* Royal Marine Light Infantry. Lost in the sinking of HMS *Monmouth* on 1 November 1914. Commemorated on Plymouth Naval Memorial.

GREENSLADE – Reginald: Private 1st Battalion Royal Warwickshire Regiment. Died 2 April 1918. Buried Wimereux Communal Cemetery, France.

HALES – William James: Private 2nd Battalion Devonshire Regiment. Son of George Hales of Church Lane, Cullompton. Husband of Louisa J. Hales of Reed's Place, Cullompton. Killed in action 30 March 1918, aged 30. Commemorated Pozieres Memorial, Somme, France.

HARDING – Arthur: Private 2nd Battalion Worcestershire Regiment. Killed in action 17 April 1918. Commemorated Ploegsteert Memorial, Belgium.

HARRIS – Samuel: Company Sergeant Major 7th Battalion Somerset Light Infantry. Died 19 October 1915. Buried Rue-du-Bacquerot (13th) London Graveyard, France.

HARVEY – Godfrey James: Sergeant 7th Battalion Royal Fusiliers. Son of Richard and Mary Harvey of 45 Somers Road, Worcester, formerly of Fore Street, Cullompton. Killed in action 29 January 1917, aged 32. Buried Hamel Military Cemetery, Somme, France.

HAWKINS – Henry Charles: Sergeant 1st/12th Battalion London Regiment (The Rangers). Killed in action 8 May 1917. Commemorated Ypres (Menin) Gate Memorial, Belgium.

HELLIER – Oliver John: Private 1st Battalion Devonshire Regiment. Son of Mrs Rosa Hellier of Higher Mill Lane, Cullompton. Killed in action 1 May 1915, aged 20. Commemorated Ypres (Menin Gate) Memorial, Belgium.

HILLMAN – Walter George Tree: Driver 88th Field Company Royal Engineers. Died 12 July 1916. Buried Basra War Cemetery, Iraq.

HITT – Ernest Edward: Private Devonshire Regiment (transferred to Labour Corps). Son of Henry and Susan Hitt of Venn Dairy, Cullompton. Husband of Frances Mary Hitt of Causeway End Cottage, Broadhembury. Died 28 March 1919, aged 35. Buried Broadhembury churchyard.

HITT – George Frank: Private 10th Battalion Royal North Lancashire Regiment. Died of wounds 23 October 1917. Buried Clyst Hydon churchyard.

HOLMDEN – William Alfred: Private 9th Battalion Devonshire Regiment. Son of the late Richard and Mary Elizabeth Holmden. Killed in action 26 October 1917, aged 40. Commemorated Tyne Cot Memorial, Belgium.

HOWE – Thomas Frederick (Fred): Lance Corporal 23rd Company Machine Gun Corps (Infantry). Son of Thomas and Annie Howe of Crow Green, Cullompton. Died of wounds 28 March 1918, aged 20. Buried Namps-au-Val British Cemetery, Somme, France. (Brother of Sidney John Howe.)

HOWE – Sidney John: Private 8th Battalion Royal Berkshire Regiment. Formerly served with Devonshire Regiment. Killed in action 23 October 1918. Buried Le Cateau Military Cemetery, France. (Brother of Thomas Frederick Howe.)

HUGHES – Walter Bernard Chammings: Private 2nd Battalion Devonshire Regiment. Killed in action 25 November 1917. Commemorated Tyne Cot Memorial, Belgium.

INGERSENT – James: Private 61st Company Machine Gun Corps (Infantry). Killed in action 23 March 1918, aged 24. Commemorated Pozieres Memorial, Somme, France.

JAMES – Wilfred: Rifleman 1st/8th Battalion London Regiment (Post Office Rifles). Killed in action 21 May 1916. Commemorated Arras Memorial, France.

JEFFERY – Albert: Corporal 2nd Battalion Devonshire Regiment. Son of Henry and Elizabeth Jeffery of Pound Square, Cullompton. Killed in action 31 May 1918, aged 29. Commemorated Soissons Memorial, Aisne, France.

KERSLAKE – Robert: Private 4th Battalion Canadian Infantry (Central Ontario Regiment). Died 8 October 1916, aged 28. Buried Adanac Military Cemetery, Somme, France.

LABDON – Percy Miller: Second Lieutenant 469th Field Company Royal Engineers. Son of Fred L. and Eunice Labdon of 'Glenthorne', Cullompton. Died 26 September 1917, aged 21. Buried Bridge House Cemetery, Belgium. Also commemorated in Cullompton Baptist Church.

LOVERING – William: Private 4th Battalion Devonshire Regiment. Son of Henry and Mary Elizabeth Lovering of Kercombe, Gittisham, Honiton. Died on 16 September 1916, aged 22. Buried Baghdad (North Gate) War Cemetery, Iraq.

LUXTON – Gordon: Private 9th Battalion Devonshire Regiment. Killed in action on 1 July 1916. Commemorated Thiepval Memorial, Somme, France.

LUXTON – Waldron Frederick: Private 1st/4th Battalion Devonshire Regiment. Died 15 December 1916. Commemorated Angora Memorial, Baghdad (North Gate) War Cemetery, Iraq.

MARTIN – Frederick Adam Sanford: Private 2nd/1st (Wessex) Field Ambulance Royal Army Medical Corps. Son of Adam Sanford and Miriam Frances Martin of 'The Pines', Minehead. Born Cullompton. Killed in action 3 June 1917, aged 20. Buried Brandhoek Military Cemetery, Belgium.

MILLS – Henry John: Private 1st Battalion Devonshire Regiment. Son of Henry John and Charlotte Mills. Husband of Bessie Mills of Higher Street, Cullompton. Died of wounds 26 July 1916, aged 31. Buried Heilly Station Cemetery, France.

NEX – Cecil Victor: Private 5th Battalion Devonshire Regiment. Killed in action 13 September 1918. Commemorated Vis-en-Artois Memorial, France.

OWENS – William: Private 1st Battalion Royal Dublin Fusiliers. Killed in action 4 October 1917. Commemorated Tyne Cot Memorial, Belgium.

PALMER – Herbert Slader: Lance Corporal 5th Battalion Dragoon Guards. Son of John Palmer of Beacon Terrace, Bradninch. Husband of Daisy Cornish (formerly Palmer) of 86 Egremont Road, Exmouth. Killed in action 31 October 1914, aged 25. Commemorated Ypres (Menin Gate) Memorial, Belgium.

PARSONS – Arthur Henry: Private 1st/7th Battalion Devonshire Regiment. Son of William and the late Mrs Parsons of New Street, Cullompton. Died 21 August 1916, aged 20. Buried Vermelles British Cemetery, France.

PARSONS – Frederick James: Private 2nd Battalion Devonshire Regiment. Son of Richard and Mary Ann

Parsons of 15 New Street, Cullompton. Died 30 September 1916, aged 21. Buried Cullompton Cemetery.

PURCHASE – Reginald Hawkins: Private 2nd Battalion Devonshire Regiment. Son of the late Mr and Mrs T. Purchase of Fore Street, Cullompton. Died of wounds 14 March 1915, aged 32. Buried St Sever Cemetery, Rouen, France.

RICHARDS – Edgar (Jock): Private 24th Battalion Royal Fusiliers. Brother of Mrs E. Herrington of Rogerstone, Monmouthshire. Killed in action 31 March 1916. Buried Aix-Noulette Communal Cemetery Extension, France.

SELLICK – Walter John: Private 1st Battalion Bedfordshire Regiment. Killed in action 7 May 1915. Commemorated Ypres (Menin Gate) Memorial, Belgium.

SHATTOCK – Thomas Henry: Engine Room Artificer 4th Class HMS *Good Hope* Royal Navy. Son of Henry James and Ruth Shattock of 'The Croft', Cullompton. Lost in the sinking of HMS *Good Hope* on 1 November 1914, aged 20. Commemorated on Portsmouth Naval Memorial.

SKOINES – Frederick Charles: Private 6th Battalion Dorsetshire Regiment. Died of wounds 11 June 1918. Buried St Sever Cemetery Extension, Rouen, France.

SNOW – Louis Binford: Private 1st Battalion Middlesex Regiment. Killed in action 2 October 1918. Commemorated Vis-en-Artois Memorial, France. (Brother of Reginald John Snow.)

SNOW – Reginald John: Private Royal Army Medical Corps. Son of John and Lucy Snow of 'Trumps Barn', Cullompton. Died 25 April 1918, aged 24. Buried St Sever Cemetery, Extension, Rouen, France. (Brother of Louis Binford Snow.)

SPARKES – Reginald R.J.: Private 1st/6th Battalion Devonshire Regiment. Son of Tom and Florence Sparkes of 7 New Street, Cullompton. Died 5 June 1919, aged 22. Buried Haidar Pasha Cemetery, Turkey.

STILING – Frederick William: Private 1st/5th Battalion Norfolk Regiment. Killed in action 2 November 1917. Buried Gaza War Cemetery, Israel.

STONE – Ernest Charles Hugh: Corporal Royal Engineers. Son of John and Sarah J. Stone. Husband of Laura Stone of Higher Street, Cullompton. Died of wounds 30 July 1919 aged 34. Buried Cullompton Cemetery. Also commemorated in Cullompton Baptist Church.

SWEET – Frank Clarence: Private 2nd Battalion Devonshire Regiment. Killed in action 31 May 1918. Commemorated Soissons Memorial, Aisne, France. Also commemorated on parents' gravestone in Cullompton Cemetery, where date of death is given as 29 May 1918.

TUCKER – Reginald John: Private 166th Company Machine Gun Corps (Infantry). Formerly Manchester Regiment. Killed in action 20 September 1917. Commemorated Tyne Cot Memorial, Belgium.

VOISEY – Sidney Henry Albert: Private 14th Battalion Gloucestershire Regiment attached 7th Battalion Royal West Kent Regiment. Died 4 April 1918. Commemorated Pozieres Memorial, Somme, France.

WALKER – William MSM: Thought to be Regimental Sergeant Major 1st/4th Battalion Devonshire Regiment. Husband of Janet Maud Walker of 55 Ravensbury Road, Fields, London. Died 10 April 1919, aged 38. Buried Baghdad (North Gate) War Cemetery, Iraq. Connection with Cullompton unknown.

WATTS – Bert: Private 2nd/4th Royal Berkshire Regiment. Son of Mr and Mrs William E. Watts of Growen Cottages, Cullompton. Died of wounds whilst prisoner of war 11 May 1918, aged 20. Buried Berlin South-Western Cemetery, Germany.

WELLINGTON – William: Corporal 9th Battalion Devonshire Regiment. Killed in action 8 May 1917, Commemorated Arras Memorial, France.

WEST – Harold: Lance Corporal 1st/4th Battalion Devonshire Regiment. Son of Herbert and Elizabeth West of 1 Mill Lane, Cullompton. Killed in action 4 February 1917, aged 19.

WHITFIELD – William: Private 2nd/8th Battalion Worcestershire Regiment. Died 2 August 1916. Buried Merville Communal Cemetery, France.

LEST WE FORGET: SECOND WORLD WAR

BENNETT – John Paul Barkell MC: Captain Royal Engineers. Died 24 April 1945. Buried Becklingen War Cemetery, Germany.

BOND – Charles Frederick Gordon: Major attached 1st Special Air Service Wiltshire Regiment. Son of Major C.G. Bond, The Wiltshire Regiment, and Mrs Bond. Husband of Evelyn Hinchcliff Bond of Kilve, Somerset. Died 10 April 1945, aged 33. Buried Sage War Cemetery, Germany.

CARTER – Richard: Leading Supply Assistant HMS *Illustrious*, Royal Navy. Son of Richard and Mary Jane Carter of Cullompton. Died 10 January 1941, aged 19. Buried Imtarfa Military Cemetery, Malta.

COCKRAM – Charles Havill: Flight Sergeant Air Gunner 37 Squadron Royal Air Force Volunteer Reserve. Son of Charles Havill Cockram and Elsie May Cockram of Cullompton. Died 23 November 1944, aged 20. Buried Budapest War Cemetery, Hungary.

DYER – Edward Harold George: Sergeant 51 Squadron Royal Air Force Volunteer Reserve. Killed in action 22 November 1943, aged 19, when Halifax Bomber No. LW286 crashed into the Ijsselmeer. Four of the seven crewmen are still reported as missing. Buried Amersfoort (Old Leusden) General Cemetery, Netherlands.

ELWORTHY – Arthur James: Sergeant 40 Squadron Royal Air Force Volunteer Reserve. Son of Stanley and Kathleen Elworthy of Down St Mary, Devon. Died 11 July 1944, aged 20. Buried Milan War Cemetery, Italy.

ENDICOTT – Leonard John: Pilot Officer 502 Squadron Royal Air Force Volunteer Reserve. Son of William and Annie Elizabeth Endicott. Husband of Eileen Endicott of Trenance, Mawgan Porth, Cornwall. Died 30 July 1942, aged 30. Buried Mawgan-in-Pydar Cemetery, Cornwall.

GOSS – George Robert: Corporal 1st Battalion Hertfordshire Regiment. Son of Mr and Mrs J.E. Goss of Cullompton. Died 28 November 1944. Buried Florence War Cemetery, Italy.

GRANT – Walter Stewart: Flight Sergeant Royal Air Force. Son of James Malcolm and Minnie Grant of Cullompton. Died 25 August 1945, aged 30. Buried Cullompton Cemetery, alongside his mother. Also commemorated on small window in Methodist Church.

GRANT-STURGIS – Robin Julian: Lieut-Commander (A) HMS *Saker* Royal Naval Volunteer Reserve. Died 16 February 1944. Commemorated Lee-on-Solent Memorial, Hampshire.

HEALE – Francis James: Driver Royal Corp of Signals. Son of William and Laura Hester Heale of Cullompton. Died 3 November 1943, aged 22. Buried Sangro River War Cemetery, Italy.

HILLMAN – Walter George Tree: Private 2nd Battalion Devonshire Regiment. Husband of E.M. Hillman of Knowle, Cullompton. Died 23 June 1942, aged 33. Buried Pieta Military Cemetery, Malta. (Son of W.G.T. Hillman killed in First World War.)

HOOPER – Lionel Albert Jeffery: Telegraphist HMS *President III* (lost in MV *Athel Sultan*), Royal Navy. Son of Albert and Florence Hooper. Husband of Phyllis Hooper of Hemyock. Died 22 September 1942, aged 21. Commemorated Plymouth Naval Memorial.

PERHAM – Donald: Stoker 1st Class HM Submarine *Seahorse,* Royal Navy. Died 12 January 1940. Commemorated Plymouth Naval Memorial.

PRING – Robert Conrad: Ordinary Seaman HMS *Gloucester,* Royal Navy. Died 22 May 1941. Commemorated Plymouth Naval Memorial.

STONE – Thomas John: Leading Stoker HMS *Tamar* (lost in SS *Lisbon Maru*), Royal Navy. Son of William and Fanny Stone. Died 2 October 1942, aged 22. Commemorated Plymouth Naval Memorial.

SYMONDS – William James: Boy 1st Class HMS *Repulse*, Royal Navy. Son of Mr and Mrs J. Symonds of Cullompton. Died 10 December 1941. Commemorated Plymouth Naval Memorial.

Chapter Eleven

EMERGENCY SERVICES

POLICING

The following is collated from recollections of former members of the Special Constabulary and regulars of the Devon and Cornwall Police and Fire Service and David Hopper (formerly Sergeant No. 648, stationed at Cullompton from June 1976 until 31 March 1988).

Policing began with the formation of the Special Constabulary in 1831 under an Act of Parliament following the Reform Bill and four years before the first regular Borough Police Forces were created. Justices were empowered to appoint Special Constables where any tumult, felony or riot had or was about to occur. The history of Cullompton's police force has progressed as follows:

Cullompton Police Officers, c.1950.
Left to right: Malcolm Barnes, Barry Denner, David Head, Robin Hiron, Martin Hookway.

1835: The first regular paid police were appointed under the provisions of the Municipal Corporations Act of 1835; Tiverton was one such Borough Police Force.

1856: On 25 November 1856, the Devon Constabulary came into being by the issue of a Royal Warrant. Quarter Sessions appointed its first Chief Constable, a Gerald de Courcey Hamilton, who held office until 1891.

1857: On 30 June 1857, the Police Committee made arrangements for renting of a Police Station at Cullompton, which fell in the then District 'B' and provided accommodation for three cells, quarters for three constables, an office for the Superintendent and a petty session courtroom. Cullompton was a significant station in those days and appears to have been a Divisional Headquarters. Under the control of the superintendent were the following: Bampton, Culmstock, North Tawton, Crediton, Axminster, Stockland, Upottery, Honiton, Woodbury, Exmouth, Sidmouth, East Budleigh, Ottery St Mary and Colyton. In the whole of this area only five sergeants were established with 28 constables.

1878: On 31 March 1878, the Chief Constable reported on the strength and disposition of his force and confirmed that in 'C' Division, Cullompton, a Superintendent Richard Collins was in charge assisted by a first-class sergeant at Bampton, a second-class sergeant at Cullompton and 20 constables.

1888: By the Local Government Act of 1888, the Court of Quarter Sessions ceased to be the Police Authority, appointed was the Standing Joint Committee with equal numbers of its members from appointees of the Quarters Sessions, and the newly-formed County Council for Devon.

1921: The Special Constabulary was reorganised. They had in times of stress been sworn in to deal with such contingencies as the Bread Riots, the Chartist Riots and the Dartmoor Prison Riots. In 1938 Major Morris, then Chief Constable, began to properly train and equip them to deal with major incidents.

1956: The authorised establishment for the regular force for this area was a superintendent, a pair of inspectors, 10 sergeants and 48 constables. Divisional control had now been relocated to Tiverton, 'C' Division. The strength of the Special Constabulary in Devon was 2500 men and 2 women, being the second largest force outside London.

1965: The establishment of the Special Constabulary pertaining to the Cullompton Section was 15, including a woman Special Constable. Special Sergeant George Lewitt was their supervisor.

1966: The Devon Constabulary and Exeter City Police amalgamated and in the following year a further combining of forces, Plymouth and Cornwall,

Cullompton Fire Brigade 1911. About 11.30 on Thursday 10 August 1911 Captain Brooks received a telegram worded 'Come at once, Plymtree Rectory on Fire, Hay'. He at once cycled round to warn several firemen and within six minutes of the alarm three horses drawing the manual engine were on their way to the scene of the fire. The men pumped continuously from noon to midnight but the rectory was destroyed.

Cullompton's Merryweather Gem Steam Fire Pump. It was purchased from Teignmouth Council in 1914 for £100 plus £5 for the equipment. It attended its first fire at Bradfield House on 23 October 1915.

joined with Devon and Exeter to create the Devon and Cornwall Constabulary. The Chief Constable that oversaw these combinations was Lt Colonel Ronald B. Greenwood (1967–79).

1974: The opening of the motorway required more officers and a new Police Station was completed.

1977: The completion of the motorway in May 1977 caused major changes as Cullompton Police Station became the first and last port of call for drivers, of private, commercial and emergency vehicles. The increase in traffic using the motorway brought extra business to Cullompton Magistrates Court, thereafter dubbed the 'motorway court'. Cullompton Police were prominent in local activities and events such as the carnival and Festival Week, all of which relied to some extent on organising skills. They also fielded teams in skittles, the Whitbread Cup for cricket and were prominent in the snooker and billiards league. Rugby and football also drew support. Use was made of other club facilities for this.

1980: Cullompton Police initiated their own registered Police Club. It was entirely self funded; Inspector John Essary, latterly head of CID and Deputy Chief Constable, former Sergeant David Hopper and retired Constables Paul Prothero and Helen Vicary were to the fore, although many others helped. The 'Club' was comparatively short-lived due to pressure of space as more room was required for operational use.

The Retained Section of Cullompton Fire Service had used the bar facility after fire practice on a Monday and many were already Special Constables as well. Bernard Land and his 'crew' of fearless individuals were to the fore. Bernard has long since retired but still exhibits his restored fire engine at local rallying events.

1980–2001: Constable David Head wound the clock at the old Police Station for many years after the move to new premises and served as Constable in the area for almost all of his 30 years. He sadly died in January 2001, a well-known figure in at least three communities. At Hemyock he was the 'village' policeman for many years until the adoption of the 'panda' scheme which closed village stations and motorised its bobbies. At his memorial service great recognition was paid to his role as a community policeman.

It was the duty of the Sectional Sergeant to inspect the Beat Books for all his section twice a year to ensure the information remained up to date. A description of the extent of a beat, villages and hamlets, acreage and population was given. The following seven villages and two towns now comprise the Cullompton Beat Section: 1. Hemyock, 2. Culmstock, 3. Uffculme, 4. Burlescombe and Westleigh, 5. Kentisbeare (included Blackborough and Sainthill), 6. Willand, 7. Bradninch, 8. Plymtree with Clyst St Lawrence and Clyst Hydon, 9. Cullompton.

FIRE SERVICE

There have been many disastrous fires in Cullompton over the years. Thatch was always the main roofing material, not only on houses but also on barns; outhouses and even walls were thatched to keep the cob, of which they were constructed, dry. By 1633, only the church and The Walronds had slate roofs, and in the 18th and 19th centuries most of the properties would still have been thatched. Once a fire had started it could soon engulf whole streets.

The worst fire on record occurred on a quiet Sunday afternoon; on 7 July 1839 as churchgoers walked home they were alarmed by cries of 'fire'. It started in a house opposite the end of New Street and rapidly spread up Fore Street, along New Street and into Crow Green until two-thirds of the town was reduced to ashes. Some 145 houses and 170 other buildings – outhouses, barns, etc. and their contents were destroyed. The loss totalled £15 000 which was an enormous sum at that time. Over 200 families were made homeless by the blaze and many took refuge in the Workhouse (now the British Legion Club), having lost the tools of their trade, mainly the cottage weavers who lost their handlooms. Fortunately there was no loss of life.

Most of the firefighting, such as it was, would have been done by engines belonging to various insurance companies and the horse-drawn vehicles would have to come from Exeter. A small hand appliance was kept in the church porch.

When the Parish Council was formed in 1894 it became responsible for the Fire Brigade and provided it with a horse-drawn manual pump. Mr G. Brooks, a local ironmonger, was appointed Captain in 1907 and his eldest daughter, the late Mrs M.R.M. Whitton wrote of her memories of that time:

The young people of today might think the method of calling out the Fire Brigade, up to 1929, ludicrous, but I assure you it was both effective and efficient, although there were practically no telephones and no sirens. In the daytime, a maroon rocket was fired from the yard behind the Captain's house, and this was audible all over the town, but it was not detonated at night, between 10p.m. and 6a.m. Then, the firemen had to be called by whatever means possible. Usually the elder daughter of the Captain, Mr George Brooks, would run up the New Cut blowing the Fire Brigade whistle to summon Mr Walter Sweet, then down to Crow Green through the lane in front of Shortlands House, to call Mr Whitfield. Meanwhile someone else went to Mr Walter Brooks to get him to catch the three horses and harness them in a field near the Cullompton Hotel (now Toad Hall). A man called Jack Dummett always rode the first horse and I remember some of the other firemen were Drummer, Progg, F. Sweet and Jack Eales. The manual engine was manned by volunteers who were paid 4d. an hour to work the pump, the supply coming

Fire Brigade

Right: *PUO 928 Dennis F8 stationed at Cullompton, 1952.*

Below: *OTA 999M stationed at Cullompton from 1974.*

Right: *Remains of the Tannery after the fire.*

Below: *Retirement of Sub-officer J. Sweet, fireman P. Lambert and fireman P. Discombe, 1970. Left to right: F. Hoskins, C. Pike, J. Willett, N. Harper, P. Discombe, D. Westcott, ADD P. Elliot, C. Hodge, Sub Officer J. Sweet, B. Land, P. Lambert, C. Gould, Leading Fireman J. Hutchings, Leading Fireman N. Gooding.*

from streams, ponds and rivers as there was no main water supply. The firemen got 9d. an hour I think.

Calls came from as far afield as Broadclyst and Clayhidon, but despite this ten minutes was the average time it took for the firemen to be on their way – often they were even faster.

In 1909 an old coach-building shop in High Street, now the site of Clark's Motors, and storage sheds opposite the station yard went up like a blazing furnace on the same night; both were properties of the same man.

Sadly, one of the horses dropped dead on the road to Kentisbeare, while answering a call, and the remaining two animals had to complete the journey without it. Sometimes the Brigade was on duty for up to 24 hours attending serious fires. In November 1908 they saved Bradfield House where a large party of distinguished guests had just finished dinner. The call was received at 11p.m. and the Brigade arrived preceded by the Constable on his bicycle at 11.25p.m. They were joined by the Tiverton Brigade and later by Exeter, which arrived by special train, complete with horses and engine!

In 1914 Mountstephen House was destroyed by a terrible fire, the occupants escaping in their night attire. Two of the Cullompton men were injured, Mr Prigg being rendered unconscious by a lump of falling cob. The assessor from Exeter complimented the Brigade highly on the smart stop they had made, saving hundreds of pounds worth of property by their good work.

The same year there was a disastrous fire at Kings Mill, and again the Brigade worked magnificently to save hundreds of tons of wood pulp. Soon afterwards Cullompton acquired a steam engine costing £100 raised by voluntary subscription, which had 1500ft of hose and threw 300 gallons a minute, instead of 80 gallons using the manual pump. Higher Kings Mill was badly damaged again five years later, and Captain Brooks had a narrow escape when the corrugated roof fell in on him, but the firemen 'one and all worked like Trojans'.

The Brigade was a very devoted body of men, with tremendous pride in their unit, indeed it was the Captain's main interest. Although the pay was small, and danger and difficulty commonplace, there was never a shortage of volunteers.

In 1924 the first trailer pump was housed at the Town Hall, where the kitchen and ladies' toilets are now. This was towed by a lorry belonging to local traders and the firemen were still called out by maroon. When the first motorised vehicles appeared they were too big for the Town Hall and were kept at Court House.

In later years the most disastrous fire occurred on 17 October 1958. A huge fire broke out at Messrs Sellwood's Tannery in Exeter Road, now the location of Somerfields. The whole building became a raging inferno and was completely gutted.

Left: *John and Wendy Hawke with the Cullompton Ambulance, 1995.*

Below: *This First World War ambulance was purchased through fund-raising.*

St John Ambulance

Left: *St John Ambulance Badgers.*

Below left: *St John Ambulance inspection night, c.1984. Left to right: Dave Buxton, Wendy Hawke, Pete Sherman, Ann ?, David Haywood, Sheila Steels, Colin Plant.*

Below: *St John Ambulance, 1960. Left to right: Mrs Flower, Mrs G. Davis, Mrs D. Glass, Mrs Morgan.*

Bottom: *Left to right, back row: ?, ?, Miss Mitchell, Mrs Morgan, ?, Mrs Palmer, ?, Mrs Rowsell, Mrs Rowe; front: G. Davis, Mrs Flower, ?, ?, Miss Salter, Mrs Glass.*

Chapter Twelve

SPORTING LIFE

CULLOMPTON BOWLING CLUB

by Ron Parker, Chairman

Cullompton Bowling Club was established in 1901 and was the only bowling club in Cullompton until 1935. When Culm Vale Bowling Club was formed our nickname became 'Cully Old Club'. Throughout its 100 years it has always been a small club, with all the work being done by members on a voluntary basis. The green was leased from the Cricket Club until a few years ago when it was bought. In the last few years alterations have included new dressing rooms plus toilets for the disabled.

There have been a few interesting stories over the years; one which springs to mind is the young boy who was helping his mother with the teas and was asked to fetch the water from the standpipe at the other side of the field. For all his hard work he was paid tuppence. When there was a drought all the washing-up water was put into watering cans to water the green.

The green is very important to every club; a good green is one everyone wants to play on and ours is a good green. The club has had many good green keepers. In recent years these have included Ken Vinnicombe and Bill Force. Now Ray Constable and the 'green committee' keep our green in good condition. It's a year-round job which involves a lot of commitment; just ask the wives!

The present membership is around 55, both male and female, from ages 13 to 80 and it is a great pleasure seeing everyone mixing together. Over the years the club has had players achieving Devon honours plus Ladies' and Men's Devon County competition success and also young players playing for the county.

As 2001 was the club's centenary year special celebration events were organised including a competition so that players from all around the UK could come and play on the club's green.

To run a club for 100 years takes something special: a strong committee and a friendly atmosphere, and the club is always on the lookout for new members.

CULM VALE BOWLING CLUB

by Mrs Queenie Broom

The bowling green at Culm Vale Bowling Club was laid using Cumberland turf in 1931. The green was part of the newly-built Cullompton Hotel sporting facilities. The whole set-up was the idea of a group of Cullompton business people including Dickie Miller, Bull Plumpton and Messrs Buscombe and Hamilton of Lloyds and Midland Banks.

The bowling team started playing on Thursday afternoons (probably due to half-day closing) and Saturday afternoons. Some bowlers from Cullompton Bowling Club split off to bolster the newly-formed team, the attraction being that the Cullompton Hotel had a bar and was used for teas and toilets, as the club had minimal facilities but an excellent green.

With the businessmen of Cullompton playing there was no need for fund-raising as the club members just brought what was needed from their own pockets. In 1957 there was just over £1 in the kitty.

Culm Vale has had two County Presidents, Sam Heard in 1973 and George Heard in 1981. George served the club as Treasurer from 1962 to 1988. The club has had success in the County Championships including: S.J. Salter (Singles Champion 1951), Len Murray and Len Spurway (Pairs Champions 1964 and 1968), Sam and George Heard and Len Murray (Triples Champions 1972 and 1975), Len Murray (Over 60s County Champion 1984), Maurice Gwynne (Two Woods Champion 1993), Andrew Heard, Joe Peake and Simon Broom (Triples Champions 1996), and Simon Broom (Under 25s Champion 1996).

Over the years several members have played for Devon in the Middleton Cup, among them George and Bill Heard, Tony Broom, Andrew Heard and Simon Broom (a player in 2001). Culm Vale also won the 2000 County Top Club Championship.

The club paid rent to various owners until 1987 when the opportunity arose to purchase its own facilities. Since then membership has expanded to around 100, including ladies, and the necessary extensions built onto the old clubhouse shell. The green is now used most days from April to September, with ten competitive games or interclub fixtures.

Above: *Culm Vale Bowling Club with Cullompton Hotel behind, c.1938. The club and tennis courts were all part of the hotel which, at that time, was a gentlemen's club. One could only join by invitation; 'ordinary' folk used Cullompton Bowling Club.*

Above: *Cullompton Bowling Club, opening day, 1991. President, Mr Les Partridge, bowling the first wood.*

Left: *Cullompton Bowling Club postcard, 24 July 1908.*

Cullompton Cricket Club

by M. Baker, Hon. Secretary

Cullompton Cricket Club was established in 1892, although it is thought that fixtures had been played well before that date. Old score books were in existence at the club's headquarters until recently but many have disappeared, possibly being in the possession of older club members. The club's present ground is at Landspeed Meadow, situated adjacent to the CCA fields. Many people think that the ground is part of the CCA set-up, but the club has owned its field and clubhouse since the 1960s. Until fairly recently the bowling green and clubhouse were also owned by the Cricket Club.

The cricket pavilion and field have undergone many changes; the original tin shed, which served as both changing rooms and equipment shed, was demolished in the 1970s and the present pavilion, erected in 1927, has been extended and refurbished. A small bar was added in the 1970s but the present structure was completed in 1983 and boasts a large bar and lounge area, changing room, toilets, kitchen, and a hall which can hold up to 150 people for functions. The actual playing area is restricted by the fields on two sides, the bowling green and the main Exeter–Paddington railway on the other. This often causes 'train stopped play' in the summer but the sight of magnificent steam engines has provided magic moments remembered by older members.

In the club's early days matches were played against local villages and pick-up sides, due to the limitations of transport. The 1960s brought a gradual expansion of these fixtures and a Sunday trip to Cockington was always looked forward to. The club's first foray into league cricket was the old North and East Devon League. This involved trips to, amongst others, Barnstaple, Bideford and Westward Ho! At the height of the summer, before the Link Road, this could mean leaving in the early morning for a tortuous two- or three-hour journey. The formation of the East Devon League meant more local fixtures and, in time, the second XI also became involved in league cricket. Although never league champions, the club usually finished near the top and were Whiteway Cup winners in 1997, 1998 and 1999. The 1st XI entered the Devon League in 2000 and immediately became champions of the E division. Restructuring of local cricket has meant that the second team played in the Devon League beginning in the 2001 season.

Many 'characters' have appeared in teams over the years including prominent local businessmen, amongst them bank managers and shopkeepers. One of these was known as 'the Major'. He transported players to away matches in various expensive cars, including a Rolls Royce, but one day failed to turn up for a match. It was later revealed that he had been involved in a huge horse-race betting ring. His place of residence, Bolealler House, fell vacant, and the story appeared in the national newspapers some time later.

More recently a well-loved club Chairman was Norman Dingle. Despite being severely disabled and walking with the aid of two sticks, Norman threw himself into club life and was the first team scorer for several years, keeping an immaculate book. On a celebrated mini tour in the 1980s the team was enjoying a pre-match pub visit in Chudleigh. One of the tour features was that on the call of 'dead ants' everyone had to throw themselves onto the floor, no matter where they were at the time. Just as they were crossing Chudleigh main street the call went up, and we were treated to the hilarious sight of Norman lying in the middle of the road, legs waving in the air and sticks flying everywhere! This is just one example of the comradeship of club life which has led to many of our cricketers continuing to play for Cullompton for many years and keeping involved behind the scenes after retirement from active playing.

Left: *Presidents' Invitation Match, September 1989. Left to right, back: Jim Organ (umpire), Jon Pengelly, Tom Stocker, Paul Elliott, Dave Brister, Ron Dolley, Tony Drury, Andy Smith, Frank Tiley, Dave Maunder, Gordon Coombes (Chairman and life member), Mark Mortiboys, Neil Ray-bould, Keith Milford, Bob Hewer, Ray Denner, Ben Wren, Mike Smith; front: Dave Percy, Mike Baker, Martin Elliott, Norman Dingle (Pres.), Mrs Brenda Dingle, Allan Garnham, Keith Martin, Mike Ingersent.*

Cullompton Rangers Football Club, 1949/50 (2nd XI Winners of Junior Division).
Left to right, back: L. Coates, J. Sharland, J. Lake, G. Coombes, C. Caines, K. Vinnicombe;
front: G. Heard, K. Hollett, C. Gooding (Captain), C. Foster, G. Perry.

Cullompton Rangers Football Club 1961/62.
Left to right, back: J. Ross, R. Wilson, W. Richardson, C. Caines, C. Butt, C. Wellington;
front: B. Long, D. Heale, D. Blatchford, K. Salter, J. Vincent, R. Weeks, T. Patch.

Cullompton Rangers FC

by Marcus Scott, Secretary

Cullompton Rangers Football Club was formed in 1945 and played in the East Devon Victory League running two sides. The first ground was the school playing fields but they soon moved to Speeds Meadow (where they are based at the time of writing) for a short period before moving to land adjoining the M5 motorway, then Knightswood on to Court Drive and finally back to their present base in 1974.

The club badge depicts the businesses which were prominent in the town when it was formed, such as the ropeworks, glove makers and woollen factory.

The most successful era for the club was during the early 1960s when they swept everything before them, winning the Devon and Exeter League Premier Division in 1961 and 1964. It was not until 1984 that success was theirs once more when they captured the East Devon Senior Cup. The standard of the First Team has steadily improved and they went on to become one of the founder members of the Devon County League in 1992. In 1997/8 they finished runners-up in the League and went on to repeat the feat the next season but also won the Devon Premier Cup for the first time in their history.

The Speeds Meadow ground is recognised as one of the best in the league boasting a spacious clubhouse and three pitches. Floodlights were installed in 1998/9 allowing the club to compete in the FA Vase which they did for the first time in 2000.

The club also run Second and Third Teams in the Devon and Exeter League as well as a thriving Youth Section made up of five teams ranging from Under 8s to Under 15s.

Of the founder members Eric Dummett is still an active member of the committee and Jim Brooks and Fred Heal, who now look after the ground, have been active at the club for more than 50 years. Marcus Scott is now Secretary after having served the club as a player, Manager and Chairman. The Chairman is Stan Hill who has had a lifetime associated with the club, being a past player and Manager.

Right: *Cullompton Rangers Football Club, date unknown.*

Below: *Cullompton Rangers 1st Team, 2000. Left to right, back: Ray Pratt (Manager), S. Guppy, N. Douglas, P. Campbell, C. Garnsworthy, E. Roberts, D. Pengelly, S. Hill, J. Cottrell, Stanley Hill (Chairman); front: M. Scott, D. Gulliver, L. Annunizata, D. Floyd, P. Robinson, A. Horrell.*

Cullompton Rugby Club, 1892/3.
Left to right, back: W. Brooks, M.T. Foster (Hon. Secretary), T. Baker, G. Rutley, J. Pring, H. Whitton, W. Forse, G. James, S. Labdon, J.H. Baker (Hon. Treasurer); middle: P. Blackmore, W. Spurway, W. Greenslade; front: S. Kerslake, W. Harding, W. Ingersent, T. Dyer.

Cullompton Rugby Team, 1951/52 (the season they won the cup).
Left to right, back: ?, S. Wood, D. Frost, ? Hardcastle, ?, D. Cockram, P. Emmett, K. Vigars, T. Kerslake, ?; front: J. Hake, K. Butt, J. Force, P. Hill, D. Casely, J. Gollop, E. Goff, T. Jones; on ground: G. Gillard, C. Holloway.

Cullompton Rugby Football Club

The club's first competitive games took place in 1892/3 and the first season the club carried the M.T. Foster spelling of 'Collumpton'. In 1896 Cullompton Football Club, later to become Rugby Football Club, headed the second division list and won the Junior Cup, having similar results the following season. The Secretary of the club was W.T. Barnard of Higher Street, and M.T. Foster, a major influence in the group's formation, became the first referee from the club.

The following is a timeline of interesting facts:

1912 Players required to supply their own jerseys
1919 Admission to games 3d. inc tax
1920 At the AGM 'A musical programme completed the evening'
1922 A groundsman was elected and paid. His was the most important job in the club.
1925 It was proposed a supporters' club be formed
1928 A discussion took place on season tickets. It was thought that 3s.6d. was too low a fee now that the club ran two teams. The fee was set at 4s.0d.
1938 The end of Dr Gidley's reign as President which extended over 28 years.
1939 During the Second World War half the side disappeared and it was not until 1946 that the club brought the game back to life.
1950 Played half the season in one field, behind the last houses in Exeter Road (now Knightswood), but because of frequent water-logging it was decided to move to Brook Meadow (now Cullompton Community College).
1969 Following the AGM, details given of a project to purchase 52 Fore Street as a clubhouse.
1978 The field, now known as Stafford Park, was purchased and soon work started on levelling the ground and preparing a pitch.
1981 The new pitch at Stafford Park was officially opened by Mr S. Hill on 6 September.
1988 Work started on building a clubhouse and the club moved from Fore Street to its new and permanent home in December.

In the early years, the club's headquarters were the Railway Hotel (now the Weary Traveller) and then from 1911 the White Hart Hotel, followed by the Dolphin Inn from 1919 and then back to the White Hart until 1931. The Half Moon (now Tavy Textiles) then became the headquarters, with changing rooms behind the stage of what is now the Masonic Hall. Can anyone remember Dicky Toogood, who lit the boiler and prepared the three tin baths for the after-match wash? Later some of the members built a concrete bath.

In 1950 the club moved to the Cullompton Hotel; there they had use of what had been the chef's bungalow, which some of the members altered inside, and installed showers. In 1970 the club bought the old Globe Hotel and the supporters' club was opened. Then in 1981, after 90 years of wandering, the club purchased its own ground and in 1988 the clubhouse was opened.

The Rugby Club has now become a venue for community events and parties. Members organise a 'Razzfest' (real ale and jazz festival) each year which is very popular and has become one of the highlights of the year for local people. In existence for over a century, the club has always been well and loyally served by its members and committee. It is not possible to list all those involved but the club is grateful to everyone who has contributed to its success.

Cullompton Rugby Football Club, 2000/01 season.
Left to right, back: D. Goff (President), D. Shippey, K. Ballantyne, P. Surridge, I. Moon, J. Baker, S. Lunn, R. Down, J. Sage, J. Canning, S. Davey;
front: A. Elliott, I. Brown, G. Richards, K. Holway, G. Meldon (Captain), M. Weeks, R. Hammett, S. Beatty, S. Harris, M. Blackmore (Coach).

Cullompton Tennis Club, 1906.

Cullompton Tennis Club, c.1950.
Left to right, back: Joyce Scorse, Sheila Heard, Bill Heard, Reg Chapman, David Creed;
front: Barbara Phillips, Muriel Coxhead, Joyce Baker, Betty Shere, Janet Spurway, Margaret Heard, ?.

Cullompton Tennis Club, 1952.

PADBROOK PARK

by Richard Chard

Padbrook Park stands at the southern end of town and is one of Cullompton's newest sporting and leisure facilities. The centre was developed by the Chard family during the 1990s on their former family farmland, and is still very much under their control.

The Padbrook Golf Course (6108 yards, Par 70) was designed by leading golf-course architect Bob Sandow, and took over two years to construct. It incorporates much natural woodland and water and had quickly proven itself to be a challenge for golfers of all standards. Affiliated to both the Devon and English Golf Unions, it competes in both county and national tournaments and its recent success in many of these proves that the golfers in Cullompton are a force to be reckoned with! The course is supported by a full range of shop, hire and practice facilities and the club professionals run regular clinics for those wishing to take up the game as well as offering advice to more experienced players.

The three-rink Padbrook Indoor Bowling Club was opened on 9 March 1992 and offers all-season playing facilities. Like the golf club, the Cullompton bowlers' success in county tournaments has been remarkable and this culminated in the 1995/6 season when Padbrook's Lady Triples Team took the English National Title. The club was especially honoured in the millennium year when one of its founder members, Maureen Robinson, was elected Devon County President and represented the town and club throughout the country.

The clubhouse is also open to those not taking part in the sporting activities. The Pavilion Suite, on the first floor, offers panoramic views over the golf course and serves a wide choice of home-made bar meals as well as a selection of local beers and ciders. This suite is available for private hire, is the perfect setting for parties and conferences and has hosted many local wedding receptions for Cullompton couples. Two other conference suites have been constructed and are now in regular use by town businesses and those from further afield.

Since its opening Padbrook has developed other facilities including a fishing lake and a health-and-fitness studio. As time goes by further developments of a hotel bedroom block and further fitness (wet and dry) activities are being considered and planned to ensure that Padbrook really can be a centre for the town to be proud of.

CULM VALLEY SPORTS CENTRE

Culm Valley Sports Centre, which was opened in 1985 by Mid Devon District Council, is situated in Meadow Lane adjoining the Community College. In 1999, with the help of Lottery funding, additional facilities were added. The improvements included an extension and air conditioning in the Fitness Studio, refurbishment of the activities room to make it into a dance/aerobics studio, an all-weather pitch and new changing rooms. The facilities now include: a four-court multi-purpose sports hall, an air-conditioned fitness studio, an air-conditioned dance/aerobics studio, squash courts, a sauna and an all-weather pitch. The Sports Centre runs a comprehensive aerobics programme, with classes catering for all interests and abilities. In addition, for many years, the Centre has been running a successful 'Active Start Scheme' in conjunction with local health practitioners. People of all ages and abilities have successfully taken the first steps to a healthier future. A wide range of activities for children of all ages is on offer, including football, ballet, gymnastics, tap dance and trampolining.

CULLOMPTON
12th MAY, 1937
- AT 6 P.M. -

CORONATION
SPORTS
SOUVENIR
PROGRAMME

E. H. KNOTT,
Hon. Sec. Sports Committee

Mothers' Union outing to Lynton and Lynmouth, July 1957. Left to right: Mrs Snow, Miss Melhuish, ?, Mrs Frost, Miss Joyce Trezise, Mrs Bessie Owen, Mrs May, ?, ?, ?, ?, ?, ?, Miss Selwood, Mrs Cockram, Mrs Broom, Mrs Earle, Mrs Bradbeer, Mrs Denner, Revd Hammond, ?, ?.

Cullompton Old Age Pensioners Club, c.1970. Left to right, back: ?, Miss Melhuish and Mrs Gooding; front: Mr and Mrs Ford, Mrs Pring, Mrs Sayer, Mrs Parsons, Mrs Earle, Mrs Stone, Mrs Yard, Mr Aldridge, Miss Kellaway, Mr Gooding, Mr Aldridge, ?.

Chapter Thirteen

CLUBS & ORGANISATIONS

CULLOMPTON TWINNING ASSOCIATION

by Mrs Joyce Owens

In 1975 a steering committee was invited to visit Ploudalmezeau in Brittany, the proposed twin town for Cullompton. In all 13 people travelled by air from Plymouth to Morlaix in a very small plane (we were visually measured for size to keep the balance). We were taken by coach to Ploudalmezeau to meet our host families. Ploudalmezeau is approximately one and a half hours' drive from Roscoff, a town very similar to Cullompton, rural and mainly a farming community. We received a very warm welcome and had a very enjoyable stay.

After many meetings and discussions between officials from both towns it was decided to exchange charters to confirm the 'twinning' in 1977. These were duly signed by Mr Jack Whitton, on behalf of Cullompton Town Council, and M. Alphonse Arzel, the Mayor of Ploudalmezeau.

Exchange visits are made on alternate years and approximately 50 people take part. The students from Cullompton Community College also participate in an annual exchange. Over the years many gifts have been exchanged. A member of the Twinning Association arranged for an English red telephone box to be placed in the town square at Ploudalmezeau. You can walk down Rue de Cullompton or sit on a bench in the Maire (Town Hall) which was presented to the town to celebrate 20 years of twinning. Many gifts presented to Cullompton can be seen in the Town Hall.

The visit to our twin town in 1978 was marred by the sinking of the *Amoco Cadiz* close to Portsall, spilling 220000 tonnes of petroleum along the coast. The smell was atrocious and the pollution disastrous to the sea life and the birds. The anchor from the ship can be seen on the quay at Portsall as a permanent reminder of the disaster. Subsequent visits have been very successful and enjoyable. Our hosts always prepare a very varied programme with visits to many interesting places, complete with wonderful French picnics. The two towns will celebrate the 25th anniversary of twinning in the year 2002; it is hoped that entente cordiale will continue to flourish.

Above: *Clock being presented to M. Alphonse Arzel, Mayor of Ploudalmezeau, by Mr Jack Whitton, Cullompton Town Council. The clock was made by Mr Ken Saunders of Cullompton.*

Left: *Twinning tree planting in CCA fields.*

WI

Left: *WI Tea at Upton Lake, 1927.*

Below: *Dr Gidley rowing on the lake.*

Below: *Members of the first Cullompton Women's Institute Committee, 1917. Left to right, back: Mrs Rutley, Mrs Sharland, Mrs Jones, Mrs Brooks, Miss Westcott; front: Miss Morris, Mrs Pyne, Mrs Gidley (President), Miss Wilkinson, Mrs May, Miss Hill.*

Cullompton & District Flower Club

by Mrs Margaret Strurcke

Mrs Margaret Russ and Mrs Jane Attlee are presented with the Constance Spry Trophy by the NAFAS President.

After some informal meetings and visits to other Flower Clubs, Mrs Helen Caterer of Exeter was invited to assist in the formation of a club for flower arrangers in Cullompton. In July 1968, with Mrs Whitton as Chairman, a club was established and affiliated to the Devon and Cornwall Area of the National Association of Flower Arranging Societies (NAFAS). By the September demonstrations and members' practice sessions were being organised.

Gradually activities were extended to include visits to gardens and other clubs and some social and money-raising functions. Competition work was introduced and by 1971 groups of members were entering the floral competition at the Devon County Show. Charitable gifts began when surplus funds became available.

Informal classes for beginners were organised and members began to have confidence to arrange flowers for festivals, charity events and area and national shows organised by NAFAS. By 1973 successes in competitions were forthcoming with a 2nd place in the Club Class at the Devon County Show and in 1975 members were 'Commended' for their entry in the Club Class at the National Show at Bournemouth. When the Nationals returned to Bournemouth in 1987 the club was awarded 1st Place and a Gold Medal for an arrangement by Mrs Margaret Russ and Mrs Jane Attlee.

Meetings took place for many years in the Church Rooms behind the Baptist Church then a move was made to the Cullompton Hotel to allow for increased membership. Following the sale of the hotel the Parish Rooms were used but parking difficulties for demonstrators forced a change to Padbrook Park. A stage, good lighting, hall space and free parking facilities attracted the club to meet in Willand Village Hall where they still assemble.

Meetings are held monthly, except in January, on the first Monday afternoon at 2.30p.m. unless it is a Bank Holiday when it moves to the second Monday. Normally there are eight demonstrations, at least one of which is by a nationally-qualified demonstrator, a members' practice day or show, a speaker and an outing each year. There are various stalls for the sale of flower arranging sundries, plants and publications, and tea is available at the end. Members also still take part as individuals or groups in demonstrating, flower-arranging competitions, church flower arranging and festivals and exhibitions. Contributions to charity are still made annually. New members are always welcome and many find that flower arranging is a very useful, creative and relaxing hobby.

Cullompton WI

by Mrs Muriel Coxhead

Cullompton WI was the first to be founded in Devon in 1917. Mrs G. Gidley, wife of a prominent doctor in the town, had formed a group of women to help with the provision of food during the First World War and when the WI movement started in this country she became a strong supporter and her group of workers formed into the WI. They continued to work hard for the war effort, and were responsible for running a National Kitchen in the old Cyclists Barracks in The Green which was just off Fore Street. This ensured that all had a reasonable standard of nutrition. The following items were on the menu: soup 2d., sausage roll 2d., potatoes 1d., jam tart 2d., milk pudding 2d., fish cake 2d., vegetable hot-pot 2d., treacle tart 2d., boiled pudding 2d., fish pie 3d.

Many social activities were enjoyed. Concerts were held at the Victoria Hall to raise money for 'Comforts' for the troops and a choir and small orchestra were formed. A highlight of the year was the annual picnic at Upton with rowing on the lake.

In later years a very successful drama group gave many performances in the Assembly Rooms and in the County Drama Festival won the Shakespeare Shield. The WI has competed in the Devon County Show with items of craftwork and cookery and on a more serious note fully discussed affairs of national importance.

The Merry Wives of Windsor, *produced by the WI in 1935. Left to right, back: Mrs Widgery, Mrs Rawlings, Mrs Clapp, ?, ?, Mrs Sayer, Mrs Atkins; front: Mrs Ingersent, Monda Stone, Mrs Dummett.*

Cullompton Dramatic Society & Pantomime Club

Above: *The first pantomime,* Ali Baba and the Forty Thieves, *1953. The principals were: Alice Harris, Frank Wellington, Dora Eveley, Eunice Butt.*

Right: *Cullompton Dramatic Society staged* The Happiest Days of your Life *in 1952. Left to right: Arthur Whitlock, Joy Browning, Wilf Coxhead, Beth Woolcott, Amy Woolcott, Frances Chapman, Reg Chapman, Guy Willatt, Eve Valentine, Michael Morgan, Peggy Willatt; seated: Brian McFarlane, Muriel Coxhead.*

Left: *Cullompton Pantomime Club produced* Jack and Jill *in February 2000. Left to right, back: Bob Hewitt, Matthew Barrow and Matthew Claremont-Davies (as the horse), Jeanette Simmons, Kyla England, Linda Phillips, Jemma Searle, Alison Harris, Elizabeth Crocker, Amy Vaughan, James Jones, Rodney Warwick; front: Ruth Buse, Bexy Claremont-Davies, Lesley Darlow, Julie Case, William Goddard, Sarah Clarke.*

Cullompton Pantomime Club

by Mrs Alison Harris

The Cullompton Pantomime Club was originally the 'British Legion Pantomime Club', started by Richard Eveley in 1953 to raise money for local charities. The first production was *Ali Baba and the Forty Thieves* which was presented in the Assembly Rooms (now the Masonic Hall). After several successful shows the club decided to become an independent group.

Through the 1960s and '70s the club continued to thrive, having a substantial cast and boasting both a senior and junior chorus numbering up to 34. One notable figure who gave much time and expertise to the group for well over 30 years was Margaret Coates. Her first involvement was as a chorus girl but her passion and gift for acting took her through many principal roles and the group benefited from her many talents as dancer, choreographer, producer and ultimately President. Her early memories include using wartime blackout material to make costumes.

There are other long-standing stalwarts whose names often crop up in the club's history, but worthy of special note is Bill Terry who was still in charge of lighting at 91. Also long-serving organist Bill Brooks.

In 1988 the club spawned a sister society, the Cullompton Allsorts Theatre, which has rapidly built up a reputation for excellent productions. The club has an enduring place in the town keeping alive the tradition of a family show that brings people lots of laughter, where good always triumphs over evil and there are always happy endings...

Cullompton Dramatic Society

by Mrs Muriel Coxhead

Cullompton Dramatic Society was formed in December 1949 shortly after Reg Chapman came to the town to teach in a local school. In conversation with Bill Woolcott, the local dentist, he said he was interested in drama as were several members of the Woolcott family and some of their friends. Founder members included Muriel and Wilf Coxhead, Muriel's father Bill Terry (who was a stalwart back-stage and usually operated all the lights and electrical equipment), Francis Chapman and Guy and Peggy Willatt. The report of their first AGM records that their first production, *A Quiet Weekend*, was at the Primary School (now St Andrew's). Subsequently performances took place at the Assembly Rooms, and there were four productions in the first 18 months.

In the years that followed, the society produced two plays a year; one in the spring and one in the autumn, and some of them were really memorable. The reviews in the local paper record that the plays were well received and that Reg Chapman was correct when he said that the Dramatic Society filled a great need. The standard of the stage sets was remarkably good, particularly when one considered the size of the stage and the limited facilities available to players and back-stage workers. Mr G. Venn and Mr Bill Yendell received great praise for the set of *A Play for Ronnie*, and this continued throughout the life of the society. One of the most enjoyable productions was *The Rape of the Belt* in 1964. The Dramatic Society held various social events, often on the tennis court behind Golds Place, now the site of the temporary classrooms at St Andrew's School.

The cast rehearsed in the dentist's waiting room at Gold's Place until Bill Woolcott died in 1960 and the practice was sold. Rehearsals then moved to Veryards for a couple of years before John Curgenven took over as producer. Rehearsals moved to his house at Uffculme and plays were produced at Willand Village Hall. The Dramatic Society withered away until 1988 when The Allsorts Theatre revived drama in Cullompton with a new production of *The Happiest Days of Your Life*, previously staged in 1952.

Cullompton Allsorts Theatre

by Mrs Jane Campbell

Cullompton Allsorts Theatre was formed in 1988 and the group has now produced some 25 plays. These have included comedies as well as modern classics and standards such as *Gaslight* and *Uncle Vanya*. The group's production of *Billy Liar* won an annual award from the National Operatic and Dramatic Association and their efforts regularly attract critical comments like 'an evening of total enjoyment' and 'achieved wonderful amounts of humour and pathos'. The group could not have succeeded without widespread moral support from people who clearly look on theatre as an asset to the town. But it isn't easy to keep going. Amateur drama in Cullompton faces the same problem as theatre everywhere in drawing a regular audience away from competing attractions. It also needs a large pool of volunteers to take part in plays, to publicise them and to set up and manage the stage and the 'house'.

Ring of Bells Morris Dancers

by Mr Ian Bloomfield

The mixed Morris Dancing side was formed in October 1999, the name being chosen after the small bell-making foundry in the town, which made bells for some of Devon's churches. Also there is a dance called 'Ring of Bells'. The side held its first dance practice at Cullompton Baptist Church Hall on 14 October 1999, moving to the Bell Inn, Exeter Road, in 2000. The colours are black shirt and trousers, top hat, rag waistcoat made up of coloured strips of material in blue for the sky, green for the grass and gold for the bells (and also because the town's badge contains blue and green). Since forming, the side has danced at several local village events and charity functions, the first official 'dance out' being at the launch of the Cullompton Festival in June 2000.

CULLOMPTON COMMUNITY ASSOCIATION

by Mrs Eileen Andrews

The Cullompton Community Association consists of a council of 26 members; half are elected and half are appointees nominated by certain of the town's organisations, managed by an executive committee of 15 which it elects from within its ranks. The work of the executive is overseen by a board of four trustees. The trustees at the time of writing are Liz Bullivant, Keith Owers, Roy Jeffery and John Vicary (who is also Chairman of the executive committee).

With the help of the National Federation of Community Associations, the Cullompton Community Association was founded in 1970. This followed in-depth research, which began in 1965 and included a questionnaire survey of community opinion and public meetings. As a result a committee consisting of four Town Councillors – John Vicary, Mrs Martinscroft, Tom Smith and Martin Neeves – was formed to take the matter forward.

It became apparent that the town wanted and needed a recreation area, a community hall, and a swimming pool, and it was felt that at least two of these aims were achievable – the recreation area and community hall. The need for a recreation area had been brought to a head by the fact that the town Football Club, Cullompton Rangers, had been moved off two previous pitches as a result of the development of Hayman's Close and Knightswood. The club was seeking a permanent site, as was the Rugby Club. Six different sites were examined and assessed with the planning authorities recommending the current CCA fields site, largely because the water meadows were regarded as unsuitable for development due to their low level – there was a need for the town to retain a flood plain for protection. In fact, there is only a 9-inch fall from the highest point on the fields to the stream.

The land, approximating 32 acres, belonged to two different farms, one owned by Mr George Heywood and the other by Mr Lionel Richards. In order to purchase the land, which cost around £11 500, 11 local business people stood surety for £1000 each. A search for dormant club and charity accounts was undertaken at local banks and permission obtained from the Charity Commissioners to merge any monies therein, where appropriate, to form one fund. This exercise discovered an account belonging to one of the pre-war swimming pool fund-raising bodies that contained some £800. Unfortunately the money had not been invested and so retained face value. After grants to other bodies the balance of approximately £550 was made over to the CCA in 1970. A sum of £1000 was returned, by the CCA, to the new swimming-pool fund in about 1990.

As a matter of interest, Lionel Richards sold the little field, the one used by the funfair and to the right of the main entrance to the CCA land, to the Town Council before the war for the purpose of building a swimming pool. However, Mr Richards bought it back from the Council at a profit during the war years.

Another reason for the choice of the site was that the Cricket Club was already in situ on land leased to them by Murray Toogood Foster and his heirs until the 1960s when the club purchased the freehold. Part of the original site is now owned by the Bowling Club. As two of Cullompton's major clubs were already using this area for recreation it seemed an appropriate location for the focus of the town's leisure activities (although the Rugby Club subsequently decided to go its own separate way).

Work began in 1971 to prepare the water meadows for public use. Volunteers donated labour and professional services, with events being held to raise the funds to purchase materials. The land drainage was a major project that required a great deal of skill and this was organised by a man from Kings Mill. In recent years the Committee has ensured that this has been upgraded, although evidence of the high water table can be seen in places on the eastern perimeter where rushes flourish.

By coincidence the Cullompton bypass was being converted to the M5 in 1972/3 and so a little tit-for-tat took place with the contractors. In return for John Vicary providing some bulldozer driver training, one was left on site and in order to practise it was necessary to be supplied with hardcore! This became the base for the car park and access road. In the process of removing an old oak tree, a paid contractor levelled the football pitch. The remains of its trunk are still being used today as an item in the children's play area.

To compensate for the loss during works of hedgerows and a few mature trees, the CCA has planted several hundred saplings over the years, under the supervision of a dedicated volunteer, Mr Percy Cross. These include many varieties, some of which form a colourful avenue to the car park. One unusual tree is the monkey puzzle which was donated by a tenant of Hayman's Close when part of the estate was demolished. The tree was approximately 20 years old and seven metres tall when it was moved and it survives as a result of the skill and expertise of Mr Alan French.

The Football Club building on the CCA site was erected by that club which also carried out major drainage work to the pitch. The building is a replacement for the temporary wooden structure they initially used.

The rough area to the north of the site by the Longbridge Meadow Industrial Estate hides the foundations of old farm buildings which the CCA hope to clear in time. The fields that border this and the stream are cut for hay, with the proceeds being used to pay for grass mowing on the lower fields which are used for events and play.

Percy Cross planting trees at the CCA fields, 1999.

A Whippet Club holds regular meetings at the Fields and the track, which runs alongside the avenue, is regarded as one of the fastest in the country. Every June a National Whippet Racing Fortnight is held on the site and some of the CCA land is turned into a campsite for the duration with other caravanners using local sites.

The field to the right of the main entrance hosts the annual bonfire and firework display, which coincides with the visit of the funfair. Most years see a circus visit the fields. In the past this has included Chipperfield's but in recent years the John Lawson Circus, which has no large animals, has been the regular visitor. There is a barbecue in the children's play area that is available on request for public, private or corporate use.

The monument with the Town Twinning plaque that stands in the field next to the play area is in fact the plinth for the old gas lamp that stood in the centre of the Lower Bullring – this is now the junction of Cockpit Hill, Fore Street and Exeter Hill. Having languished for 40 years in the old DCC layby on the Willand Road, it was brought to its present location ten years ago by the Young Farmers.

The picnic area and land bordering the stream to the east is a part of the CCA site but is leased to Mid Devon District Council. This now forms the Riverside Walk which is popular with residents and visitors alike.

In addition to the land, the CCA bought a property on the corner of Church Street from the Boys' Club, to be used as a community centre. In former times the building was a public house known as the Rising Sun. The CCA spent £15000 renovating the property but over the years the building required further major repairs. With insufficient funds to do the work the CCA were forced to sell the building to Cullompton United Charities, who still use the property as Community House. The Cullompton Community Association land belongs to the people of Cullompton and is held in trust for their benefit. The CCA welcomes ideas for projects that will enhance use of the land, provided that such projects fall within the parameters of the Charitable Trust.

Cullompton United Charities

by Peter Labdon

United Charities is a fund of property and investments providing an income to help those in need living in the parish. It is mainly the result of bequests left to the parish during the 17th century, together with some 19th- and 20th-century additions. The 13 charities were amalgamated in 1921. Some dictated how money was to be spent: Sir John Acland's charity fund was intended to provide 13 penny loaves of bread each Sunday to be given to the poor; the Whiteheathfield Charity was to buy linen cloth to be made into shirts and shifts for the 'most needy and impotent'; John and Henry Hill's Charity was to provide kersey, the local cloth, to be made into large coats with the letters J.H. on the arm (in 1817 61 such coats were distributed); and Marjorie Arundell's Gift was to distribute linen to 16 poor widows.

In 1953 these charities were combined with three others, the Trott's Almhouses, the John Lanes Charity and the Charity of George Spicer, to create the current United Charities.

The trustees have available income from land, including a pony paddock at Stocking Close, opposite the Rugby Club, and a three-acre field at Higher Langlands, Knowle Lane, together with interest from investments. The main capital was obtained from the sale, in July 1973, of land (previously allotments) at Crow Bridge to the Raglan Housing Association for the construction of sheltered housing. Property includes Community House in Church Street, seven houses at Higher Street and two houses at Stoneyford.

The trustees are responsible for the maintenance, repair and letting of the nine Almshouses, and also the maintenance of Community House. They are also able to use income from the investments for the assistance of those living in the parish of Cullompton who are sick or in need. There are limitations imposed by the Charity Commissioners as to what help can be given, but the following are examples: assistance with relief for carers of those who are sick; the provision of equipment to help those who are ill, including nebulisers, special chairs and hearing aids; assistance for the Day Centre; assistance for the elderly (e.g. provision of 'Piper Lifelines' or nursing care); assistance in paying for equipment or clothing, fuel or furniture for those in hardship or distress; assistance in the purchase of tools or books for people under 25 starting in a trade or profession; and assistance to other charities with similar aims (i.e. St John Ambulance).

Generally the trustees receive requests through social workers, doctors and nurses, clergy and others involved with caring for those in Cullompton. The trustees purchase the necessary goods or services for the applicant. They are not allowed to pay directly for relief of rates or taxes, or commit themselves to making recurring grants.

Trott's Almshouses The 16th-century terrace of six one-bedroomed almshouses at the junction of Station Road and Higher Street was built with money left to the parish by John Trott who died in 1520. For part of their history during the early-19th century they were used as a bell foundry, but were returned to their original use at the beginning of the 20th century. They have been updated to include gas heating, fitted bathrooms and kitchens and are available to couples or single persons from the parish.

Weaver Wood This modern bungalow was built in 1988 and is designed specifically for disabled people with full wheelchair facilities. It was designed with stone external facing and a slate roof to blend with the almshouses. The name is taken from one of the charities comprising the United Charities, the Weaver Wood Charity of 31 October 1668.

Stoneyford This turn-of-the-century pair of substantial brick built houses at Stoneyford has also been modernised. The property is available to retired agricultural workers from the parish of Kentisbeare as well as Cullompton.

Community House This property was purchased from the Cullompton Community Association in May 1982. Used during the early part of the century as the Boys' Club, the building was subsequently used for a youth club and other community groups. The trustees have carried out alterations and improvements to both floors of the building. Originally the intention was to create a suitable venue for the Day Centre, providing meals and fellowship for the retired. Use of the building has now considerably increased and with the installation of a stair lift in 1993 both floors are now well utilised.

ROYAL BRITISH LEGION

The British Legion was formed after the First World War and part of the Old Workhouse in The Green was rented. In 1934 a building fund was started and the compensation paid during the Second World War, when the property was occupied by the troops who were stationed in the town, was paid into the fund. Fund-raising continued after the war and in 1964 the decision was taken to purchase the premises, together with three nearby cottages, to provide an extension. Volunteers did the necessary demolition work and, once professional builders had completed the construction of the new premises, they moved back in to complete the plastering and decoration.

The Army built a corrugated iron cookhouse and this was subsequently adapted to become a skittle alley for the club. The Legion club in the centre of the town is still the focal point of the Legion's activities in the area and is always on the lookout for new members who, by paying their membership fees, are helping the Royal British Legion bring the support and help which our ex-service personnel and their families need.

Above: *Opening the RBL extension, 1964. Left to right: W.H. Terry, Joe Chowings, George Roberts.*

Left: *RBL Entertainment Gang. Left to right, back: Eileen Andrews, Mara Moore, Joan Heard, Joyce Parsons, ?, Euni Butt, ? Marlow, ?, Mrs Luxton; front: Dorothy Andrews, Dora Eveley.*

RAOB Christmas party, 1951.

ST ANDREW'S LODGE 4097

by Terry Kerslake

Freemasonry started in Cullompton with the Phenician Lodge No. 608. The warrant of the lodge was dated 21 April 1809 and meetings were held at the White Hart Hotel. The lodge was only in existence for 19 years and was erased in 1828. Its number was changed in 1814 to 615. From 2 June 1809 to 14 April 1810 there were 30 members, the first being Richard Blake who was the Past Provincial Grand Master of South Africa. The present lodge is a daughter lodge of St Peter's in Tiverton and was founded in 1920, founder members including two doctors, two teachers, a former commercial traveller, two builders, a licensed victualler, a naval officer, a Post Office clerk, a draper and an insurance agent.

The meetings were held in the Half Moon Hotel but in 1939 the Army requisitioned the Lodge supper room so, there being no other entrance, it was impossible to reach the lodge. Permission was sought from Captain Bibb, RE, to allow the members to pass through the room. The premises of the Uffculme Lodge were also requisitioned and they used the lodge twice before holding meetings in Tiverton which proved to be more suitable. The premises, which include the Assembly Rooms, were bought in 1967 after the closure of the Half Moon.

YE CULM VALLEY LODGE 3708

On the roll of the grand lodge of England of The Royal Antediluvian Order of Buffaloes (1921–2001)

by Mr M. Smith

The story of Ye Culm Valley Lodge really starts in Broadhembury. Ye Hembury Lodge 598 used to meet there in the Drewe Arms until 1999 when they amalgamated with Ye Culm Valley Lodge due to a shortage of brothers. Numerous brothers from Cullompton travelled out to Broadhembury each week. Consequently it was suggested that another lodge be started here in Cullompton. An application was made to the Grand Lodge and Ye Culm Valley Lodge came into being on 5 July 1921, the founder members being Bro. James Bowles CP, Bro. Harris CP, Bro. Jewell CP and Bro. Jenkins CP. The Provincial Grand Primo Bro. J. James ROH, together with his officers, presided over the opening ceremony held at the King's Head Hotel at which there were 46 in attendance. The takings for the night were £6.7s.6d.

A year on the lodge was regularly opening with 20 or more in attendance. Indeed, so successful were we here in Cullompton we were asked to open another lodge, this one being in Tiverton. Consequently on 11 September 1923 Ye Twyford Lodge 4928 opened in the Black Horse Hotel, Tiverton. Sadly this lodge closed in 1995.

The lodge carried on going from strength to strength and in fact formed its own Concert Party in the mid 1920s and regularly held shows and concerts in the parish rooms for the townsfolk. Both adults and children alike eagerly awaited the Christmas parties that were held every year.

During the war years the lodge managed to keep going, albeit with shorter meetings. This was due to blackout restrictions and reduced numbers, as brothers were called up for their military service. Many lodge nights had to be cut short due to air-raid warnings when brothers engaged in Civil Defence suddenly disappeared at a rate of knots. Occasionally their numbers would be swelled when brothers who were stationed in the area paid visits. The meeting held on 9 June 1942, however, which celebrated our 21st birthday, was attended by 67 brothers, many coming from outlying areas, which during those times of petrol rationing, etc. was no mean feat. This celebration was held a month early as there were several brothers on leave from the Forces at the time. Monies taken on the night amounted to £4.4s.0d.

It was during this period that the lodge changed its meeting place from the King's Head to the Globe Hotel in Fore Street, Cullompton. It was also decided to change lodge nights to Wednesdays; this was to allow those brothers who were involved in the Home Guard and Civil Defence to attend their weekly parades. During 1943 it was decided to hold a Christmas party for the US Army. Each brother was asked to invite one US serviceman from the nearby barracks and on 8 December 1943 an enjoyable evening of Christmas entertainment was had by all who were in attendance.

Throughout the war years it was decided that members who were away in HM Forces should be sent a Christmas present. This was to be 10s.0d. for those stationed in the UK and 400 cigarettes for those stationed abroad.

Throughout the late 1940s, '50s and '60s the Town Council's carnival committee regularly asked to borrow the 'Royal' chairs from Ye Culm Valley Lodge for use by the Carnival King and Queen, which the lodge had no hesitation in sanctioning.

It is also interesting to note that throughout this period the lodge paid regular monthly visits to other lodges in the area. By all accounts these visits were more of a social affair than anything else. The coach, or should I say charabanc, full of brothers and their wives and girlfriends, would travel to Exmouth, Honiton, Exeter and Okehampton, where the host lodge would lay on entertainment and refreshments. With these visits and reciprocal visits to Ye Culm Valley Lodge, the social side of things was quite hectic. There was also a lodge trip at least once a year to places like Lynton and Lynmouth, Dartmouth and Weston Super Mare, the annual dinner dance, the Christmas party, to which many of the town's children would be invited, and several other functions throughout the year which certainly kept the entertainment committee on their toes.

In August 1952 the county was numbed by the flood at Lynmouth and the lodge made a donation of £7.10s.0d. to the Lynmouth Flood Relief Fund. It was in the December of the same year that the lodge moved its meeting place from the Globe Hotel to its own premises in Tiverton Lane, which it initially rented from the Young Conservatives but purchased outright in 1956. It shows how active and respected the RAOB were in the town at the time as they were invited by the Town Council in January 1953 to have two members elected onto the town's Coronation Committee: Bro. Donald Young CP and Bro. Clifford Hodge CP were duly nominated and elected.

In the late 1950s and early 1960s the Order in general started to look more towards supporting outside charities. It had previously concentrated on its own orphanages and convalescent homes, and looking after the widows and children of deceased brothers (indeed these are our main priorities today).

On 4 October 1961 Bro. Jim Brooks became the first brother to attain recognition for his 40 years' service to both the lodge and Order. Subsequently several brothers have achieved this feat; in fact two of our existing members, Bro. George Venner, ROH, and Bro. Bob Clarke, ROH, have 60 and 70 years' service respectively in Ye Culm Valley Lodge.

In July 1967 the lodge presented a bench to the town. This was actually made by Bro. Charlie Williams, CP especially for the occasion, and was gratefully received on behalf of the town by the Chairman of the Parish Council Dr B. Hammond. It was sited in Higher Bullring, close to the Memorial. The bench fell into disrepair due to vandalism in January 1968 and although the Council had agreed in committee to have it repaired it was sadly dug up and destroyed.

Due to falling numbers and lack of support the RAOB Club, Tiverton Lane, was beginning to be a liability for the lodge and it was decided in October 1981 that we should sell up. Consequently on 6 January 1982 we moved to the Rugby Club, which was then in the middle of town, where we stayed for exactly a year, before moving back to our original 'home', the King's Head, on 5 January 1983. Apart from a brief spell in the Market House, when the King's Head was closed for six months, we have met there ever since.

Today we still meet on Wednesday evenings at the King's Head, where we have a regular attendance of around 12 to 15 brothers. Our fund-raising activities have been witnessed around the town, from the Community College and Pre-school groups, to St John Ambulance and Community Midwives. Indeed, over the last five years we have donated in the region of £6000 to local and national charities and good causes.

Chapter Fourteen

Life in a Country Town

Work

The agricultural sector has changed much over the last century; long gone are the days when it was possible to make a reasonable living with 'four acres and a cow' and even small farms employed several workers. To survive, agriculture has had to change to improve efficiency, which has meant accepting new farming techniques including mechanisation. Today very few farms employ anyone outside the immediate family. A newspaper cutting from the *Western Times* in 1930 sets out the wages payable for agricultural workers from 26 March of that year:

The wages payable for the employment of male workers shall not be less than at the following minimum rates:

	Per week s.	d.
21 years of age and over	*32*	*6*
20 and under 21 years	*29*	*0*
19 and under 20 years	*26*	*0*
18 and under 19 years	*23*	*0*
17 and under 18 years	*20*	*0*
16 and under 17 years	*17*	*0*
15 and under 16 years	*14*	*0*
14 and under 15 years	*11*	*0*

For the purpose of this clause the expression 'week' shall be deemed to mean a week consisting of the following number of hours:

In the week in which Good Friday falls, 43
In any other week in summer, 52
In the week in which Christmas Day and Boxing Day fall, 32
In any other week in winter, 50

The wages payable for the employment of female workers shall be not less than wages at the following minimum rates:

	Per hour d.
20 years of age and over	5
19 and under 20 years	$4\frac{1}{2}$
18 and under 19 years	4
17 and under 18 years	$3\frac{1}{2}$
16 and under 17 years	3
15 and under 16 years	$2\frac{1}{2}$
14 and under 15 years	2

In addition, most farmworkers occupied a tied cottage and were provided with as much milk as they needed as well as potatoes and root vegetables.

Boxer Salter and his wife being driven by Mr Aldridge on their golden wedding.

Corn in stitches from Old Hill.

View from Exeter Road, with Woodmill Farm in the background.

Above: *Puppy walkers at Silverton Foxhounds Show, 27 April 1924.*

Left: *Hunting at Growen. Jack Heard is looking over hedge on the left, Master John Pearcey is in the centre and Ern Saunders is standing on the hedge at the rear on the right.*

Leaving Cullompton Hotel, which was opened in 1930 as a Gentlemen's Club and is now Toad Hall.

Harvest

Above: *Corn being threshed by a contractor who travelled from farm to farm in the autumn.*

Left: *Stitching the corn. The corn was left in stitches until dry and then made into a rick, August 1945.*

In the cornfield waiting for the rabbits to run.

Cutting the corn with a binder with John Pearcey on the tractor and Derek ? on the binder, August 1945.

COUNTRY PURSUITS

For young children in the years immediately after the Second World War, one of the greatest pleasures was to join a crowd of other youngsters in the fields at harvest time. They would follow the tractor and binder to the cornfields and, as the corn was cut and bound into sheaves, would run around in the stubble chasing rabbits as they tried to escape into the hedges. As the boys were only armed with sticks, very few rabbits were ever caught but it kept them happy for hours. They sometimes helped to stack the sheaves into bundles of six or eight which were left to stand to dry off before being collected for threshing. The stitches or stooks of sheaves made wonderful tunnels to crawl through and the children returned home exhausted and scratched by the stubble. The local farmers must have been very tolerant to put up with them as they were much more of a hindrance than a help.

A fish caught by a visitor at Upton Fishing Lake, 2000.

Although very few rabbits were caught in the cornfields, more success was had by the men and boys who kept ferrets. The ferrets were kept in hutches and taken out to the rabbit warrens. Nets were spread over the openings along the burrows and then the ferrets were put into a rabbit hole to chase them out into the nets. Rabbits were such pests that farmers willingly gave permission for men with 12-bore shotguns to come on their land to shoot them. Rabbit pie or rabbit stew were favourite meals – until myxomatosis was introduced.

Foxes also cause problems for the farmers, and fox hunting has been a popular pastime for centuries. In the past many country parsons were keen followers of the hunt. Although not as famous as John Peel and Jack Russell, Cullompton had the Reverend William Sykes, MA, Vicar of Cullompton between 1834–57. Today, there are three hunts in the Cullompton area – the Silverton, East Devon and Tiverton Foxhounds. For many years John Pearcey of Growen was master of Tiverton Foxhounds. The puppies are 'walked', that is given basic training in walking to heel, etc. by local farmers and friends, and the photograph *on page 141* shows puppies and their walkers at the Silverton Hunt Puppy Show in 1924. Today it is often the case that 60 riders, men and women, from many walks of life, still turn out for a hunt plus many followers in cars and on foot. They usually meet at a local farm or pub where they park the horse boxes, have a stirrup cup and pasties, etc. before setting off for a day's hunting. It is now quite usual to see members of the anti-hunt organisations attending to protest and demonstrate their opposition.

The sequel to hunting is the annual point-to-point. For seven years in the late 1950s and early '60s the local point-to-point was held at Newlands, on the Honiton Road, at that time farmed by Mr Jack Cann. Before that it was held at Upton at the top of Old Hill, farmed by Norman Down. In recent years the point-to-point has been held in Silverton. To qualify to compete a horse must have taken part in seven days of hunting. In the past, most farmers trained their own horses for pointing, but now that the owners are frequently not farmers, there are local trainers. There are also some trainers in Cullompton such as Chris Down at Upton, Gerald Cotterell at Dulford and Rod Millman who trains horses for National Hunt racing.

Shooting was a popular pastime and there were several local shoots – one based around Bradfield and another at Hillersdon. Pigeons were shot during February. Standing under trees waiting for them to fly in was a very cold pastime as it was usually frosty.

Fishing is popular with all age groups and the local boys are often seen fishing in the river at Stoneyford. In the past many of the youngsters caught eels in the local rivers. In 1943 Kenneth Luxton, a local businessman and member of a fishing group, informed his fellow anglers that he had rented the fishing rights of the Culm from Stoneyford Bridge to Last Bridge at the bottom of Old Hill. He accepted a quote from the Fish Farm at Dulford to restock the river and the fish were delivered at 11.30a.m. on 16 April. There were 700 trout in all, approximately 9 inches long. They were mainly brown trout, but about 100 were a mixture of rainbow and Loch Leven. The little fishing group did get some sport from this venture, but not as much as they had hoped.

In those days of food rationing quite a lot of poaching occurred and the stock of fish soon dwindled! Today, many local fishing lakes provide sport for keen fishermen, both for local people and as a popular part of the tourist industry.

Postcard of a lively Market Day in Cullompton, c.1900.

Cullompton Young Farmers Club Milking Classes held at Rull, 1937. Left to right, back: Betty Shere, Doreen Knowles, Pauline Retter, Sylvia Southwood, Kit Chave, Kathleen Gush, Joan Chave; front: Tony Retter, Miss Lloyd (instructress), Mary Elworthy, Marjorie Shere, Gertie Jarvis, Mr Colin Russ (Devon County Council), Barbara Knowles, Margaret Elworthy, Kathleen Baker and Ivy Southwood.

CULLOMPTON YOUNG FARMERS CLUB
by Miss Marjorie Shere

The club's first meeting was held in the Parish Rooms on 27 February 1933 and the boys sat on one side of the room and the girls on the other. It was agreed that Miss Mary Elworthy would be an efficient and popular Chairman. Mr F. Cligg was elected Vice-Chairman, Miss K. Chave Hon. Treasurer and Miss Ivy Southwood Hon. Secretary. It was also agreed that the club would be affiliated to the County Federation of Young Farmers Clubs. The first club leader was Mr Raymond Cole, followed about a year later by Mr Robert Lawrence (or 'Uncle Bob').

The club moved via the White Hart Hotel to the Cullompton Rugby Club and the boys were eventually allowed to sit beside the girls. One of the first items agreed by the club was the keeping of calves for the first Show and Sale in the spring of 1934 which became an annual event. Stock, bought by the club and reared by members, was shown and then sold at Cullompton Market. Cash prizes were given to those producing the best animals in various categories. The Show moved to Mr W. Hill's field, then Tiverton Junction Market and eventually to Honiton Market. It enabled young farmers to learn about stock-keeping and showing. In the 1970s the number of stock-keepers began to decrease as more non-farming members joined the club.

In the beginning the club was very active in the education of its members, including such practices as sheep shearing, milking and thatching. Many such skills have now been lost or formalised in college or training boards courses. The club took part in ploughing matches, quizzes, public speaking contests, drama competitions and various sporting activities. It was also active in raising money for charity and in 1976 it was decided to nominate a charity for the year.

In the early years of the club, young people in the countryside had little choice but to join Young Farmers or stay at home. This has gradually changed; many young people go to college and, for those who do stay at home, there is no shortage of outside interests which can be pursued. The club finally closed at the end of 2000 after 67 years.

REGENERATION
by Linda Holloway

The Civic Trust Appraisal In March 1995 The Civic Trust Regeneration Unit was commissioned by the Rural Development Commission, Cullompton Town Council, Mid Devon District Council and Devon County Council to prepare a Regeneration Strategy for Cullompton. Three community workshops were held which enabled local people to contribute their ideas. Positive and negative perceptions of the town were established, and people were encouraged to identify and prioritise their ideas for improvement. A business survey was carried out and a questionnaire was distributed to the residents of the town.

A steering group comprising approximately 20 people drawn from the community, local businesses, councils and the RDC, helped to co-ordinate, monitor and manage action throughout the course of the study.

The principal idea was that the Report would contain a practical programme of action that would 'promote and facilitate a range of projects which would benefit the social, economic, environmental well-being of Cullompton and the surrounding area.' It was to be used as a basis for promoting regeneration during the following five years but it was recognised that it would be subject to change and dependent on funding arrangements.

After the Report was published in August 1995, members of this reference group formed the initial membership of a Regeneration Group.

The Regeneration Group The first meeting was held in July 1996 and Mr Gerard Edwards agreed to be Chairman. The idea was that the group should become a regular forum, open to all members of the public, for the discussion of issues concerning the regeneration of the town. It was recognised that most of the projects suggested in the Report were heavily dependent on funding from the County and District Councils and that this would not be easy to come by. It was therefore agreed that there were also additional projects that could be pursued which could make a difference to the town.

Since then, the group has focussed on subjects large and small. They have added their voice to planning issues and commented on the distribution of documents by the County and District Councils for consultation. They have organised promotional events, such as the 'Best Dressed Window' at Christmas, encouraged shops to open at lunchtime and for late-night Christmas shopping, and installed a Community Notice Board at Somerfield (jointly funded with a grant from the Rural Development Commission).

The group has aimed to work in partnership with Councils and other groups, for they believe this is the most effective way to achieve success. The Cullompton Website and Closed Circuit Television system are two examples of this. Members of the Council and the Regeneration Group continue to work jointly on two projects – a Development Manager and an indoor swimming pool. Other projects have been achieved that were not in the original study, such as the Farmers Market. The artificial playing pitch (astro-turf) was already under way at the time of the study.

Cullompton Website The website was set up in the autumn of 1998 (at www.cullompton.org). Tracey Frankpitt, a member of the Regeneration Group, carried out much of the research for the idea with Judy Morris and Roger Mudditt. They visited a similar project at Ottery St Mary to learn from their experiences. Roger Mudditt then set up the first demonstration which convinced the Town Council that the project was worthy of support. It was jointly sponsored by the Cullompton Regeneration Group, St Andrew's Church, Cullompton Town Council and Hippotek Internet. Cullompton was one of the first towns in the area to create its own website.

It is managed by a committee and maintained by a handful of enthusiasts including Steve Hellier, Paul Gubb and Michael Thompson. It features items of community, tourist and business interest and receives approximately 230 hits per week.

Farmers Market In 1997 Tracey Frankpitt went to a Regeneration Group meeting with her idea for a Farmers Market. The idea was for the market to sell locally-produced goods to local people. She was very much the driving force behind it and due to her enthusiasm convinced others that it could work. She was ably supported by other members of the group. Richard Priestley organised many aspects of the market including insurance and the buying of tents and a banner. The Regeneration Group made available £1600 of funding to enable the purchase of the five large walk-in tents each able to hold four or five stalls.

Tracey worked hard to find local producers to come to the market to sell their wares. Philip King got the promotional leaflets printed and distributed and seven members turned up at 7a.m. to put the tents up. They continued to do this for the next two months, until an arrangement could be made with other voluntary groups, who then received payment towards their funds for their hard work. A supportive neighbour arranged for her electricity to be used to run the generators for the refrigerators.

The first market was held on Saturday 13 June 1998 at the far end of the Station Road Car Park. It was opened by the then Chairman of Mid Devon District Council, Mr David Pugsley of Cullompton and although the weather was appalling, with very heavy rain most of the morning, people still attended in vast numbers. Members of the group who were helping to direct traffic into the car park had to call for reinforcements. Many of the producers sold out quite quickly and had to return to their farms to pick up more stock. It was hard work for everyone, but was hailed as a success. Tracey was pleased to report that for the first Saturday in a long time Cullompton High Street was full of people who had come to visit the market and then walked to the main street shops.

The Cullompton Farmers Market was the first not to be set up by a local authority and Tracey was in much demand advising others on how this could be done. She appeared on the radio, television, and in the national papers talking about the Cullompton project. The producers of the radio programme 'The Archers' consulted her to get their facts right and Cullompton's market was mentioned in one of the episodes. The market continues to thrive as a co-operative venture and is now under the management of Mr Roger Mudditt.

The Cully Cobbler There have been quite a few parish magazines over the years: the *St Andrew's Parochial Magazine* was produced regularly through the late-19th century and through to after the war. A modern version of the *Parish Magazine* eventually ceased to be produced in the late 1980s. The Regeneration Group had identified the need for a newsletter and perhaps a separate trade, services and information directory. Phillip King found himself volunteering to produce a magazine if he could find some assistance. This initially came in the form of Colin Bentley. Phillip said at the time that the aim was 'to provide a newsletter that was informative and interesting, mildly controversial and hopefully at times amusing.' He hoped that it 'would bring a diverse and fragmented community together and help newcomers to the town to find their feet.'

The first issue was produced in December 1997 with a print run of 3100 copies. It was entirely independent and self-funded from advertising revenue and it was distributed free of charge to over 2500 homes. The name came about because it was 'rather hastily cobbled together'. The magazine lists useful contact numbers and facilities and gives information on local issues, keeping people in touch with what is going on in the town. Many groups and organisations use the magazine to promote their events, there are items on health, cookery and legal matters, and residents have the chance to air their views in letters to the Editor or by writing articles of interest.

Producing a magazine of this size became more a full-time job than a hobby, particularly after Colin moved on to other things. Eventually though, help was found in the form of Angela Fuller who dealt with the advertising, Jenny Radford who sorted out distribution, and Steve and Sarah Reardon handling the accounts. *The Cobbler* is now produced every two months and delivered to over 6000 households in Cullompton, Kentisbeare, Plymtree, Dulford, Westcott, Mutterton, Willand and Uffculme.

CCTV A bid submitted by Councillor David Hathaway in 1998 was unsuccessful, but in 1999 Councillor Michael Thompson, a retired police officer, put together another bid to the Home Office. This was successful and the Home Office granted £21 000 to install cameras in the main street. After much hard work sorting out the details and getting permission from property owners, the cameras and recording equipment were installed in December 2000.

SNIPPETS

Royal Occasion On Wednesday 26 September 1990 Diana, Princess of Wales, visited Cullompton. Local people including St John Ambulance members, Guides, Brownies, Scouts, Cubs, playgroup children and pupils from all of the schools, lined Meadow Lane and the area leading to the John Tallack Centre. Everyone was excited and eagerly awaiting her arrival. When the cars eventually arrived there was loud cheering and waving of flags to give the Princess a very warm welcome. The Chairman of Cullompton Town Council, Mrs Marian Dummett, accompanied by her husband Eric, was presented to the Princess who then watched a display by local branches of the British Red Cross Youth and Juniors, a group which had the Princess as its patron.

She then visited the John Tallack Centre to see a training session for 14 playgroup leaders attended by young mothers. (She was also patron of the Pre-school Playgroups Association.) The course tutor, Mrs Kay Gordon of Tiverton Road, welcomed the Princess and explained the workings of the training session. Following this she cut the ribbon to officially open a double-decker bus converted by Hemyock's Clean Cut Youth Club, which was to provide facilities for homeless, elderly and unemployed people. The project had received a £1000 grant from the Prince's Trust.

The Princess abandoned her official timetable to spend some time talking to many of the hundreds of people who had gathered to welcome her. By the time she left Cullompton to continue her travels to Tiverton and Exeter, she was half an hour behind schedule, but all who had met her agreed that it had been a memorable occasion.

Clockwise from top: *The Prince of Wales, later Edward VIII, passing through from Bradninch to Ottery St Mary, 1921. There was no other royal visit until the Princess of Wales in 1990; Princess Anne's visit on 13 October 1998 to open The Woodmill Brain Injury Rehabilitation Trust unit (which replaced the Woodmill Hospital) at Cullompton. Left to right: Mr Graham Andrew; Town Mayor Councillor Mrs M. Coxhead; Mr Mike Bull; Chief Executive Mid Devon District Council, Councillor David Pugsley; Chairman Mid Devon District Council, Mr Fred Symons; Vice Chairman Devon County Council, Lord and Lady Clinton; High Sheriff of Devon, Air Vice Marshal Attlee; Diana, Princess of Wales' visit in September 1990 to inspect the Red Cross unit and the John Tallack Centre.*

The Bleeding Hawk of Hillersdon This is a mummified hawk, the property of Mr Patrick Grant-Sturgis of Hillersdon House. It is said to ooze blood whenever England is about to be at war and to continue until it is past. The hawk was brought to Hillersdon in 1887 by an explorer, Mr W.J.A. Grant, who acquired it in Egypt, where it is reputed to have been found in the tomb of a priestess. Mr Grant had a notable career and on one occasion when he and his companions were starving in some remote place, it is said they drew lots and ate one of their number. The last few years of his life were spent in great pain at Hillersdon, but death relieved his sufferings in 1935, at the age of 84.

In 1924 he told a press reporter that the hawk began to bleed just before the Boer War; 'spots of blood were coming up in the form of bubbles upon it.' It ceased this manifestation just before the treaty was signed and remained dry as dust until about ten days before the outbreak of the First World War. Then it oozed continuously till Armistice. At some date between the end of the First World War and 1924 a general visiting Mr Grant expressed the view that England was on the verge of another conflict. Mr Grant examined the hawk and it was perfectly dry; he predicted that no war was imminent.

In 1939 the house was requisitioned by the Government and the contents put into storage. It is not known whether the hawk bled during the Second World War. The house was sold and sadly the hawk was removed with all other possessions when the Grant-Sturgis family moved out.

Mysterious Knocking In February 1925 crowds of people gathered outside a house in Exeter Road, the home of Mr J. Harris, to hear the mysterious knockings at his front door, which had been taking place on and off for about four weeks. At first Mr and Mrs Harris had thought it was youths playing a prank, but it became so pronounced that eventually they made the police aware and a constable kept watch.

Not only could Mr and Mrs Harris hear the knocking but passers-by could also hear it and the mystery could not be solved. In the presence of the crowd rat-tat-tat would recur at intervals, so loud that it could be heard at some distance. It was suggested that the knocker had become magnetised and a needle was put against it but the knocking continued. The door was examined by the police and later by a carpenter and mason but no cause could be found and the knocking continued. It became the talk of the town and police had to keep the road clear due to the number of people that congregated each day to witness the phenomenon.

Cullompton Highwaymen Mr John Barnes moved to a Cullompton inn with his wife Mary and several children in around 1677. Previously he was a taverner at the Black Horse in South Street, Exeter. He ran up large debts and matters came to a head when a local blacksmith pleaded for money owed to him. Barnes suggested they enter into a partnership to rob a coach on its way from Exeter to London transporting a large amount of money and protected by guards. The plan was to waylay the coach on a long steep hill leading out of Honiton towards Chard. To lessen the burden for the horses the guards walked up the hill beside the coach and, when Barnes and his henchmen suddenly sprang from their cover, virtually no resistance was offered. The guards were held at gunpoint, the money found and loaded onto horses, and the gang were soon off with their haul which amounted to about £600, sufficient to set each man up for the rest of his days.

Unfortunately Barnes' debut as a highwayman was marred by one oversight; he was well remembered in Exeter, which was the city the coach had come from and the guards recognised him. The innkeeper and his colleagues were soon arrested and taken to Exeter Gaol. They managed to escape and the blacksmith got away, but the others, still partially encumbered by their irons, were soon recaptured.

At the County Assizes held in Exeter on 5 August 1678 both John Barnes and an accomplice, a worsted comber, were found guilty and sentenced to death. Although a group of Exeter ladies petitioned to the court for him to be spared due to concern for his wife and children, the plea was rejected and he was hanged, possibly at Heavitree gallows, on 13 August 1678.

Our second highwayman, Tom Austin, was born into a reputable Cullompton farming family and, upon his father's death, their farm fell into his hands. Being a man of good family and property, he was able to marry quite a well-to-do woman and so found himself quite wealthy within a short period of time. However, within four years he had squandered away his money and found himself in debt.

After tricking money from his neighbours and finding himself still wanting, he took to performing acts of robbery and murder which ultimately cost him his life. Some distance from Cullompton, on the road between Wellington and Taunton, Tom assumed the role of highwayman and waylaid Sir Zachary Wilmot. In the struggle that followed Sir Zachary was gunned down and Tom fled home carrying 46 guineas and the unlucky traveller's valuable sword.

These gains were quickly spent and on paying a visit to his uncle and finding him away, he smashed in his aunt's head with an axe and slit the throats of her five young children. He stole 60 guineas and returned home. When asked by his wife why he was covered in blood he took up a razor and slashed her throat and then took the lives of his own two children. Soon after, his uncle happened to call at the farm, unaware of the carnage that awaited him at his own home, saw the bloodshed, and quickly overpowered Tom and took him to the local magistrate. He was committed to Exeter Gaol and in August 1694 hanged.

The Galpin Family by Ross McBride My great-great-grandmother Elizabeth Galpin was born in Cullompton in 1853, and came from a long line of the Galpins. The earliest ancestor I have been able to trace is Thomas Galpin who had five children between 1731 to 1742, all mentioned in the parish records. Many of Elizabeth's ancestors were master weavers, with the females being loom girls. Some died of debility and dementia by the time they were 60 – not surprising if you have visited the working wool mill at Uffculme and heard the noise.

As employment in the wool trade started to wane the Galpins began to choose other professions. One branch moved to Chard and took up lace making, and later they moved to Nottingham, still following the same profession. Later members of this branch emigrated to South Africa. Others became agricultural labourers, domestic servants, postmen and blacksmiths.

One of Elizabeth's aunts emigrated to Australia under the assisted passage scheme (to provide wives for settlers). She arrived in Geelong Port Phillip on 2 October 1848 and was married in 1849 to a John Thompson. Another aunt ended her days in Tiverton Workhouse after she was widowed. Elizabeth had three sisters and three brothers. Her eldest brother, William, married and stayed in Cullompton. He was an agricultural labourer and lived at 33 New Street. Her sister Sarah married a Charles Salway, who was a cabinet maker and they lived round the corner at 10 Exeter Hill. Elizabeth's father, William, was still employed in the woollen industry as a woollen handloom weaver when she was born. He had a long life and in 1891, when he was retired, he was receiving parish relief and living with his daughter Sarah and her husband.

Elizabeth herself married John Bowles in Cullompton on 1 July 1873. He was an agricultural labourer and shortly after they married they moved to Exminster. Here he worked at Bowhayes. They had two children, Mary (1874) and Sarah (1878). Elizabeth's life was not without tragedy, however, as John was killed on 10 June 1884. Whilst out walking he came across a runaway cart pulled by two horses and tried to stop it. Unfortunately he was trampled and killed.

Elizabeth married again shortly afterwards and her second husband would not take on both children so Mary, the eldest (my great grandmother) was sent into service at the age of nine. Her sister Sarah stayed at home and later married and emigrated to Canada. As far as I know there are no Galpins now in Cullompton – the line seems to have died out in this area in the middle of the 20th century.

The Hake Family by Ron Hake We were a family of four, Audrey, John (Jack), Rene and Ron the youngest, all born and brought up in a small cottage at 26 Higher Street, with our parents John (Jack) and Maud Hake. As a small boy in the 1930s a visit to my grandparents, Harry and Emma Hake (*overleaf, bottom*), across the road at 23 Higher Street, meant dipping a wet finger into a sack of sugar and licking the finger dry or eating a piece of cheese sliced with a wire cutter. They lived in an old thatched house, part of which was a small grocery and sweet shop. Learning to ride a 1930s Coventry Eagle motorbike around the orchard at the back of the house was great fun until my friend Reg Holey crash-landed into the chicken run and Grandfather would not let us use the orchard again.

Mr Bending, a retired railway man, lived a few doors up the road and when he knew I was learning to ride a motorcycle, he offered me his 1920s belt driven motorcycle and side-car for nothing. He felt he was too old to ride it. I declined his offer because I wanted something more modern.

In the 1930s, there was little road traffic, mainly horse-drawn and the odd steam lorry and car and motor cycles so we were able to have trolley races. We went four abreast starting from the top of Higher Street/Station Road to the River bridge and from the Station Railway bridge to the Weary Traveller Inn, all done in great safety apart from grazed knees. Mr Drew the blacksmith of Higher Mill Lane (*overleaf, centre*), helped make our trolleys by drilling the front axles and the metal chassis from old pram wheels – he kindly did this for nothing.

During the war, schooling was interrupted once a week so that the older boys could collect waste paper from shops and offices around the town which we would then load onto a barrel loaned by Hellier the Undertakers of Cockpit Hill, and push to the paper mills as part of the war effort. No-one complained.

We were always on the lookout for and waiting to hear news of planes which had been shot down around Cullompton and as soon as school was over we got on our bikes and cycled to the crash area and looked for pieces of the plane and any bullets – we nearly all had a collection of shrapnel and ammunition. On one occasion we saw the body of a German pilot still in the cockpit.

Miss Florrie Paul who had a shop on the corner of High Street and Higher Mill Lane was well known for her cooked ham on the bone and as her grocery boy, I delivered groceries by bicycle for two hours after school every day and all day on Saturday. For this my wage was 5s.0d. a week and any broken biscuits. I made sure there were always broken biscuits. Thursday was white pudding day and although it was early closing I had to deliver the pudding as far as Newlands Farm on the Honiton Road. When not delivering I had to stand by and open the door for customers to come in and out of the shop and quite often I had to cut and shape the butter. Christmas time was exciting because tips averaged 1s.0d. to 2s.6d. per house. I remember Mrs Labdon (*overleaf, top*) of St George's Well always gave me a 5s.0d. tip.

Above: *Mr and Mrs Will Labdon (behind) with Mrs Labdon's parents at home in Belle Vue Terrace, c.1900.*

Right: *Higher Mill Lane Forge. Left to right: Harry Drew, Sam Blackmore, John Thomsitt.*

Harry and Emma Hake with daughter Bessie at their cottage in Higher Street which has now been demolished. Part of the house was a small shop. Photograph, c.1930s.

To earn extra pocket money, Derek Westcott and I spent many an evening at the rear of the cinema rewinding reels of film by hand and repairing joins in the film which had been shown the same evening.

Two or three times a year on a Sunday, I walked with my mother to Silverton, where we had tea with an aunt – no buses ran on Sundays. My spare time was spent trout fishing with Derek Westcott and John Hopkins in the River Culm Mill Stream between Head Weir and Higher Mill. Picnics and swimming in the river at Head Weir and High Banks off the end of Duke Street/Old Hill were very popular pastimes for children and adults in the summer months.

Sometimes I would go with my friends to the cinema and also helped my father who worked at Forces Farm and the slaughterhouse on Colebrook Lane. He taught me to plough with a horse, hedging, etc. and occasionally I took a cow to the bull at Padbrook Farm and was told to wait outside – it was all part of my education. The hard work and long hours were not for me and when I left school at 14, I travelled daily by bus to work in Tiverton.

My brother Jack (born 1915) was selected by the local charity to become an indentured apprentice plumber for William Plumpton & Sons, Higher Street, and as part of the contract our parents had to promise to provide him with 'sound food'. He qualified after five years and as the workers had no form of transport other than a bicycle, he cycled, sometimes many miles a day, to carry out a job, tying the tools on the handlebar. On one occasion, he cycled to Rackenford and back. In the 1960s he set up his own plumbing and heating business. He enjoyed rugby. All the players used the Cullompton Hotel as a changing room and a social centre for the club and they held regular dances there which were very popular. The weekly washing of kit was all done by hand and every Monday, Netta, his wife, washed 15 rugby shirts. When he gave up rugby he took up bowls and played for Culm Vale Bowling Club, subsequently becoming president and later when women were allowed by play, his sisters Rene Richardson and Audrey Phillips also became members. Both played for Devon.

Rene and Audrey began their working life at the glove factory in Exeter Road. Two days before the Second World War, Jack and other Cullompton territorials marched out of the town to join the main Devonshire Regiment. He was a keen member of the British Legion and was the Chairman for many years.

From the 1950s through to the 1970s the Annual Horticultural Show was held in the secondary school on Exeter Hill and another show in the Unitarian Chapel. This was the centre of great competition in the town. Jack was a very keen gardener and there was always competition between Jack and Percy Widgery for both vegetables and flowers.

Jack and Netta were members of the Cullompton Church. Netta became a staunch member of the Mothers' Union and Jack was a sidesman for many years. He was also a founder member of the Church Badminton Club which played in the Church Rooms. He served on the Church Council for many years. The highlight of the Cullompton Church social calendar was the fête held on the first Thursday in July in the Vicarage grounds and Jack helped organise fund-raising events for the restoration and repairs of the church. In later years, he was a member of the Town Council and of the Cullompton United Charities.

Whilst Jack and Netta never left Cullompton, their two children moved away, Sarah to follow a career in the Probation Service in Surrey and Barry to work as a lecturer in Holland.

Mrs Katie Coombes' Memories (aged 101) Mrs Coombes came to England from Ireland at the age of 21 and worked in service at Hembury Fort. Her wages were 2s.6d. a week plus board. She stayed five years and then she packed her clothes in a cloth bundle and went home to Ireland. She returned to marry the gardener at Hembury Fort and four years later had a daughter.

She worked in the fields planting and picking fruit and when the need arose helped with the threshing and farm work. When the council houses at Colliton were built Mrs Coombes moved there and she and her next-door neighbour cycled each day to work at the paper mill in Cullompton. They broke up books and waste paper and sorted new paper for about 19 years. When the cycling got too much they went to work at Maunders and a bus collected them. There were about 100 women working there and they had to hand pluck all the chickens and clean the wings. Mrs Coombes was close to her father, mother and her three sisters and two brothers. She followed her mother everywhere and can remember her father singing to them for entertainment. In Ireland they smoked clay pipes as this was cleaner than wood. For their leisure they went to dances and whist drives but never went out of the village.

Mrs Clark's Memories (aged 95) Mrs Clark remembers looking after her five children and her husband who worked on a farm at Newlands. She remembers the children walking to school in Cullompton and that her time was spent cooking and mending clothes. She also used to mend the children's shoes. There was no time for going out on trips. She especially remembered one year, when there was heavy snow, having all the groceries and provisions delivered by sledge.

Mrs Wellington's Memories (aged 93) Mrs Wellington remembers starting school in Cullompton at three years old. Her teacher was Miss Gunn and there was another teacher named Miss Smith who used to 'go mad with a pointer'. Of the First World War she remembers men from the Belgian army marching through Cullompton on their way to Plymouth. The children in town waved black and yellow flags. There were injured soldiers at Bradfield and they were brought into Cullompton where concerts were held behind Clampitts.

In the area of Ploudal Road there was a lace factory before the jam factory and Mr Bill Brooks' father had a flour mill also in that area. The horses which pulled the fire engine were kept at the back of Clampitts. If the children got in the way when they were being caught they would be shouted at and clipped around the ear.

There seemed to be a lot of tiny shops in houses. There were little cottages where the schoolhouse in Exeter Road is now. A Mrs Bidgood sold home-made faggots and chiddlings, which someone named Tiddley Rowe would deliver. On the way round he would drink the gravy and fill up the basin with water from a pipe coming from the hedge in Back Lane.

A slaughterhouse was situated where Stile Close is now and children used to go there to get a pig's bladder to use as a football. Where the fish shop was in Exeter Road was then a workhouse for tramps. This was later a grocers and then a butchers. Mrs Rosie Wells' sweet shop was next door. In the area of the tannery there was a fish-and-chip shop – people would go to the house to help chop the chips. In Ways Lane there was a house selling fish and Sarah Duffin's house in Crow Green was Mr Taylor's greengrocers. Community House housed a kettle maker and there was a shoe shop next door.

Mrs Wellington left school at 13 and went into service. She left soon after and went to work at Fox's factory. She worked from 6a.m. to 6p.m. for 10s.6d. of which she gave her mother 10s.0d. Her mother insisted that all the family went to church each Sunday and they went to a chapel in the grounds of The Walronds. A family named Plumpton lived there at that time and they were Roman Catholic. This was before the present Roman Catholic church was built. Of the Second World War Mrs Wellington remembers American tanks being kept alongside Exon Buildings and their camp being where the Community College is. She married Frank in Cullompton Church and had five sons.

Mr Chowings' Memories (aged 91) Mr Chowings worked as a butcher for Battens before the Second World War. He would attend the cattle market in the Bullring, pick out the animals he wanted, pay for them and then the farmer would take them back to the farm and keep them until required for slaughter. There was a slaughterhouse behind the butcher's shop, but they also slaughtered animals in the one in Colebrooke Lane. He was paid 6d. per lamb.

After the war he returned to Cullompton and ran a van delivery service, in association with Mr Trezise, to surrounding villages. He could take up to £200 per week. He lived in Goblin Lane then moved to High Street, where he rented a house behind Moss Chemist with his family. His two children went to St Andrew's then to grammar school in Tiverton. They went on the train from Cullompton Station, changing at Tiverton Junction and boarding a bus to the school.

Lower Bullring with Cockpit Hill on the left, and (inset) *Batten's on the corner of Crow Green and Exeter Hill.*

Chapter Fifteen

2000 & Beyond

The Town Council organised various millennium projects to celebrate the year 2000:

Aerial Photographs Towards the end of 1999 the Royal Marines, based at Lympstone, very kindly agreed to take aerial shots of the town while they were flying over the area. We were then able to purchase these photographs, some of which residents bought to keep as a memento. The money raised was put towards the Christmas illuminations in the town centre. Each of Cullompton's three schools received an enlarged and framed copy.

Open-air Performance In June the Rugby Club was the venue for the Common Players' performance of the *Three Musketeers*. The Town Council met the cost and a good-sized crowd of children and adults enjoyed the fine weather and lively entertainment.

Document Exhibition with Flowers In partnership with St Andrew's Church a document exhibition with flower arrangements was organised in October. Documents were borrowed from the archives at the Devon Record Office, although some were too delicate to put on show. Many of the flowers were arranged by members of the Cullompton and District Flower Club. Entrance was free but voluntary contributions went to the Church Tower Restoration Fund.

Millennium Exhibition This exhibition depicted life in Cullompton during the millennium year. Various groups, including both primary schools and pre-schools, St John Ambulance, churches, craft groups and the WI recorded their year in pictures and words. The exhibition was held at the end of November for three days leading up to the turning on of the town's Christmas lights.

Christmas Lights The previous year the Council had contracted a specialist company to provide the Christmas light display. The results were so well received that it was decided to do the same in the year 2000. To make it a particularly special evening, one of the town's oldest residents, Mrs Kate Coombes, was invited to perform the 'switching on'. She was ably assisted by three of Cullompton's youngest schoolchildren; Robert Stockman, Tori Wheeler and Dean Weatherall.

Town Book Many of the Council members felt it was important to produce something lasting, that could be kept for future generations. The Town Book seemed an ideal opportunity to gather together pictures and memories of the history of the town before they were possibly lost. We also wanted to record a little of what life in Cullompton has been like in more recent years, leading up to the present day.

To give a flavour of the varied work the Council is involved with and what the future possibly holds for Cullompton it was decided to include the following report from the Parish Meeting, 2001. It gives the reader an insight into a year in the life of the Town Council and the matters with which it is concerned. It may also make interesting reading for future generations, especially if they find that, as often happens, the same items are still being discussed:

We have more to report to you each year as the range of duties of the Town Council becomes more complex and the range of our responsibilities increases. Cullompton Town Councillors hold full Council meetings once a month with an additional planning meeting on the third Thursday. There are also various committees, each of which meet on average 6 times a year. These deal with issues of Personnel, Properties, Financial Management, Promoting Cullompton projects and Rural Roads and Footpaths. We have working groups on the Town Book Project, The Website, Traffic and Environmental Issues and Best Value Car Parking.

Members also represent the Town Council on The Devon Association of Parish Councils and the Mid Devon Association of Local Councils; The Development Manager Working Group, The CCA; The Regeneration Group; The Swimming Club; The Police Parish Liaison Group and The Police Consultative Group; the Citizens Advice Bureau; Culm Valley Education; the Rural Transport Forum and the Culm Voluntary Car Service.

The year has been dominated by two major issues – both of which are still on-going: Firstly the Darwin

Main: *Aerial view of the parish, showing its rural location.*
Inset: *July 2000. Framed copies of aerial photographs were presented to each of Cullompton's three schools at the Festival Service at the Parish Church. Pupils from Willowbank Primary School are pictured receiving their picture from the Town Mayor Councillor Mrs Linda Holloway.*
Left to right, back: Harry Gibson, Nathan Davey, Daniel Cole, Phillip Ecclesfield, Naomi Abrahams, Rosemary Ecclesfield, Sammy Cole; front: Jack Davey, the Town Mayor, Luke Abrahams.

Town Council, Mayoral Reception, March 2001.
Left to right, standing: Judy Morris (Town Clerk), David Hathaway, Steve Hellier, Mike Thompson, Deputy Town Mayor Graham Barden, Brian Mitchell, David Glenn, Jane Fenlon (Administrative Asst); front: Mrs Marian Dummett, Mrs Muriel Coxhead, Mrs Jane Campbell, Town Mayor Mrs Linda Holloway, Mrs Eileen Andrews, Mrs Pat Gleeson, Geoff Munn. Not in picture – Wally Johns.

Estates application for a foodstore, non foodstore and petrol filling station at land off Station Road. The application has now been 'called in' by the Secretary of State, and a Public Enquiry will be held to decide the outcome. Secondly, we have been working with representatives of the Regeneration Group, The Community Council of Devon, the Business sector and Local Authorities towards the appointment of a Development Manager. Contributions have been secured from local businesses and the Councils, but we await the result of our application to the Regional Development Agency for the final outstanding amount required. Other projects which also focus on the promotion of the town are a Town Guide leaflet to include information and a map, a Visitors Street Plan, a town 'brown sign' and the Town Book, to be published at the end of the year.

Through the year we have continued to put pressure on developers and the authorities to provide cycle and pedestrian links. We have also been lobbying for provision of an internal bus service linking the residential and industrial estates with the town centre. We continue to seek solutions to traffic congestion problems and provision of safe crossing places for pedestrians.

We have tried to ensure that landowners understand their responsibilities to ensure fenders and streams are unblocked, to avoid unnecessary flooding problems. We have put pressure on Devon County Council to solve the problems of flooded pavements.

We are trying to secure safety schemes and 20 mph speed limits for certain areas of the town. Devon County Council and Margram have been asked to ensure that the M5 junction roundabout is maintained properly and that the design of the whole junction is reconsidered. Negotiations continue to acquire land for the cemetery extension. Now that the lower part of New Cut has been enhanced we are trying to ensure the remainder is refurbished as soon as possible.

We have continued to feed back information to Stagecoach to try to improve the frequency and timings of the local bus services. We continue to support the opening of a Railway Station with appropriate services for the people of the area.

Where the Local Plan is concerned, the Town Council expressed its concern with regard to some of the proposed uses of land being too restrictive. It is our view that it is wiser to keep the options as open as possible so that opportunities are not missed. Unfortunately, Mid Devon District Council did not agree with us in all cases.

We have handled a number of complaints about the poor standard, or in some cases the complete lack, of grass cutting and shrub maintenance on some of the new estates. After repeated discussions with the responsible authority, MDDC, they have promised that there will be improvements this year under the new contracts and arrangements with developers.

Last autumn a Heavy Goods Vehicle Origins and Destinations Survey was carried out. Once the results have been analysed we will be asking a spokesman to present them to the Council.

During the year we have given grants to local groups and organisations, funded the visit of the Common Players performance of 'The Three Musketeers' last June, provided free car parking during Festival Week and at Christmas and provided Christmas lights and decorations for the centre of town.

We have installed fencing and a gate at the Upcott field and provided welcome signs at the gateways to the town. It has been agreed to fund a street light at St Andrew's Lane. In response to public demand we have arranged for domestic refuse skips to be available at the Station Road Car Park for the 4 months of the year not already provided by Devon County Council. This will cost about £500 for each of the 4 Sundays. We are concerned that there should be a separate collection of green waste and so have arranged for a skip to be provided for one day a month from March to October.

We have been pleased to be part of the continued development of the Cullompton Website. This is the result of a very successful partnership of the Town Council, the Regeneration Group and St Andrew's Church. It attracts much praise for its high standard.

I'm sure that many of you are aware that Cullompton is now the proud owner of a CCTV system. With the support of the Town Council and the Regeneration Group, Mike Thompson has worked tirelessly on this project, and now, nearly 18 months after the bid to the Home Office was submitted, the system is installed. The Town Council has agreed to employ tape changers for the system and pay for the maintenance and insurance.

For many years now, we have been asking Mid Devon to provide limited free parking for people doing their shopping in the town; this has been without success, except that we have persuaded them to keep the charges relatively low. Last year, however, we resolved not to renew the lease of the St Andrew's Car Park to Mid Devon District Council and with the financial assistance of some of the town's traders there is now the facility of a Shoppers Car Park with free parking for a maximum of 2 hours. We continue to make every effort to improve the facilities and amenity of our town for all of us who live here, and for those who visit us.

To make it easier for members of the public to raise matters with Councillors, we have introduced a Public Question Time item on the Council main meeting Agenda. Also, in December, we held the first of our regular Council Surgery Coffee Mornings – we feel these offer an ideal opportunity for you to bring your complaints and concerns, and maybe even your praise, to us in person and we plan to hold them regularly.

During my year as Mayor I have endeavoured to encourage a teamwork approach to problems and projects. There is much to be gained through working in partnership with other groups in the town and learning from others' experiences outside of Cullompton. There have been some outstanding successes as a result of such initiatives. I feel sure we can build on this in the future.

Town Mayor Mrs Linda Holloway

In Conclusion

Children from Cullompton St Andrew's School first performed this poem as a pageant for Cullompton Festival Week on 25 and 26 June 1986. Willowbank Infants School provided the dancers. The pageant was performed in the Bullring in front of the Baptist Church. The poem was written by Brian J. Hooper, Headmaster of St Andrew's.

CULLOMPTON'S STORY

Cullompton's story starts we know,
Nearly two thousand years ago.
Although a road that passes through
Saw ancient Britons – painted blue –
Pass up along the old Portway
That stretched up to the Bristol Channel,
The Romans in their tin and flannel
Built the first fort upon the rise
Below which St Andrew's 'state now lies.

CENTURION

Sinister, dexter, sinister, dexter, haltus.
Pile up your pilem in a heap
And climb up there, it's not too steep,
The view around is really good
Though almost all you'll find is wood.
But from up here we'll surely see
The wild tribes of Dumnonii,
Who sally forth to fight and pillage
From their stronghold near Hembury village.

LEGIONARY

Here Cent, we've come a long way
Didn't we oughta
Dig a hole and look for water?

CENTURION

On top of the hill just dig straight down,
But not too far or you might drown,
So now get cracking, dig that well.

LEGIONARY

On top of the hill? You go to...

CENTURION

Tell you what, in years to come,
When folk round here are not so dumb,
This well filled in, will still appear
In new crop markings every year,
And experts passing by will say –
When picking up your broken mug –
'Tis here the Romans must have dug.

And so the Romans came and went
They left the site without a dent
Except for bits of pots and stone,
That soon by brambles overgrown
Became a field boundary
That lasted till Nineteen Eighty.
But when the legions from here fled
The drear dark ages came instead
And we know little more until
King Alfred wrote down in his will.

KING ALFRED

Now take a letter, Aelfric do,
I have some things to say to you.
I have some land in far off Devon
I wish to leave, before to heaven
I shall go. So write this down
My lands include Cullompton Town.
'Tis a place that I passed by
When I to Exeter did fly
To quell that city fair in Devon,
In the year Eight Seventy Seven.

The Saxon rule came soon to ruin
When Harold, not knowing what he was doing
Promised his help to cousin Willy
By swearing...

KING HAROLD

... I was rather silly,
For Bill came over straight from France;
My army never stood a chance.
He clobbered it on Senlac Hill,
If I had ducked, I'd be king still.

But William had won the day
And crowned himself then right away.
He needed knowledge of his land,
And wanted it all right to hand.
He sent his men to gather pay,
The Saxons thought it was Domesday.

NORMANS

Now then you serfs, what have you hidden?
Bring us your taxes when you're bidden,
And tell us if you have a mill,
Or plough, ox, or we'll use you ill.

SAXONS

We have some fields near the Church,
But please don't leave us in the lurch
By taking all our goods and chattel
And leave us sheep and hens and cattle.

NORMANS

The Normans, knowing little Saxone
Called the village here Cruremtone.
The town belonged to several Lords,
Baldwin, Osbern and the Cliffords,
Until in Thirteen Seventeen
A market fair came on the scene,
For Buckland Abbey's pious glance
Gave us a week to sing and dance.

And now that all the selling's through
Come gather round you townsfolk do,
And see our younger ones perform
As they dance here this summer morn.

Willowbank Infants
Country Dancing
Now all this dancing makes us dream
Of water that is pure and clean
For all the people living here
Who up to now must all drink beer.
It really would cheer all our hearts
To have a drink that reaches parts
That when indulged by strongish liquor
Leaves all our senses somewhat thicker.
And Buckland's most congenial abbot,
Finding it hard to kick the habit,
Gave to the town, with pure source,
A new, but open, water course
That still flows gently through the street,
Though now enclosed beneath our feet.

A building project fifty years was taking
That saw St Andrew's in the making,
'Twas started in Fourteen Twenty,
The work was hard, the labour plenty.

Mason
Come on now lads, this won't take long.
I know that you are big and strong
To lift these stones to build the walls,
For I remember my Dad's calls
To your grandfathers when they started
And their digging was half-hearted.

They left the tower for another time –
Their grandchildren in Forty Nine
Finished the tower right on time
And when they old and weary got,
They all gave thanks for one John Trott
Who in the year Fifteen Two Two
Left money for almshouses too.
Old John Trott's house is built to stay;
We hope it never goes away.
Indeed up by our Lower Street
And Higher Street most grand
John Trott's almshouses stand.
And people now partake their luncheon
And in its shelter as they munch on
Fish and chips and egg and chicken
Bought from over in 'Kev's Kitchen'.

In Fifteen Hundred and Fifty Two
When John Lane's ships sailed the ocean blue,
He used his wealth in proper style
To give our church another aisle.

In September Sixteen Forty Four
Charles's army passed the door
Of gaping townsfolk in their homesteads,
Some cheered the king, but some were Roundheads.

Royalist
God save the King, long may he rule us.

Roundhead
God save old Noll. Now don't be foolish,
The King must never more hold sway,
'Tis time for Parliament to say
What shall happen in this land.
God save Cromwell, ain't he grand!

The year Sixteen and Eighty Five
Saw men more dead than were alive,
For Monmouth raised rebellions sound
Expecting us to rally round,
But on a plain in Somerset
The rebel army beaten yet
Was caught and taken off to rot
In prisons where they'd be forgot.
And some on route for other shores
In our own church were shut indoors.
They left it in such sorry state,
The cleaners were paid at the top rate.

John Wesley, that God-fearing fellow,
Preached in Cullompton – how he'd bellow.
He really frightened many a lad
Who swore he'd never more be bad.

A war with France then followed fast
For more than twenty years did last.
Cullompton men watched all amazed
As the Hayridge Volunteers was raised.

Recruit Sergeant
Now come on lads, let's see who's willing
To join the Colours, here's a shilling.

Yokel
I've never had twelve pence that's mine
So show me where I have to sign.

Recruit Sergeant
Well done lad. Now you're in, no flagging,
We meet each week at the Green Dragon.

The Dragon was a local bar
Where Kemps and Labdon's Yard now are,
Famous for its grog and gruel
And also for a fatal duel
That took place on a dreadful day
Before Queen Vic came here to stay.
She wasn't Queen then – no, less
Only a small royal princess.

A tragedy in Queen Vic's reign
Left the town in sadder vein
For in the year of Thirty Nine
A fire burned while people dined,
But not until Eighteen Sixty One
Was anything about it done,
For in that year for townsfolk's aid
Was formed the Voluntary Fire Brigade.

Within the last one hundred years
The town has changed so fast,
For our young men went to the wars
They thought they would not last,
But many sons failed to come home
And died on foreign turf
Their names are mounted on a stone
Where we recall their worth.

After the war, the traffic's hum
Came swiftly on our ear
For all who would be Cornwall-bound
Had still to pass through here.

Pedestrian
I've stood here now for many a day,
It really is too bad,
For my home's on the other side,
These drivers are so mad.
They never stop until at last
We have a traffic jam.
I get so furious with them,
I almost just said...

Damaging evidence was found,
That showed the folk the way,
A survey too was carried out,
To build a motorway.
The motorway brought peace at last
As now all traffic thunders past,
Except for when it thunders through
And then the air sometimes turns blue!

But motorways and parkways too
Have also left their mark
With large estates now springing up
At North Farm and Oak Park.

Cullompton's history carries on
Its character still changes,
And as we close this little piece that ranges
O'er its history
We hope that all we've said and done
Will bring to light its mystery.

SUBSCRIBERS

David and Dawn Abrahams, Hele, Exeter, Devon
Joshua John Andrew Ace, Cullompton, Devon
David B. Addison, Cullompton, Devon
Tony, Joan and Lauren Ainsworth, Cullompton, Devon
David Aird-Hughes, Sampford Peverell, Devon
Tonia Akhurst, Cullompton, Devon
Mr Francis G. Aldridge
Cllr Eileen Andrews, Cullompton, Devon
Hilary Anstis (née Hodge), formerly of New Street, Cullompton
David J. A. Arbery, Cullompton, Devon
Mr N. R. Arm, Cullompton, Devon
J. Arnold, East Butterleigh, Devon
Chris Ashby
Joyce A. Avery (née Clarke), Washington State
Anthony W. Bailey, Cullompton, Devon
Mike Baker, Cullompton, Devon
Corey John Bale, Cullompton, Devon
Rick Banfield, Cullompton, Devon
Graham and Karen Barden, Fore Street, Cullompton, Devon
Prof. Maurice S. Bartlett, Exmouth, Devon
Mr Peter Batten, Bournemouth
Sidney R. Batten, Willand, Devon
Tom Batting, Cullompton, Devon
Stuart I. Bennett, Cullompton, Devon
Mrs P. A. G. Bird
Stuart and Shirley Blaylock, Cullompton, Devon
Ian and Mary-Ann Bloomfield, Cullompton, Devon
Vera and Reginald Bowden
John H. Bowles
Rodger V. Boyce, Cullompton, Devon
Brady, Middleditch, Cullompton, Devon
Gill Bridson, Cullompton, Devon
Mr and Mrs Arthur Brooks, Bodmin, Cornwall
Allen J. H. Broom, London
David J. Broom, Kerswell, Cullompton, Devon
Margaret R. Broucke, Cullompton, Devon
Mollie D. G. Brown, Cullompton, Devon
Derek R. Budd, Cullompton, Devon
Mr B. A. Bunker, Wallington, Surrey
Darren J. W. Burns, Cullompton, Devon
K. J. Burrow, Bucks Cross, Devon
Colin M. S. Butt, Cullompton, Devon
Laura and Norman Cable, Willand, Devon
Grant Cann, Newland, Cullompton, Devon
Jack F. Cann, Kentisbeare, Devon
Michael Ivan C. Carter, Cullompton, Devon
Christina A. Chambers, Cullompton, Devon
G. D. and H. Chambers, Plymtree, Devon
Gary Chambers, Cullompton, Devon
Richard Chard, Cullompton, Devon
Mumtaz and Alan Cheshire, Winkleigh, Devon
Vera E. Clapp, Cullompton, Devon
Richard D. Clapp, Doxey, Stafford
The Claremont-Davies family, Cullompton, Devon
The Cleaver family, Cullompton, Devon
Charlie Clist, Cullompton, Devon
Anthony and Iris Cole, Cullompton, Devon
A. J. and W. J. Coleman, Clyst Hydon, Cullompton, Devon
Nigel and Anna Coleman
Joan and Harold Cook, Cullompton, Devon
Beulan M. Coombe, Cullompton, Devon
Mrs Joan Cotterill (née Keen), Brixham, Devon
L. Gerald Cottrell, Dulford, Devon
Mrs Muriel Coxhead
Barbara J. Crispin, Hele, Bradninch, Devon
Colin Crispin, Bradninch, Devon
Robert Crispin, Bradninch, Devon
Paul Crispin, Bradninch, Devon
Joyce G. Cross, Cullompton, Devon
Margaret E. Crowe, Cullompton, Devon
Dr and Mrs John Cruickshank, Knowle, Cullompton, Devon
Paul and Linda Curtis, Cullompton, Devon
Mary and Den Darwen-Bradbury, Padbrook, Cullompton, Devon
Terry and Marilyn Davies, Cullompton, Devon
Peter and Kit Davis, Stoneyford, Cullompton, Devon
Ron and Betty Day, Uffculme, Devon
Stan and Joan Deakin, Cullompton, Devon
Mr and Mrs W. R. Denner, Cullompton, Devon
Kay Dimbleby, Clyst Hydon, Devon
Pauline M. Discombe, Cullompton, Devon
Mr Peter W. D. Discombe, Cullompton, Devon
Fay Down, Upton, Cullompton, Devon
Mr J. L. Drew, Cullompton, Devon
Frederick C. Drew, Bradninch, Devon
Mrs Sarah Duffin, Cullompton, Devon
Eric and Marian Dummett M.B.E., Cullompton, Devon
David E. Dunn, Exeter, Devon
Gary K. Dunn, Cullompton, Devon
Roy and Janet Dunn (née Fone), Cullompton, Devon
Elaine J. Dunn (née White), Kentisbeare, Devon
Tony Eames, Plymtree, Devon
Sally Eaves, Hartland, North Devon
Carolyn Eaves, Haverfordwest, Pembrokeshire
John Eaves, Neyland, Pembrokeshire
Barry and Ann Edmonds, Cullompton, Devon
Gary and Michelle Edwards, Cullompton, Devon
Mr Ray and Mrs Gwen Edworthy
Mr Dane R. Ell, Cullompton, Devon
Mr Robert Ell, Cullompton, Devon
Mr Gary R. Ell, Tiverton, Devon
Ian Ellicott, Kentisbeare, Devon
Janet Ellicott (née Graves), Willand, Devon
Mr and Mrs Les Ellis, Cullompton, Devon
Richard S. Elstone, Cullompton, Devon
Steve and Liz Ewings, Cullompton, Devon
Ashton and Sheridan Farrant, Cullompton, Devon
Sally and Colin Farrelly, Plymouth, Devon
David and Karen Febry, Searchlight, Fulford Barnyard, Cullompton, Devon
Bett Field, Cullompton, Devon
Mr and Mrs S. J. Firbanks, Cullompton, Devon
The Fisher family, Blackborough, Devon
Chris Fleming, Portsmouth (grandson of Harold Denning)
Mrs N. V. Forse, Cullompton, Devon
Harris Fowler, Solicitors, Cullompton, Devon
Tracy Frankpitt, Mutterton, Devon
The French family, Dulford, Cullompton, Devon
Suzanne D. Frost, Cullompton, Devon
Eric A. Frost, Cullompton, Devon
Gavin J. Frost, Cullompton, Devon
Mike and Julie Frost (née Chilcott), Cullompton, Devon
Marian Fulker, Cullompton, Devon
Patrick and Helena George, Cullompton, Devon
Liz Gibbins and Mark Cornish, Rose Cottage, Plymtree, Devon
Harry J. Gibson, Cullompton, Devon
Rosemary E. Glanville, Talaton, Devon
The Glenn family, Cullompton, Devon
Mrs Christiana T. Glover, Cullompton, Devon
Mr and Mrs G. D. V. Glynn, Hillersdon House, Cullompton, Devon
James and Emily Goff, Adelaide, Australia
Derek E. Goff, Cullompton, Devon
Frazer Goff, Sydney, Australia
Bill and Mandy Goff, Cullompton, Devon
Trevor and Sharon Goodall, Cullompton, Devon
Mr G. W. D. Goodhind, Leigh-on-Sea, Essex
B. and P. K. Gordon, Cullompton, Devon
Kevin R. Grant, Willand, Devon
Mrs P. J. J. Griffiths (née Discombe), The Green, Cullompton, Devon
Susan Groves, Cullompton, Devon
Alan and Lorraine Gubb, Cullompton, Devon
Ian B. Gunn, Cullompton, Devon
Netta Hake, Cullompton, Devon
Gillian Hake, Tiverton, Devon
Ron Hake, Tiverton, Devon
Jane S. Hamilton, Cullompton, Devon
Mrs Tracey D. Hammett, Willand, Devon
Janet C. Hancock (née Phillips)
Glen N. Hanks, Cullompton, Devon
Hann and Seddon Estate Agents, Cullompton, Devon
Stephen M. Harris, Cullompton, Devon
Jeremy K. Harris, Butterleigh, Devon
Adrian J. Harris, Cullompton, Devon
B. J. and J. M. Harris, Cullompton, Devon
Dr John Hart, Orway, Cullompton, Devon
Amanda Hawkins, Cullompton, Devon
Philip Hazeldine, Kentisbeare, Devon
Mary S. Heard, Cullompton, Devon
Chris and Jenny Hellier, Cullompton, Devon
Norman and Barbara Hellier, Cullompton, Devon
Steve and Alison Hellier, Cullompton, Devon
Ashley Hellier
Dorothy Ackland Hill, Cullompton, Devon
Stanley J. Hill, Cullompton, Devon
Mike and Sarah Hill, Cullompton, Devon
Stan and Cherry Hilton, Cullompton, Devon
M. J. and R. V. Hines, Langford, Cullompton, Devon
Michael and Sheila Hitt, Cullompton, Devon
Felicity and Anthony Hoare, Cullompton, Devon
Marilyn L. Holley, Sampford Peverell, Devon
Michael Hooper, Cullompton, Devon
Tessa M. E. Horobin, Cullompton, Devon
Lesley Howell (née Owens), St Stephens, Cornwall
Norman F. Hunt, Cullompton, Devon

Mike and Jeanette Ingersent
Mr Frederick and Mrs Barbara Jane, Cullompton, Devon
Roy Jeffery, Cullompton, Devon
Richard Johns, Grays, Essex
Michael Johns, Crowthorne, Berkshire
Peter and Emma Jones, Cullompton, Devon
Christine Jones, Cullompton, Devon
Tricia Jones (née Bradbeer), Montford Bridge, Shrewsbury
Douglas William Alfred Keen, Cullompton, Devon
Muriel E. Kellaway, Cullompton, Devon
Joyce and Derrick Kellaway, Cullompton, Devon
Fiona Kelly, Cullompton, Devon
Mr and Mrs Maurice Kemp, Cullompton, Devon
Sandra P. Kemp, Cullompton, Devon
Mrs Dorothy Kennedy, Cullompton, Devon
Janet Kennedy, Manaton, Devon
Mr Stuart W. L. Kerslake, Paignton, Devon
Kenneth E. Klee, Cullompton, Devon
Mike Knight, East Grinstead, West Sussex/formerly of Cullompton
Gordon A. Knight, Cullompton, Devon
Mr and Mrs P. Labdon, Cullompton, Devon
Jennifer and Owen Land, Cullompton, Devon
Bernard Land, Cullompton, Devon
Mr R. E. Langford, Cullompton, Devon
Mick Lawrence, Helston, Cornwall
Mrs Pat Leach
Mrs Maude Lee, Cullompton, Devon
Geoffrey H. Lee, Uffculme, Devon
Mrs P. Leighton (née Gill)
J. Lemon, Woodbury, Exeter, Devon
Mr and Mrs M. C. Lotz, Langford, Cullompton, Devon
Mrs Pippa Lovering
Brenda E. Luke
Margaret Luscombe, Willand, Nr Cullompton, Devon
Justin and Claire Lush, Cullompton, Devon
Stephen J. Luxton, Taunton, Somerset
Jean and George Manfield, Cullompton, Devon
Miss N. Manfield, Tiverton, Devon
Elsie Manning, Cullompton, Devon
Christine A. Manning, Cullompton, Devon
Penny Marshall, Cullompton, Devon
Mr Paul H. Matthews, Cullompton, Devon
Frances Maunder, Cullompton, Devon
Reith M. May, Cullompton, Devon
Mr and Mrs J. Maynard, Clyst Hydon, Devon
Mr and Mrs P McMillan Browse, Cullompton, Devon
Dennis and Jean Meecham, Honiton Road, Cullompton, Devon
Colin and Julie Metcalf, Willand, Devon
Jennie Middleton
Krista M. Midwinter, Coulsdon, Surrey
Laura L. Milton, Cullompton, Devon
Mrs R. V. Moore, Cullompton, Devon
Paul Alec Morgan, Cullompton, Devon
Steve and Judy Morris, Cullompton, Devon
Ivan D. and Christine E. Munn, Cullompton, Devon
Mr and Mrs R. E. Needham, Plymtree, Devon
Rose Neeves (née Bradbeer), Shrewsbury
Brian C. F. H. Newman, Cullompton, Devon
Janet Newton (née Goff), Cullompton, Devon
Clive S. Nicholas, Cullompton, Devon
Nick and Barbara Nicholson, Cullompton, Devon
Sidney A. Norman, Cullompton, Devon
Judith Northam-Nowell, Cullompton, Devon
Brian W. Organ, Cullompton, Devon
Ben and Carol Ouellette, Smithville, Canada
Joyce Owens, Cullompton, Devon
John and Ann Parkin, Shuffshayes, Langford, Devon
Joyce and Jack Parsons, Cullompton, Devon
Leslie R. F. Partridge, Cullompton, Devon
Mr P. Patterson, Cullompton, Devon
Christopher and Steve Pengilly, Cullompton, Devon
Susan and Roger Perry, Cullompton, Devon
Philip Perryman, Creech St Michael, Somerset
Russell and Nikki Phillips, Cullompton, Devon
Alan and Ruth Phillips, Cullompton, Devon
Clifford J. H. Pike, Kentisbeare, Cullompton, Devon
Rachel Pinder, Staple Hay, Taunton, Somerset
Mr and Mrs E. Pollard, Cullompton, Devon
Ruth Powell, Exeter, Devon
Lionel Pratt, Cullompton, Devon
Lionel W. Pratt, Cullompton, Devon
Christopher J. Pratt, Woodbeer Court, Plymtree, Devon
Graham Prescott Domestic Appliances, Willand, Devon
Gordon Pring, Cullompton Town Crier
Mr and Mrs R. Puddicombe, Plymtree, Devon
David Pugsley, Cullompton, Devon
Gladys M. Radford
Karen and Marcus Rees, Cullompton, Devon
Norman H. Rendell-Reynolds,
Revd Michael J. Resch, Cullompton, Devon
Lionel F. Richards, Cullompton, Devon
Ring of Bells Morris Dancers, Cullompton, Devon
Claire and Steve Roberts, Beckenham, Kent
John R. and Brenda M. A. Roper, Cullompton, Devon
Colin G. and Judith E. E. Rorie, Clyst Hydon, Devon
Lillan Rorie, Langlands Road, Cullompton, Devon
Mrs Mary Rowe, Cullompton, Devon
Dr N. P. and C. R. Rushton, Lower Moorhayes, Cullompton, Devon
Jennifer P. Rutley
Adrian G. Rutley, Cullompton, Devon
Magery Salisbury (née Fear), Cullompton, Devon
Dianne J. Sanders, Willand
Roy and Beatrice Sanders, Moorhayes Farm, Cullompton, Devon
Jeremy I. Sanders, Cullompton, Devon
John S. Schultze, Tatworth, Chard
M. and N. Scorse, Cullompton, Devon
Audrey M. Shearing, Kentisbeare, Devon
Elizabeth A. Shere, Silverton, Devon
Richard Shere
Mr Andrew J. Shere, Kintore, Aberdeenshire
Marion Shere (née Ford), Budleigh Salterton, Devon
Mr and Mrs J. Silby, Cullompton, Devon
Mr and Mrs Cyril Smith,
Malcolm Smith, Cullompton, Devon
Lucinda Smith, Cullompton, Devon
Kathleen C. Spear M.B.E.
Isabelle J. Spiller, Trull, Somerset
D. Sprake, Willand, Devon
Michael Thomas Squire, Cullompton, Devon
St Andrew's Primary School, Cullompton, Devon
Yvonne L. Staddon, Cullompton, Devon
Jeanne Staddon, Pinhoe, Exeter, Devon
Alan and Brenda Stanbrook, Cullompton, Devon
Fiona J. Standford, Cullompton, Devon
Mrs Phylis Starr, Trethomas, South Wales
Sir Michael and Lady Stear, Dulford, Devon
Mr Donald Stevens, Heavitree, Exeter, Devon
Mr and Mrs Anthony, and Les Stevens, Cullompton, Devon
Mr and Mrs Michael Stevenson, Cullompton, Devon
Martin E. Stocker, Cullompton, Devon
Tim Stone, Dawlish, Devon/formerly of Cullompton
Eleonor Stone (née Hamilton), Nailsea, Avon
Master Archie J. Stoneman, Cullompton, Devon
Mr Anthony and Mrs Joyce Stride, Cullompton, Devon
Peter and Pam Tait, Hemyock, Devon
Gwendoline W. Talbot, Cullompton, Devon
Mrs M. Tancock, Cullompton, Devon
Sonia Tankard (née Yendell), formerly of Cullompton, Devon
Mr Pat Tanton, Cullompton, Devon
Paul and Katrina Tapp, Cullompton, Devon
Daniel J. G. Thomassen, Cullompton, Devon
Thorne and Carter, Cullompton, Devon
Peter Trayte, Cullompton, Devon
Mrs Penny Trevelyan, Heavitree, Exeter, Devon
Alan Troke, Westcott, Cullompton, Devon
Andrew Troke, Westcott, Cullompton, Devon
Rachel Troke, Westcott, Cullompton, Devon
Christopher and Marguerite Tucker, Cullompton, Devon
Jan, Jerry and Benjamin Tucker, Cullompton, Devon
H. Van-Bussel, Cullompton, Devon/Holland
Derrick L. Vigar, Cullompton, Devon
Anne S. Vile, Cullompton, Devon
Peter and Helen Vile, Lower Mill, Cullompton, Devon
Angela and Gerry Wall, Knowle, Cullompton, Devon
John F. W. Walling, Newton Abbot, Devon
Joy Walters, Hemyock, Devon
Colin and Wendy Ward, Probus, Cornwall
Mr and Mrs N. Watts, Kentisbeare, Cullompton, Devon
Shirley and David Webber, Kentisbeare, Devon
Mike Webber, Cullompton, Devon
David Weetman, Cullompton, Devon
Michael and Teresa Wegner, Cullompton, Devon
Ellie Wegner, Cullompton, Devon
Malcolm F. Wellington, Cullompton, Devon
Mike and Sharon Wetherell, Cullompton, Devon
Roger A. J. White, Langford Green, Cullompton, Devon
Michael A. Whitfield, Cullompton, Devon
Mike and Jan Widgery, Cullompton, Devon
Mr Henry Williams, Cullompton, Devon
Linda C. Wilson, Kerswell, Cullompton, Devon
Jenny Winford, Berkhamsted, Herts.
Richard and Debbie Woof, Cullompton, Devon
Richard Young, Cullompton, Devon

ALSO AVAILABLE IN THE SERIES

The Book of Addiscombe • Various
Book of Bampton • Caroline Seward
Book of Bickington • Stuart Hands
Blandford Forum: A Millennium Portrait • Various
The Book of Brixham • Frank Pearce
The Parish Book of Cerne Abbas • Vale & Vale
The Book of Chittlehampton • Various
The Book of Constantine • Moore & Trethowan
The Book of Cornwood and Lutton • Various
The Book of Creech St Michael • June Small
The Book of Dawlish • Frank Pearce
The Ellacombe Book • Sydney R. Langmead
The Book of Grampound with Creed • Bane & Oliver
The Book of Hayling Island and Langstone • Rogers
The Book of Helston • Jenkin with Carter
The Book of Hemyock • Clist & Dracott
The Book of High Bickington • Avril Stone
The Book of Ilsington • Dick Wills
The Book of Lamerton • Ann Cole and Friends
Lanner, A Cornish Mining Parish • Scharron Schwartz & Roger Parker
The Book of Loddiswell • Various
The Book of Lustleigh • Joe Crowdy
The Book of Manaton • Various
The Book of Meavy • Pauline Hemery
The Book of Morchard Bishop • Jeff Kingaby
The Book of Minehead with Alcombe • Binding & Stevens
The Book of North Newton • Robins & Robins
The Book of Paignton • Frank Pearce
The Book of Pimperne • Compiled by Jean Coull
The Book of Plymtree • Tony Eames
The Book of Porlock • Denis Corner
Postbridge – The Heart of Dartmoor • Reg Bellamy
The Book of Priddy • Various
The Book of Rattery • Various
The Book of Silverton • Various
The Book of South Stoke • Various
South Tawton and South Zeal with Sticklepath • Roy and Ursula Radford
The Book of Sparkwell with Hemerdon & Lee Mill • Pam James
The Book of Stithians • Various
The Book of Swanage • Rodney Legg
The Book of Torbay • Frank Pearce
Uncle Tom Cobley and All: Widecombe-in-the-Moor • Stephen Woods
The Book of Watchet • Compiled by David Banks
The Book of West Huntspill • Various
Widecombe-in-the-Moor • Stephen Woods
The Book of Williton • Michael Williams
Woodbury: The Twentieth Century Revisited • Roger Stokes
The Book of Woolmer Green • Various

SOME OF THE MANY FORTHCOMING TITLES

The Book of Addiscombe, Vol. II • Various
The Book of Barnstaple • Avril Stone
The Book of Bridestowe • R. Cann
The Book of Buckland Monochorum • Hemery
The Book of Carshalton • Stella Wilks
The Book of Chagford • Ian Rice
The Book of Chittlehamholt with Warkleigh & Satterleigh • Richard Lethbridge
The Book of Colney Heath • Bryan Lilley
The Book of Down St Mary • Various
The Book of Dulverton with Brushford, Bury & Exebridge • Various
The Book of Dunster • Hilary Binding
The Book of Hurn • Margaret Phipps
The Book of Lulworth • Rodney Legg
The Book of Markyate • Richard Hogg
The Book of Mawnan Smith • Various
The Book of Newdigate • John Callcut
The Book of Newton Abbot • Ian Rice
The Book of North Tawton • Various
The Book of Northlew with Ashbury • Various
The Book of Peter Tavy • Various
The Book of Publow with Pensford • Various
The Book of Sampford Courtenay with Honeychurch • Stephanie Pouya
The Book of Staverton • Pete Lavis
The Book of Studland • Rodney Legg
The Book of Wythall • Val Lewis

For details of any of the above titles or if you are interested in writing your own community history, please contact: Community Histories Editor, Halsgrove House, Lower Moor Way, Tiverton Business Park, Tiverton, Devon EX16 6SS, England, e-mail: sales@halsgrove.com

In order to include as many historic photographs as possible in this volume, a printed index is not included. However, the Community Histories are currently being indexed by Genuki. For further information and indexes to volumes in the series, please visit: http://www.cs.ncl.ac.uk/genuki/DEV/indexingproject.html